A Plain Account of Christian Faithfulness

A Plain Account of Christian Faithfulness

—— *Essays in Honor of David B. McEwan* ——

EDITED BY
Rob A. Fringer
AND
Dean G. Smith

WIPF & STOCK · Eugene, Oregon

A PLAIN ACCOUNT OF CHRISTIAN FAITHFULNESS
Essays in Honor of David B. McEwan

Copyright © 2020 Wipf and Stock Publishers. All rights reserved. Except for brief quotations in critical publications or reviews, no part of this book may be reproduced in any manner without prior written permission from the publisher. Write: Permissions, Wipf and Stock Publishers, 199 W. 8th Ave., Suite 3, Eugene, OR 97401.

Wipf & Stock
An Imprint of Wipf and Stock Publishers
199 W. 8th Ave., Suite 3
Eugene, OR 97401

www.wipfandstock.com

PAPERBACK ISBN: 978-1-5326-5557-9
HARDCOVER ISBN: 978-1-5326-5558-6
EBOOK ISBN: 978-1-5326-5559-3

Manufactured in the U.S.A.   04/29/20

For our dear friend, colleague, and teacher, David B. McEwan,
with the utmost love, respect, and thanks.

Contents

List of Contributors | ix

Preface | xiii
—Rob A. Fringer

Introduction: The Life of a Faithful Servant | xv
—James McEwan and Shona Van Garderen

Section 1: Biblical Perspectives on Christian Faithfulness

1. The Fewest of All the Peoples: God's Incipient Faithfulness to Israel | 3
   —Joseph Coleson

2. Faithful Teaching: Jesus, the Model Teacher | 20
   —Kent Brower

3. Acts as a Faithful Source for Understanding Paul and His Christophanic Experience | 36
   —Rob A. Fringer

4. You Have Been Called to Faithfully Follow Christ's Steps: A Missional Reading of 1 Peter | 49
   —Svetlana Khobnya

Section 2: Theological and Historical Perspectives on Christian Faithfulness

5. The Faith of Christ: Theological Implications | 65
   —Thomas A. Noble

6. The Sacramental Life: Towards a More Holistic and Faithful Understanding of Holiness | 81
—Dean G. Smith

7. Wynkoop: On the Presuppositions of Christian Faithfulness | 96
—Johan Tredoux

8. Faithfulness to the Gospel: An Interpretation from the Early Church Fathers | 112
—David Rainey

9. The Ideal of Faithfulness in Western Culture | 130
—Diane Speed

10. Holiness as Happiness: A Plain Account of Sanctification | 147
—Glen O'Brien

Section 3: Pastoral Perspectives on Christian Faithfulness

11. The Church and Urban Justice: A Faithful Wesleyan Perspective on Caring for People with Lived Experience of Poverty within Cities | 167
—Deirdre Brower Latz

12. Faithful Preparation for Ministry: Exploring a Synthesis of Educational Models | 184
—Bruce G. Allder

13. Faithfulness in the Face of Differences: John Wesley's Catholic Spirit and One-Heartedness | 205
—Richard Giesken and Erik Groeneveld

14. A Faithful Father's Acceptant Love and Healing of Shame-Proneness: The Prodigal Son and John Wesley | 221
—Neil Pembroke

Contributors

Bruce Allder, EdD (Griffith University), Senior Lecturer in Pastoral Theology and Liturgy at Nazarene Theological College, Australia and New Zealand, and the Asia-Pacific Regional Education Coordinator for the Church of the Nazarene.

Kent Brower, PhD (University of Manchester), Senior Research Fellow and Senior Lecturer in Biblical Studies at Nazarene Theological College, Manchester, England.

Joseph Coleson, PhD (Brandeis University), Emeritus Professor of Old Testament, Nazarene Theological Seminary, Missouri, USA.

Rob A. Fringer, PhD (University of Manchester, NTC-Manchester), Principal and Senior Lecturer in Biblical Studies and Biblical Language at Nazarene Theological College, Australia and New Zealand, and Honorary Research Fellow in the School of Historical and Philosophical Inquiry at the University of Queensland.

Richard Giesken, DMin candidate (Asbury Theological Seminary), Associate Lecturer in Biblical Studies and Missiology at Nazarene Theological College, Australia and New Zealand, and Pastor of Redlands Church of the Nazarene.

Erik Groeneveld, DMin (Sydney College of Divinity, NTC-Australia), Lecturer in Practical Theology and coordinator of the Leadership Training Program at the Evangelical College, The Netherlands, and Netherlands Coordinator and Lecturer for European Nazarene College.

Svetlana Khobnya, PhD (University of Manchester, NTC-Manchester), Senior Lecturer in Biblical Studies and Languages at Nazarene Theological College, Manchester, England.

Deirdre Brower Latz, PhD (University of Manchester), Principal and Senior Lecturer in Pastoral and Social Theology at Nazarene Theological College, Manchester, England.

James McEwan, MMTec (University of Newcastle), lecturer in Music Production and Audio Engineering at SAE Institute, Brisbane, and Program Committee Member and Program Developer for SAE Institute Australia. He is also David McEwan's son.

Thomas A. Noble, PhD (University of Edinburgh), Research Professor of Theology at Nazarene Theological Seminary, Missouri, USA, and Senior Research Fellow in Theology at Nazarene Theological College, Manchester, England.

Glen O'Brien, PhD (La Trobe University), Associate Professor of Church History and Theology and Research Coordinator at Eva Burrows College, University of Divinity, Melbourne, Australia.

Neil Pembroke, PhD (University of Edinburgh), Associate Professor of Christian Studies in the School of Historical and Philosophical Inquiry at the University of Queensland, Australia.

David Rainey, PhD (King's College London), Senior Research Fellow in Theology at Nazarene Theological College, Manchester, England.

Dean G. Smith, PhD (University of Queensland), Senior Lecturer in Theology and Philosophy and Dean of Students at Nazarene Theological College, Australia and New Zealand, and Director of the Australasian Centre for Wesleyan Research.

Diane Speed, PhD (King's College London), Dean and CEO of the Sydney College of Divinity, and former Senior Lecturer in English at University of Sydney, Australia.

Johan Tredoux, PhD (University of Manchester, NTC-Manchester), member of the PhD Supervisory Team at Africa Nazarene University, Kenya, and Chaplain at Research Medical Center, Missouri, USA.

Shona Van Garderen, MCCJ (Griffith University), a current coordinator for the Human Research Ethics Committee of Queensland Health, of which David McEwan is a member. She is also David's daughter.

Preface

—Rob A. Fringer

Let us hold fast to the confession of our hope without wavering, for he who has promised is faithful. And let us consider how to provoke one another to love and good deeds, not neglecting to meet together, as is the habit of some, but encouraging one another, and all the more as you see the Day approaching. (Heb 10:23–25, NRSV[1])

It is with great pleasure and excitement that I introduce this volume of essays dedicated to David B. McEwan. I first met David in June 2013 at Nazarene Theological College, Manchester, England. David was there teaching a postgraduate course (probably on John Wesley), and I was there working on my PhD through the University of Manchester. About five months earlier, I had accepted a position as Lecturer in Biblical Studies at Nazarene Theological College (NTC) in Brisbane, Australia, where David was Academic Dean. Over the next two weeks of my time in Manchester, David and I had several walks, several talks, and several meals together. I quickly came to appreciate his breadth and depth of knowledge, which went well beyond the topic of John Wesley, and his faithfulness to Christ, the church, and to Christian education. A friendship developed in this short time that continues today.

Two years after arriving at NTC, I was elected principal, and David was among those who supported me during this transition. I have relied on him time and time again, finding in him great wisdom, encouragement, and genuine concern for my wellbeing. When David informed me that he would be retiring from his Academic Dean role after twenty years of service, I knew I had to find a way to honor his service to NTC and to the greater

---

1. Unless otherwise stated, all Scripture references throughout this book are from the NRSV.

church in a way that he would both value and appreciate. This book, which brings together excellent articles from scholars from around the globe, who also happen to be great friends, colleagues, and former students of David's, was my answer.

As I pondered the theme, the word "faithfulness" kept coming to the forefront. The title—*A Plain Account of Christian Faithfulness*—is a play on John Wesley's famous book, *A Plain Account of Christian Perfection*, of whom David B. McEwan has spent his academic career studying, teaching, and writing about. It also reflects the "faithfulness" that David has shown in his years of ministry and teaching.

The book is a mix of biblical, theological, historical, and pastoral essays, each focusing on aspects of faithfulness from a Wesleyan perspective. It is my hope that these chapters will do for you, the reader, what David had done for so many—that they will open your heart, mind, and soul, challenging you and beckoning you deeper in your faith journey with the Triune God (Father, Son, and Holy Spirit).

Introduction

The Life of a Faithful Servant

—JAMES MCEWAN AND SHONA VAN GARDEREN

Birth and Early Years

While many people know David as a pastor, lecturer, or friend, few perhaps know the whole story of who he is and the journey on which he has been. Our father is a private man, but we wanted to share in this introduction an overview of what has shaped him into the person he is today.

David Bernard McEwan was born on the 20th of August 1950, in the town of Irvine, North Ayrshire, on the Scottish coast. David's younger sister, Kirstie, was born in 1955. Their parents, Bernard and Mary, were also from small coastal towns in Scotland. Mary was a nurse and Bernard had been in the Royal Air Force before transitioning to his career as an exhibition cake decorator. Bernard became quite successful in his profession, receiving national and international recognition for his work.

Bernard's work required the family to relocate twice, first to London in 1957, and then to Kent in 1963. David attended a number of schools during these periods including George Spicer Primary School, Minchenden Grammar School, and Bromley Grammar School for Boys. Some famous alumni from Bromley include Sir George Martin CBE (a.k.a. "the fifth Beatle"), Ken Wood (the founder of Kenwood appliances), and Billy Idol. While there had been the possibility of entering a medical career, David ended up graduating with a Higher National Diploma in Food Technology from the London South Bank University in 1970.

During his teenage years, David developed a passion for one of his lifelong loves—motorcycles. He loved his motorcycle and spent much of his time riding with friends around the area. Triumph motorcycles were, and are, his favorite and in his younger days he often fixed them up himself.

His first bike was a 200cc Triumph Tiger Cub. He had a few major bike accidents when younger, which required having both knees reconstructed. If you listen carefully, you can hear them clicking as he walks.

David loved blues music and some of his friends formed a band that played in the local pubs; he would follow them and often took his tape recorder to record the sessions. Growing up in the greater London area, David had the opportunity to see several well-known bands play in their early days such as the Rolling Stones and Cream. The music scene must have been the trigger for David to learn the guitar, and while it is not something he's well known for, his skill was good enough to play for church and Bible College events later in his life.

Australia Part 1

David immigrated to Australia in 1970 when he was twenty, as a £10 pom, and went to live with relatives in Sydney. They introduced him to the Church of the Nazarene, and he began attending services. During this season of his life he experienced Christ's redeeming grace and became a believer. His time at church inspired him to enter the ministry and enroll at Nazarene Theological College (NTC), at the time based in Sydney. He would later graduate with a Diploma of Ministry.

David made trips with the church to Brisbane and on one such occasion went to help on a youth project. At the same time, a young woman named Christine Rouen was also working on the project. Christine and David were introduced to each other by the leader, but that was all that happened during the trip. Christine decided she liked David and wrote to him later, and so began their long-distance relationship. David would drive up from Sydney on a Friday night and stay in Brisbane to visit with Christine till Sunday afternoon, he would then drive back to Sydney to be at college on Monday morning. He later ended up moving to Biloela as part of his career in supermarkets and thus the relationship continued long distance. David and Christine were engaged on the day of David's graduation and married in 1974.

After graduating, David accepted his first ministry position back in his home country of the UK, where he pastored several churches from 1975–80. During his first posting, he and Christine lived in Partick in Glasgow, Scotland in a traditional Scottish tenement. They were then transferred to Stockton-on-Tees in northern England where they lived in a traditional end-of-terrace house. The church was next door to the local synagogue and mosque. Kumba (Aboriginal for Sunshine) had become part of their lives at this time as a five-week-old Labrador puppy who traveled down from Scotland with them when they moved. They then moved down to Bristol as the final posting before returning to Australia. They had to leave Kumba behind, which was a great loss to both.

Australia Part 2

David and Christine returned to Australia in 1980 to pastor the Logan Church of the Nazarene in Brisbane, and a year later their son James McEwan was born. When he was only three years old, the family travelled to Kansas City, USA for David to complete his Master of Divinity at Nazarene Theological Seminary. His friend from college, Bruce Alder, along with his family, also moved there at the same time.

Anecdotes from others have revealed David to be a dedicated student who excelled in his studies and would often assist others. One colleague said:

> David's single focus on his studies and his breadth of reading is an attribute that has made him one of the foremost Wesleyan theologians in the global Church of the Nazarene. As a good Wesleyan theologian, he has always sought to be practical in his application of theology. His amazing intellect has given him the ability to quickly analyze a huge volume of material and succinctly go to the heart of the issue expressed. As you know, he does not suffer fools lightly, and quickly moves on to other interests if the conversation appears to be going nowhere. Having said that, he is amazingly patient with parishioners who need to talk.[2]

On his return to Australia in 1986 at the completion of his MDiv, David began pastoring the Wantirna Church of the Nazarene in Melbourne. He had the ability to take the small struggling church and help it become a vibrant community. While still regarded as relatively small, the church got involved in mission and community connections that punched far above their weight for the size. During this period his daughter Shona McEwan was born.

David has always been a gifted preacher and teacher. As such, he would hold Bible studies mid-week in Melbourne. He had hoped to develop a series of home groups with their own Bible studies, but people would rather sit under his teacher ministry in a larger group than divide up into smaller groups; they loved his teaching so much! His first experience in

2. Allder, "David McEwan," email, 2018.

formal ministry in Britain had significantly shaped him as a pastor, taking seriously the pulpit ministry and visiting parishioners on a regular basis.

David is a real history buff, particularly British history. In the McEwan house, Braveheart is considered one of the worst movies of all time due to its historical inaccuracies. On a family trip to the UK in 1994, the family endured four weeks of being dragged to every castle and historical monument found across the isles. All of this was captured on video for posterity. If you were to watch one of these videos, you would think that David was vying for a job as a presenter on the BBC, with his high-quality narration and historical details on each location. Often the rest of the family would disappear out of the castle, having seen everything, whilst David was still only filming the first room!

In 1997 David took a position at Nazarene Theological College as Academic Dean and lecturer, requiring the family to move to Brisbane. This was a big move for us kids, happening during our formative years; so, to say we were reluctant at first is an understatement! However, we soon settled into life here in Brisbane, and it enabled both of us to grow enormously with help from our parents. David's love of music extended to his son James, who has become an accomplished musician, with David often choosing the family car on the sole criteria of it being able to haul around a bass guitar, amplifier, and sometimes even a double bass as well.

David also reacquainted himself with motorcycles in Queensland, having never owned one whilst in Victoria. There have been a few different bikes over the years, and a few accidents to boot, landing himself in hospital more than once. He also joined a motorcycle "gang" (Ulysses), with the club motto of "Growing Old Disgracefully." Shona inherited his love of motorbikes, going for her first ride at six years old and continuing to enjoy rides together on weekends well into adulthood.

His family has grown and expanded to include new children (Aaron Van Garderen, husband to Shona, and Candice McEwan, wife to James) as well as the recent addition of the first grandchild, Lukas Van Garderen. David is a doting grandfather (Papa, as Lukas likes to call him) and has been a great source of wisdom and guidance to all his children.

NTC was a small, struggling institution that was having difficulty establishing itself academically and within the church community. David grabbed hold of the challenge to develop the academic credibility of the college, and over a period of years he worked the academic processes with skill and insight. The college moved from an accredited Diploma in Ministry to a Bachelor of Ministry to ultimately offering a range of undergraduate and postgraduate awards. The amount of material required in preparation to achieve this was enormous. Yet, David was able to process all this in an amazingly timely fashion. His productivity level has been extremely high, almost like a tenacious bull terrier when he catches a vision of what needs to be done. He is a hard man to keep up with sometimes.

Never one to rest, David has continued to apply himself. He completed his Doctorate through the University of Queensland in 2006. He has become Director and Research Fellow at the Australasian Centre for Wesleyan Research. He has authored three books (2011, 2015, 2017), and has also contributed numerous book chapters and articles. He became pastor again for the Logan Community Church of the Nazarene (almost thirty years since his first run). Not even impending retirement seems to slow David down, as he has many other achievements beyond the scope of this introduction.

Section 1

Biblical Perspectives on Christian Faithfulness

1

The Fewest of All the Peoples
God's Incipient Faithfulness to Israel[1]

—Joseph Coleson

Trying to exemplify David McEwan's kind of common sense in my own fields of biblical and Near Eastern studies has involved revisiting some of the theological formulations, and even some of the "facts" we already knew, or thought we knew. This chapter addresses two such topics, Israel's population in the two generations of their exodus from Egypt under Moses and their entering into Canaan under Joshua, and the manner of Israel's entry into and initial settlement of the Canaanite Highlands. In presenting these issues and suggesting a way forward, I am not really blazing any new trails. Critical discussion of the two irreconcilable sets of "facts" within Israel's Exodus traditions is at least a century old. Mendenhall[2] published the philological key to Israel's population sixty years ago, and the geographical, historical, and archaeological contributions have been available for twenty-five years now. Younger's *Ancient Conquest Accounts*, published in 1990, furnishes the paradigm for understanding what Israel did in entering Canaan under Joshua and, equally important, what they did not do.

Biblical and ANE scholars have known; we just have not managed (if we have tried) to make our work known to the world beyond our guild(s). This has left believers, seekers, and skeptics alike to adopt, or reject, the same ancient misunderstandings—to attack or defend a straw man, with both "victory" and "defeat" irrelevant to the real historical and theological issues. An accurate account of Israel's exodus and entry populations, and of the manner of Israel's entry into Canaan, though, will allow us to understand the

---

1. For the twenty-plus years of our friendship, I have admired David McEwan's level-headed, common-sense approach to Wesleyan history and theology. I am both blessed and privileged to contribute to this volume honoring David's faithfulness.

2. Mendenhall, "Census Lists," 52–66.

reality of Israel's beginnings, as continued acceptance of inflated numbers and military results never will do. This "new" understanding highlights a central tenet of divine activity: From small beginnings, "the fewest of all the peoples," God has birthed and sustains an eternal family.

Israel's Exodus Population: The Present Texts of Numbers 1, 26

The familiar data lead to the prevalent understanding that one generation of Israel left Egypt about three million strong, and the next entered Canaan in similar numbers.

Numbers 1 is a census report, the tribal tallies of Israel's fighting men, twenty years old and older, who left Egypt in the Exodus with Moses. As it stands, the Hebrew text of 1:46 lists a total of 603,550 men. Numbers 26:51 records the total of the next generation, most of whom would enter Canaan, as 601,730. Several tribes' numbers vary significantly, but the two totals are nearly equal.[3]

The usual procedure for estimating Israel's total population is to assume one wife for one soldier, on average, for a sub-total of married persons of about 1.2 million. If, on average, each "military couple" had two living children not yet adults, the total reaches 2.4 million. The count of 600,000 fighting men does not include military-aged men unable to fight, nor men too old for service, nor Levites, so a reasonable extrapolation for both censuses would be about three million Israelites. But is 600,000 itself either a reasonable, or an accurately transmitted, total?

The Less-Familiar Biblical Data

The points introduced here are but a sampling of the relevant data and conclusions on and around this issue. The sets of census numbers as they now appear in the biblical text are vastly outweighed, both in number and in significance, by biblical data sets that make the census numbers impossible as they stand. Yet both data sets are present in the current biblical texts. Our question will be: Can they be reconciled?

---

3. The priestly tribe of Levi is excluded from both censuses.

Exodus 13:17

"When Pharaoh let the people go, God did not lead them by way of the land of the Philistines, although that was nearer; for God thought, 'If the people face war, they may change their minds and return to Egypt.'"

Why would they do that? Egyptian sources refer to the Way of the Philistines as "The Way(s) of Horus"; it was the main military road from Egypt to Canaan. It ran east by northeast just off the Mediterranean coast of the northern Sinai Peninsula. During this period, Egypt claimed hegemony over Canaan and maintained a string of forts along this highway, spaced about a day's journey apart.

In the fifty years since the Six-Day War of 1968, significant archaeological investigation has been carried out along this most direct, most convenient, and most important route between Egypt and Canaan. Several of the Pharaonic fortress camps have been excavated, and others surveyed. The largest were designed and built to accommodate about four hundred troops each. Since they were fifteen to twenty miles apart, the Israelites, had God led them that way, would have come upon them one by one. Each time, then, the Israelite force of 600,000 would have invested a garrison of four hundred men. Even untested troops are not likely to run from a battle in which they outnumber their foe fifteen hundred to one. Yet, lest Israel falter and turn back from the Egyptian forces stationed along this military road, God led them another way.

Exodus 14:7

This verse should be translated, "[Pharaoh] took six hundred picked chariots, even all the chariots of Egypt with officers over all of them" (my translation).

"All the chariots" did not include those stationed in Upper Egypt, nor even every chariot in Lower Egypt. It simply means every chariot Pharaoh could mobilize quickly in the northeastern Nile Delta, where this narrative is set.

Six hundred chariots constituted a formidable force. Yet here, too, the Israelites would have had an insurmountable edge in forces-in-the-field. As nasty a fighting machine as the ancient chariot was against soldiers on foot, in this scenario each chariot would have faced one thousand Israelites. We may trust that Moses, a scion of Pharaoh's house, would have known how to deploy his overwhelming numbers so as to defeat even the best fighting machine of the day. Yet the appearance of Pharaoh and his six hundred chariots threw Israel into a panic.

Exodus 17:6

When Israel faced death from lack of water, God told Moses, "'I will be standing there in front of you on the rock at Horeb. Strike the rock, and water will come out of it, so that the people may drink.' Moses did so, in the sight of the elders of Israel."

At various locations in the southern Sinai Peninsula, underground streams run just behind thin layers of the granite hillside walls of sandy, gravelly canyon floors, a few feet above the surface of the ground. A sharp blow with a stout staff at the right point can shatter the granite and release the stream. This does happen. But enough water from one such opening to supply three million people and their livestock? To say nothing of the (impossible) length of the queue along the new river's bank, or of the (unreported) "miracle" that no one drowned in the sudden gush of such a volume of water released upon a gathered crowd unawares.

Exodus 17:8

"Then Amalek came and fought with Israel at Rephidim."

Amalek was a confederation of nomadic clans, ranging across much of the Sinai, and into the southwestern areas of what became known as Israel's Negev. We may think of them as one group of the ancient precursors of what more recently have been called the Bedouin tribes.[4]

From earliest times in this region, absent a strong central government, most pastoralists have been quite ready to attack any group traveling through their territory, if they thought victory certain and quick. When passing near unwalled towns, they did not hesitate to steal whatever (or whomever) they could carry off. Just as predictably, most were careful to avoid encounters with any they thought likely to put up a stout defense.

The total Bedouin population at the time of modern Israel's returning control of the Sinai to Egypt in the early 1980s was about 70,000 persons. Sinai's total population at the time of ancient Israel's exodus cannot have been greater than that, and not all would have been Amalekites. Moreover, not all Amalekites would have been close enough to participate in this surprise

---

4. In this period, Amalek did not have camels, but depended upon sheep and goats for their livelihood.

attack upon Israel. The Amalekites could not have numbered more than a few thousand men. If Israel fielded 600,000, they enjoyed at least a sixty-to-one advantage. No pastoral group in history would have picked a fight with so overwhelmingly superior a foe. They would have hidden as quickly as possible, or even moved out of the area until the threat had passed.

Exodus 23:29–30

Toward the end of the Covenant Code, referencing the promise to drive out the Canaanites, God said, "I will not drive them out from before you in one year, or the land would become desolate and the wild animals would multiply against you. Little by little I will drive them out from before you, until you have increased and possess the land."

The land area allotted to the several tribes of Israel on both sides of the Jordan River was about 6,000 square miles. If Israel's settlement generation numbered three million persons, their average density would have been five hundred persons per square mile. Could any district have experienced an increase in predatory animals sufficient to put many humans at risk?

Numbers 3:43

This verse deals with redeeming firstborns by God's selection of the tribe of Levi to serve the tabernacle and its offices. "The total enrollment, all the firstborn males from a month old and upward, counting the number of names, was twenty-two thousand two hundred seventy-three."

If we divide this number into the total number of fighting men, taken as 600,000, the ratio is about twenty-seven to one. Yet these are the total number of male firstborn of (essentially) all ages, while the warriors included only those twenty years old and above. Doubling the total number of males in Israel's population would not be an unreasonable move, then, but would Israel's firstborns each have had twenty-seven (or fifty) siblings?

Deuteronomy 7:7

Here, God called Israel "the fewest of all the peoples" (my translation).

Egypt then was the largest and most powerful of the Mediterranean/western Asian nations, with one to three million inhabitants. Israel's population cannot have equaled (or exceeded) Egypt's.

Some biblical references (e.g., Deut 7:1) note seven nations/people groups in Canaan that Israel would displace. The total of these nations, compiled from the several lists, is ten. I see no reason to reject Dever's recently published figure of 100,000 as Canaan's total population at this time.[5] Divided among ten people groups (a bit simplistic), they averaged ten thousand each. If Israel totaled three million persons, any assertion that they were "the fewest of all the peoples," even if intended rhetorically, would have been absurd.[6]

Joshua 6

God gave Joshua a unique stratagem for taking Jericho. The priests were to carry the ark of the covenant and lead Israel's troops in marching around the city in silence, once a day for six days. On the seventh day, all were to march around the city seven times.

We are not concerned here with the why of this approach, but in the logistics of the march. Ancient Jericho sat atop the ten-acre hillock now known as Tell es-Sultan, at the western edge of modern Jericho. If all Israel's troops were involved in this daily maneuver, as the text leads us to believe; if they traversed an oval path more or less parallel with Jericho's defensive walls; if their formation was roughly a rank-and-file resembling a many-spoked wheel; and if their numbers totaled 600,000, the outer "circle" of men would have marched/walked about thirty miles (48 km) each day, about twice the ordinary day's journey of an army on the move. On the seventh day, they would have covered about 210 miles (338 km). The narrative does not mention miraculous aid in these efforts.

Population is a factor here, also. Using Dever's estimate of one hundred persons per acre,[7] Jericho's ten acres had a normal population of about one thousand people. Possibly, we should double that, as some in Jericho's nearby, dependent unwalled villages would have sought refuge inside the city (others would have fled the vicinity). Even pressing every man and boy into service, Jericho could not have had more than seven or eight hundred defenders. Israel's army would have outnumbered them at least seven hundred fifty to one. In the face of such odds, what ancient king, unable to expect relief from his neighbors, would have committed

---

5. Dever, *Beyond the Texts*, 317–22.

6. I know of no one (except Mark Twain in his declining years) who accuses God of being an inept rhetorician. (Whether Deuteronomy is early or late is immaterial here.)

7. Dever, *Beyond the Texts*, 294, 297.

his people either to certain death or, somehow surviving a catastrophic defeat, to certain slavery?

"Extraordinary" Events: A Special Consideration

We touched on this point obliquely in considering the water from the rock at Rephidim (Exod 17:6). I am refraining here from using the word "miracle." To moderns, the terms "miracle" and "miraculous" refer to almost any purported appearance or act of God, and even many people of theistic faith have trouble believing events such as this one can or do happen. The ancient worldview and mindset held the opposite; everything existed, and every event happened, because of the direct will and action of God (or the gods).

The ancients did, however, distinguish between the everyday and the extraordinary, just as we do. One of the measures of a god or a goddess, and of Israel's Yahweh as against the pagan deities, was God's (or the god/dess's) extraordinary acts on behalf of God's (or their) adherents, and/or against opponents or nonbelievers. How these "extraordinary events" happened is beside the point here. Even if all of them are explainable in natural terms today, they still were regarded and recorded as Yahweh's extraordinary actions on Israel's behalf. Two examples will illustrate this point.

Example #1

If water had been needed for three million persons and their livestock at Rephidim, the author would have reported not only that Moses struck the rock at God's command, but also that God prevented anyone from dying due to the sudden unleashing of such a torrent through a single opening. The text does not report this.

Example #2

No ingenious arrangement of any queue could have allowed three million people to walk from one camp to the next during the daylight hours of a single day. Also, crossing the Red Sea and the Jordan River, and passing through several bottleneck points along the Sinai routes, would have required something like only ten persons per rank. At (an impossibly tight) two meters of ground per rank, and 300,000 ranks, the column would have been about 370 miles (595 km) long.[8] If this had been Israel's situation,

---

8. If they *had* taken the way of the Philistines, those in the lead would have reached

the relevant passages in Exodus and Numbers would have reported God's unusual measures for moving them all together from each place to the next. But they do not; the camp-to-camp journeys themselves were not "extraordinary" events.

Mendenhall's Solution

To this point, we have the two census lists of Numbers 1 and 26 recording a population for Israel's exodus/entry generations impossibly greater than other biblical evidence allows. No matter how one values, or does not value, the Bible, this presents an interesting conundrum in the text. Many have tried to defend/explain the census lists while ignoring the several dozen other biblical (and extrabiblical) statements, data, and implications that are falsified if the present texts of the census totals stand uncorrected. The usual defending-the-Bible motivation is not realized by this approach; rather, the problem is aggravated. A more reasonable approach is to accept the logic/demonstration of the many other data sets and investigate the transmission of the census lists. Of these approaches, we find Mendenhall's most credible.

In his definitive study, "The Census Lists of Numbers 1 and 26," Mendenhall set out two assertions he said everyone agrees on. First, *in the census lists* the Hebrew word *'elef* does not mean "thousand," as the Hebrew text itself traditionally has understood it, and as virtually all translations have rendered it. Rather, *'elef* refers to "some subsection of a tribe." Second, the numbers as they stand "are impossible." He demonstrates that *'elef* in these lists means something like "squad," or "platoon." For example, rather than reading Reuben's total (Num 1:21) as 46,500 men, we should read forty-six "units" (squads/platoons) totaling 500 men. Simeon (1:23) had, not 59,300 men, but fifty-nine "units" totaling 300 men. And so on.[9]

Mendenhall concluded that these squads or platoons averaged from five to fourteen men each. Moreover, one or more squads constituted the men "recruited" from each family or from several families of a given clan. After Israel was mostly settled, these would constitute the contingents from each town, considering that most towns comprised families or groups of related families, i.e., clans. Two or three unwalled hamlets may have banded together to provide one or two squads when called upon. Based on his considerable evidence and this line of reasoning, and by a process of simple addition, Mendenhall arrived at a total of 598 units/squads/platoons in the

---

southern Canaan before the end of the column left Goshen.

9. Mendenhall, "Census Lists," 60–62.

list of Numbers 1, totaling 5,550 men for all Israel. The figures of Numbers 26 are only slightly different, 596 units totaling 5,750 men.[10]

Mendenhall's approach in solving the census list problem is sound, but he then proceeded to assign these lists to the time of Gideon. What about these numbers makes them "reasonable" for Gideon the judge, but "unreasonable" for Moses the deliverer? I respect Mendenhall too much to accuse *him* of this, but the figure of Moses as legendary founder lost too deeply in the midst of antiquity to say anything about him is based too often on a kind of circular reasoning: The numbers are impossible; therefore, Moses could not have existed. But Mendenhall's solution shows precisely the opposite: *read correctly*, the population numbers of the two census lists do allow for a reasonable Exodus scenario, logistics and all.

I see no reason to reject the repeated assertions of the text, *read correctly*, that 5,550 is the total of all the men of all the tribes (except for Levi) who were eligible and fit for military service. The formula for every tribe in the list of Numbers 1 is identical, or nearly so, with that of Reuben, "their lineage, in their clans, by their ancestral houses, according to the number of names, individually, every male from twenty years old and upward, everyone able to go to war" (1:20). Such a specific piling-up of this type of phrasing surely was not intended to give the impression that only one-tenth to one-third of all eligible men were included in this census. Given (as Mendenhall reminds us) that census-taking was a well-known, regular practice in the ancient Near East, and given the situation at Sinai as Israel prepared to leave for the land God had promised, it is only reasonable that any census would have included all eligible men, per standard practice across the Near Eastern world during these periods.

Other considerations strengthen this conclusion; we only can mention them here. Various Egyptian records concerning pastoralists allowed into Egypt have been available for a long time, now. Rainey has established a connection between the *Shasu* of several Eighteenth Dynasty Egyptian inscriptions and the Hebrews.[11] The Austrian surveys and excavations in the northeast Nile Delta seem to have confirmed Israel's presence there; Hoffmeier has marshaled this and other evidence.[12] Putting it all together, we can say with confidence that reasonable objections to the plausibility of the exodus and entry narratives do not exist. What is correctly regarded as impossible for three million persons becomes entirely plausible for twenty-five thousand.

10. Mendenhall, "Census Lists," 62.
11. Rainey and Notley, *Sacred Bridge*, 103.
12. Hoffmeier, *Ancient Israel in Sinai*, 54, 243.

Joshua's "Conquest" of Canaan

Though they also require consideration of other vital historical and theological issues, the questions surrounding the accounts in Joshua and Judges of Israel's entry into and settlement of Canaan are bound, *a priori* and inseparably, to our question of Israel's population. Just as with those figures, many commentators seem either to misread or to ignore the pertinent evidence in the same ways. This leads, on the one hand, to the claim that Joshua and Judges contradict each other; we cannot view either as "historical," even in the limited ancient scope of that term. Too often, the response is "Can, too!" without any serious attempt at making a solid case that these books are complementary, not contradictory.

Both Joshua and Judges are clear about what Israel did, and did not, accomplish under Joshua in entering Canaan. Both also are clear, though not chronologically precise, about how quickly (or slowly) several tribes controlled their allotted territories. Moreover, in Joshua and Judges the narratives do not require the modern discovery of a forgotten nominal meaning of one Hebrew word, as Mendenhall did for *'elef*. We need only pay attention, read correctly what these narratives intend, and slide over nothing (of course, this is easier said than done).

The Reality of Joshua's Military Actions

Joshua had to take Jericho and Ai (Josh 6, 8). These two towns blocked Israel's access to the Highlands; bypassing them, leaving a constant military presence at Israel's back, was not an option. Frightened by Israel's initial successes, the four Gibeonite towns, in the heart of the southern Highlands, tricked Israel into accepting them as vassals (Josh 9). The king of Jerusalem, their erstwhile overlord, could not let this stand, and summoned his allies to help him reconquer his faithless vassals (Josh 10).

Joshua, now under treaty obligation to defend the Gibeonite towns, mounted a night advance from Gilgal to Gibeon. Israel's army attacked the Canaanites at dawn from the east, driving them from their siege of Gibeon. In the follow-up campaign in the south, Israel defeated the forces of seven other Canaanite cities in the Highlands and the Shephelah, effectively ending Canaanite resistance to Israel in the southern Highlands. It is important to note that Joshua did not destroy (burn) any of these cities.

A northern coalition mustered to fight Joshua, led by the king of Hazor, suzerain of most of the cities and districts of the Jezreel and the Galilee (Josh 11). Joshua's defeat of this northern coalition secured the same result as in the south. No Canaanite force now could stand against Israel, nor prevent the beginnings of Israelite settlement in the Highlands.

Joshua 10–11 are almost universally misunderstood as reporting wholesale genocide carried out upon Canaanite towns one by one, as Israel took them in battle. Joshua 12 often is read as confirmation, but it is not. Rather, Joshua 12 is eulogistic, a somber poetic listing of the thirty-one Canaanite kings, responsible for their cities' and people's safety, who put their faith in the wrong deities, and paid the ultimate price for their common mistake.

Beyond this somber testimony, Younger has shown that the statements in Joshua 10–11 which seem, on their face, to be clear reports of genocidal slaughter are, in fact, no such thing. They are stock phrases, of a piece with a multitude of such expressions, from a variety of genres of campaign accounts, from the late second millennium to the early first millennium, from Egyptian, Hittite, and Assyrian sources.[13] Read as intended across this spectrum, including these reports of Joshua's two Canaanite campaigns, they are simply proclamations of complete and emphatic victories on the battlefield. For Joshua and Israel, these routine expressions (syntagms) meant neither more nor less than, "(With God's help) we have thoroughly defeated both the Canaanite coalition armies that came against us. Serious opposition to Israel's settlement of the Highlands, as God instructed us, is no longer possible."[14] For thirty years now—more especially, going forward—readings of Joshua 10–11 that disregard this Ancient Near Eastern (ANE) origin and *sitz im leben* of these stock syntagmic phrasings cannot be regarded as serious readings.

The Meaning of *Haram*

Deuteronomy 7:2 records God's instruction (through Moses) that when God had given Israel victory over the peoples of Canaan, they were to enact *haram*; NRSV is representative of most translations, "You must utterly destroy them." Verses 2b–3, however, define what *haram* was to mean with respect to the people themselves, "Do not make ('cut') a covenant with them, and do not act graciously toward them. Do not intermarry with them; do not give your [sing.] daughter to his son, and his daughter do not take for your [sing.] son" (my translation). The intimacy of intermarriage, uniting families, emphasized here by the singular possessive pronouns, defines

---

13. Younger, *Ancient Conquest Accounts*, esp. 197–232.

14. This is my paraphrasing summary of the collective meaning of the syntagms of Joshua 10–11.

what it would have meant (eventually did mean) to "act graciously" toward them. This is not instruction to kill, once the inevitable fatalities of battle have ceased. It is a proscription against the admission of non-Yahwists into the Israelite family.

Verse 5 completes the definition of *haram*. Israel was to destroy, not the people, but the apparatus of Canaanite worship, largely directed toward Baal and Asherah, the central god and goddess of fertility. "Their altars you shall break down, and their standing-stone pillars you shall shatter, and their Asherah-poles you shall hew down, and their idol-images you shall burn with fire" (my translation). These are not humans, but places, structures, and objects consigned to physical destruction. This instruction (vv. 2–3, 5) is the *definition* of what God wanted Israel to do to accomplish *haram*, and it contains not even a hint that killing people is part of it.

Tribal Allotments and the Beginnings of Settlement

Joshua 13–21 is the record of assigning tribal allotments, including the special arrangements for Levi, the priestly tribe. These chapters report almost nothing but the bare records of these allotments; "settlement" details are conspicuous by their absence. Joshua 22–24 records three successive farewells. Several passages emphasize that much of the land was yet to be possessed (e.g., Josh 13:1–7; 23:4–5).

Judges 1:27–35 lists towns and districts that six of the twelve tribes were not able to secure initially, vivid confirmation that Israel's initial settlement success was limited to the Highlands. Israelite expansion, with concomitant absorption of most Canaanites, came later.

The archaeology of the Late Bronze/Early Iron Ages does not contradict this understanding. Most Canaanite towns, whether mentioned in Joshua, the various extrabiblical sources, both, or neither, were not deep in the Hill Country, but along its periphery or in the adjacent geographical districts. Moreover, archaeological surveys across most of the Galilean, Judean, and Samaritan highland districts over the past half-century attest a significant increase in the number of small towns and villages during Iron Age I, most of them on previously unsettled sites.

Understood as intended, Joshua and Judges *together* present a plausible scenario, Israel's gradual infilling of the largely empty Highland countryside. As Israel "became strong" (Judg 1:28), they absorbed the Canaanites. By Solomon's time most of his subjects, whatever their ancestry, would have self-identified as "Israelite." Whether this was "good" or "bad," from the perspective of Israel's un/faithfulness to Yahweh, is another question, but it did happen.

God's Faithfulness

We are asserting the veracity of two important biblical narratives: 1) God rescued from Egypt and brought into Canaan a people, Israel, whom *God* characterized as "the fewest of all the peoples" (Deut 7:7)—as it turns out, a people numbering only about 25,000 persons; 2) Israel did not commit genocide upon the Canaanite peoples, but established themselves first in the virtually empty Highlands, then spread out from there, through the archaeological periods, Iron Age I and Iron Age II. How may this enrich our understanding of God's faithfulness?

The Text

An important satisfaction in clarifying these issues—and this really is apropos of strengthening our confidence in God's faithfulness—is the simple fact of establishing a more accurate reading of the biblical text. Even at this late date, the Hebrew, Aramaic, and Greek texts retain numbers of uncertain readings, and many more unclear readings (these are not the same thing). Establishing the greatest possible accuracy, reliability, and clarity of the text always is good; it should be one goal of all scholarly study in and of the Bible.

Our Skeptical Age

In recent decades even many conservative and/or evangelical Christians have come to doubt that a people called Israel really inhabited the latter half of the second millennium, that God brought them out of Egypt into Canaan, that people named Moses and Miriam, Joshua and Rahab, Ruth and Boaz, David and Bathsheba and their son Solomon, are more than invented fictions tucked into the dim recesses of time to give the later Jewish nation the epic past every people needs. The reasons for this doubt are not far to seek. There are many, of course, but the two we have addressed are the most in-your-face for many moderns looking for a reasonable faith in the God whose revelation to us begins between the covers of the Bible—after all, we ourselves could not be present for these events. Three million Exodus Israelites are an obstacle; 25,000 are not. A God-commanded genocide is a moral repugnance to most—so it is to God; also, it is not in the biblical text.[15] We may dismiss that slander against God's character.

Archaeological and historical/geographical lines of evidence bolster the plausibility of the biblical narratives' assertions that Israel lived for a time under oppressive conditions in Egypt's northeastern Nile Delta district. Of course, "plausibility" is not proof, but it does confirm the necessary circumstances and possibilities. Given that God exists and intends a redemptive *telos* for this earth, the believer violates no historical or theological canons of reason in accepting that Israel left Egypt under unusual conditions, as "extraordinary events" broke Pharaoh's will to continue detaining them. Whether by employing natural processes, or by setting them aside, God acted faithfully, fulfilling the ancestral promises and delivering Israel.

Denying this "God hypothesis" obliges one either to ignore strong evidence on many fronts, or to build some other construct to account for a real Israel leaving a real sojourn in Egypt's Goshen, and turning up two generations later in Canaan's Highlands.[16] Alternative hypotheses are not scarce, but each is both inaccurate at critical junctures and insufficiently comprehensive of all the data. A current example is instructive.

The Case of William Dever

Dever is one of the best-known, best-respected archaeologists the United States has produced. In 2017, calling it his "magnum opus," he published *Beyond the Texts: An Archaeological Portrait of Ancient Israel and Judah*.[17] This work will be important for Near Eastern archaeology and for biblical studies for several decades.

Dever's data is well-chosen, comprehensive, pertinent, and almost uniformly accurate. His erudition is on display; his conclusions are in most respects sound. However, he consistently dismisses out-of-hand any

---

15. The same principles of understanding hold for Deuteronomy 20 and 1 Samuel 15. Israel could make peace with faraway cities, but was not to make peace with nearby (Canaanite) cities. Rather, Israel was to conquer them, as their own settlement process went on, and eliminate their capacity to throw off Israelite rule and/or to subvert Israel's faith in Yahweh (Deut 20). The same was true for Saul's campaign against Amalek (1 Sam 15); the syntagmic formulations expressed a well-known hyperbole across the entire ANE—not genocide, but military subjugation, as treatments of substantial numbers of survivors further along in many of the narrative (and other) reports substantiate (e.g., the further notice of Amalek in 2 Sam 8:12).

16. History and archaeology certify the plausibility of the timeframe.

17. Dever, *Beyond the Texts*, xii.

possibility that the Pentateuch or Joshua could reflect anything resembling historical reality. Two examples must suffice.

First, Dever certainly will have read Mendenhall and understands that the biblical texts claim a population for Israel's Exodus generation of about 25,000, not three million. Yet he avoids acknowledging this evidence even exists, and ridicules all of Exodus–Joshua as fictional, with a dismissive gibe calling it "an epic tale of thousands and thousands."[18]

Second, Dever dismisses, extensively but (it seems to me) cavalierly, any Israelite Exodus from Egypt or entry into Canaan, because the narratives are fiction produced much later. Yet he suggests perhaps an "Exodus group" *was* part of the "motley crew" that brought about "agrarian reform" in the Highlands[19]—just at the time Joshua situates Israel's entry to initiate *God's* program of agrarian reform outlined in the Pentateuchal legislation.

Agrarian Reform

Dever's "agrarian reform" as the real story of Iron Age I in the Highlands is spot on. This is part of why I consider *Beyond the Texts* a very important work, and why we have spent time with him here, even while wondering why he resists so adamantly the (first) and biblical version of this very phenomenon, which his own archaeology so strongly affirms. To understand God's agenda of agrarian reform for Israel as an expression of God's faithfulness, however, we take a step back to look at the bigger picture.

In most of ancient Israel's world, politically and theologically there was only one "man" in every kingdom—the king. Any other man was only "the *king's* man." But God created humans as *God's* women and men, in and for equality, for mostly egalitarian relationships of mutual benefit and *shalom*, and God intended Israel as a fresh start on God's creation intentions. Israel defaulted eventually, of course, but the Pentateuchal instruction had that model in mind, and it did succeed by fits and starts, here and there, during the period of Israel's settlement of the Central Highlands. For a brief period, Israel lived as God intended, showing her Canaanite neighbors, at least, a better way than the palace/temple monopolies that had enslaved and impoverished them or their ancestors, to the advantage of the "noble" and priestly few.

We do not have space here to detail the evidence for this agrarian reform in the Highlands of Canaan; Dever has done it better than we could, anyway. But, make no mistake, this incipient recreation, this early hint of

18. Dever, *Beyond the Texts*, 121.
19. Dever, *Beyond the Texts*, 226, 233.

eschatological *shalom*, was not a historical fluke or anomaly. It was God's gift to Israel, though they could not keep it.

The Faithfulness of God's People

God's faithfulness to early Israel was not solely for their benefit; God also had a longer-range purpose in view. Israel was an experiment, if you will, a new beginning not seen since Eden. In anthropological techno-speak, Israel was to be a non-hierarchical agrarian subsistence economy and culture, with God-given and God-guaranteed *shalom*, "each man [family] under his own vine and his own fig tree" (1 Kgs 4:25, *my translation*). This is strange language to many today, but it was a new beginning, appropriate for the western Asia of ancient Israel. It was not what the world will look like when God's eschatological purposes are fully accomplished, but it was a start.

John Wesley did not speak in terms of Israel's "agrarian reform." He understood, though, that not only "religion," but also all the social, economic, and political systems of eighteenth-century England, needed the beckoning vision of this eschatological *shalom*. Our faithfulness, as followers of Jesus through Wesley, will consist partly in pondering, designing, and implementing what such beginnings of eschatological *shalom* could look like in our twenty-first-century world.

This may seem strange as an aspect of God's people witnessing faithfulness in and to our own age, but I think it is a valid understanding and response. Another important reason for my interest in data- and detail-heavy investigations such as I have summarized here is what I see as the accelerating growth of the "factual desert" within our own cultural landscape.

To use another metaphor, with the rise of modernity and the benefits of a widespread general education in the West, previous generations could take for granted the existence of a pool of common cultural knowledge. Many individuals, even those with only rudimentary schooling, could access it with ease. But today this pool of common knowledge is drying up, and the rate of its "evaporation" is accelerating.

Employing yet another metaphor, Strawn documents this, suggesting potential remedies, in his recent incisive work, *The Old Testament Is Dying*. My point here is that the multiplied *impacts* of the historical and theological distortions generated by this growing ignorance of our cultural heritage now seem to multiply their *importance* almost exponentially. This is a detriment to Christian growth in faith, and a hindrance/stumbling-block in the path of many who may want to consider the possibility that God exists, who even may wish to ponder the amazing claim that God desires personal relationships with humans in a divine-human community. Correcting two of our most egregious errors in Old Testament understanding could be a good place to begin addressing this problem. Moreover, such work is great fun, and deeply satisfying. Yahweh *is* the God of unfailing lovingkindness (*hesed veʾemet*).

Bibliography

Dever, William G. *Beyond the Texts: An Archaeological Portrait of Ancient Israel and Judah*. Atlanta: SBL, 2017.
Hoffmeier, James K. *Ancient Israel in Sinai: The Evidence for the Authenticity of the Wilderness Tradition*. New York: Oxford University Press, 2005.
Mendenhall, George E. "The Census Lists of Numbers 1 and 26." *Journal of Biblical Literature* 77 (1958) 52–66.
Rainey, Anson F., and R. Steven Notley. *The Sacred Bridge: Carta's Atlas of the Biblical World*. Jerusalem: Carta, 2006.
Strawn, Brent A. *The Old Testament Is Dying: A Diagnosis and Recommended Treatment*. Grand Rapids: Baker Academic, 2017.
Younger, K. Lawson. *Ancient Conquest Accounts: A Study in Ancient Near Eastern and Biblical History Writing*. Sheffield: JSOT, 1990.

2

Faithful Teaching

Jesus, the Model Teacher[1]

—KENT BROWER

Jesus was a teacher. Not only is he regularly addressed as such, the content of three of the Gospels centers around his teaching. It is also arguable that the earliest material that circulated in the early church, perhaps in written form, was a collection of Jesus's teaching used by Matthew and Luke in the composition of their Gospels.[2] At least one extrabiblical document, the Gospel of Thomas, contains logia, some of which are not paralleled in the canonical Gospels and others which are manifestly secondary developments of this canonical tradition. The Jewish historian, Flavius Josephus, calls Jesus "a wise man who performed surprising works, a teacher of men who gladly welcome strange things," a not unambiguously favorable estimate of Jesus.[3] The unanimous testimony of the extant ancient sources, biblical and non-biblical, literary and historical, bear witness to the fact that Jesus was a teacher.

This, in itself, is a rather unremarkable, even banal, statement. Although the Gospels agree that Jesus is a teacher, they do not consider this to be his ultimate and highest designation. In fact, Jesus as teacher is often placed on the lips of Jesus's opponents, reflecting either sarcasm or a

---

1. David McEwan has been a faithful teacher for decades. His commitment to the kingdom of God, shown in his integrity, commitment to excellence, pastoral concern for his students, and earthing of his teaching in the inclusive life of a local church, are all modeled on the ministry and mission of the master teacher, Jesus. This brief offering is a humble recognition of David's faithfulness in ministering in NTC-Brisbane. But it is also to someone who I am delighted to call a friend. David's faithfulness in service even in challenging circumstances has blessed many.

2. The "Q" Hypothesis has been severely challenged by many recent NT scholars. See Goodacre, *Case Against Q*.

3. Bruce, *Jesus and Christian Origins*, 39. See Van Voorst, "Josephus," 509–11.

reductionist identity, supremely seen in the greeting of the betrayer to Jesus (Matt 26:49; Mark 14:45).

This short study will begin with brief remarks on Jesus as teacher in Matthew, Luke and John, before considering three themes in Mark. The study is neither exhaustive nor comprehensive. Rather, the three themes identified are aspects of Jesus's activity as teacher that might be important for faithful Jesus followers.

Matthew

Of the gospels, Matthew probably makes the most stylized use of Jesus's teaching, organizing it into five major blocks, the most familiar being the Sermon on the Mount. Precisely why the teaching is so collected in Matthew is unclear. Some have suggested that the teaching material points to a new Torah with Jesus being a new Moses.[4] The author is undoubtedly aware of the expectation of a prophet like Moses to come before the rescue of Israel. But this is not the controlling interpretative model for Matthew.

Matthew thinks Jesus's teaching is authoritative, seen clearly in the antitheses of Matthew 5. But rather than a new Moses, Jesus's authority is based on the identity already established in the prequel to the Sermon including the birth, baptism, and temptation narratives as well as the mission summarized in Matthew 4:23 as teaching, preaching and healing. According to W. D. Davies, in Matthew's view, Jesus is not Moses come as Messiah, so much as Messiah, Son of Man, and, supremely, as Emmanuel, God with us, "who has absorbed the Mosaic function"[5] just like he has absorbed the function of other OT images that prefigure Jesus's divine-human identity.[6]

The pronouncements that Jesus makes in the Sermon and throughout Matthew cannot be isolated from the identity of Jesus already established by Matthew.[7] Jesus addresses the Torah in a thoroughly Jewish fashion but is not introducing a new, more rigorous Torah or even a more rigid halakhah, despite the challenging statement, "unless your righteousness exceeds that of the scribes and Pharisees, you will never enter the kingdom of heaven" (Matt 5:20).[8] As Snow notes, "It is unlikely that Jesus advocates a more rigorous obedience to the legal demands of the Mosaic law than the Pharisees

---

4. See Allison, *New Moses*.
5. Davies, *Setting*, 93. See Snow and Ermakov, *Matthew*.
6. See Hays, *Reading Backwards*.
7. See Kupp, *Matthew's Emmanuel*.
8. See Guelich, *Sermon*, who argues that Jesus came to bring a new covenant not a new law.

practiced. Jesus envisages a righteousness that transforms the heart and mind, a radical righteousness, that gives rise to righteous behaviors which he describes in verses 21–47."[9]

Luke

Luke's focus is on Jesus as the proclaimer and bringer of salvation with texts linking salvation to justice (see Luke 1:77; 2:30; 3:6; 19:9). Right from the outset of his ministry, Jesus's sermon in the synagogue at Nazareth (Luke 4:16–30) announces the good news of the great reversal that is coming (see also Luke 6:17–26). In this initial sermon, Jesus is shown as citing an OT passage which, he claims, is fulfilled in his own mission and purpose, but the notion of God's justice runs deep through Scripture and is embedded in the Lukan Jesus's teaching and activity. While Jesus acts as a typical teacher in the synagogue at Nazareth, expounding Scriptures in a haggadic fashion, even here Luke shows little specific interest in the fact of Jesus as teacher. The point of the incident is different: Jesus himself is the eschatological bearer of God's promised salvation—the proclaimer and enactor of the good news of the kingdom.

Of the four Gospels, he gives the least attention to Jesus as teacher. This does not mean, however, that Luke does not know Jesus as teacher or does not use the teachings of Jesus. On the contrary, Luke includes a great deal of Jesus's teaching, some of which is found only in this Gospel. Luke uses parables specifically in Jesus's engagement with the Pharisees, most notably in chapters 16 and 17. Like Matthew's usage, Luke uses the teaching to advance a specific facet of Jesus's mission and person. But except for the Sermon on the Plain (Luke 6:7–49), Luke does not consciously present Jesus as a teacher who promulgates systematic teaching to his followers.

Jesus welcomes the outcasts and transforms those who follow him into participants in the mission of God. Much to the chagrin of the Pharisees, he dines indiscriminately, but purposefully, with "the righteous" and "the sinners."[10] Jesus explicitly states that "I have come to call not the righteous but sinners to repentance" (Luke 5:32). Jesus does, however, devote significant attention to the question of wealth and the great reversal (see Luke 1:53; 8:14; 12:21; 18:22–24). The possession of wealth is a severe hindrance to following Jesus. He has some strong words for the rich (see Luke 6:25–27), yet not without hope.

---

9. Snow and Ermakov, *Matthew*, 98.

10. See Thompson, "Gathered at the Table," 76–94. See also Mullen, *Dining with Pharisees*, and Blomberg, *Contagious Holiness*.

Jesus answers the question of the rich, "What must I do to be saved?," through negative and positive exemplary stories (see Luke 14:6–24; 19:2–10) of how they are to use wealth in bringing good news to the poor.[11] The rich man in Luke 18:22–24 epitomizes the hold of wealth. But this is not hopeless either. The pariah Zacchaeus responds to Jesus's call to deal with his wealth, and Jesus announces, "Today salvation has come to this house, because he too is a son of Abraham. For the Son of Man came to seek out and to save the lost" (Luke 19:9–10). In sum, participation of the rich in the people of God and their feasting at the Messianic banquet depends on how they participate in enacting the good news to the poor through compassion and justice.[12] The poor have the good news proclaimed to them, but there is salvation even for the rich.

John

As is well-known, the picture of Jesus as teacher in the Fourth Gospel is different. The synoptic Jesus speaks in sayings, parables, and short comments; the Johannine Jesus speaks in lengthy discourses. John devotes a significant portion of his Gospel to Jesus as a teacher. The teaching is particularly concentrated in the setting of the Upper Room, directed specifically to the disciples. The richness of this section cries out for attention, but this short comment will focus on the question of truth.

John rarely presents Jesus as teaching truth in terms of factual knowledge. Nor is it an abstract concept. The ironic question of Pilate, "What is truth?" (John 18:38), asked in a philosophical fashion, is answered eloquently, not in words, but in the dramatic deeds of the passion. Even his prolonged dispute with "the Jews"[13] in John 8, which at first glance might seem to be a factual debate, is about the interpretation of the Torah. This is not a theoretical hermeneutical discussion but seeks to uncover the direction and purposes of God. Jesus is the one who interprets the text and proclaims the liberating

11. See Wi, *Path*.
12. See Wi, *Path*, 154–73.
13. The dispute between Jesus and his opponents in John is fierce and strident. Modern readers find the language challenging, at the very least. But John's use of "the Jews" to describe Jesus's opponents must be firmly earthed in the fact that this is an intra-Jewish dispute: Jesus and all of his initial followers were Jews who were followers of the Jewish Messiah. Andrew Lincoln sees this as a type of courtroom drama. Lincoln reminds us that "Despite the horrendous misuse of the passage in the Gospel's later reception, in the Gospel itself it has nothing to do with anti-Semitism. . . . Loose characterization of the language of John 8 as the polemics of hatred and as inducing violence miss the point." Lincoln, *John*, 73. Anti-Semitism in any and all of its forms, including those purportedly based on Scripture, is to be utterly rejected.

truth for those known to him. "Knowledge of God through Jesus, therefore, becomes the criterion by which previous knowledge of God through the Mosaic law is to be judged and not vice versa."[14]

For John, Jesus is the Word made flesh (John 1:14), God becoming human and living as a human in our midst.[15] Jesus, the incarnate one, is full of grace and truth (John 1:14), the characteristic of Yahweh set out in Exodus 34:6—"abounding in steadfast love and faithfulness."[16] Jesus himself is the embodiment of who God is (John 14:6). Thus, truth is not teaching about God transmitted by Jesus but "is God's very reality revealing itself—occurring!—in Jesus."[17] Instead of teaching eternal truths about God in a Greek fashion, Jesus claims that "he who has seen me has seen the Father" (John 14:8).

Jesus thus states that his very being and mission is the Truth. To know the truth, then, in John's terms, is not an acquisition of intellectual knowledge but being totally and finally related to the one who is the Truth as a follower. But John goes even further: the intimate relationship between the Father and Son is a relationship into which the followers of Jesus are invited (John 17:21–23). This is participation in the missional being of the Triune God (John 20:21–23). Thus, the ministry of the Holy Spirit is not one of leading us into all-intellectual truth (John 16:13). Instead, the Spirit leads us into an ongoing and continuing relationship with he who is the Truth so that we might be participants in the *missio dei*.[18] This participation comes about because the Johannine Jesus invites his followers into the mutuality of the hospitable Triune God. Followers of the Johannine Jesus, thus, are to embody and participate in the life of the Triune God and, therefore, display to the world the one who is the Way, the Truth, and the Life. As Andy Johnson notes, "participation in the life of the Father and the Son entails experiencing their mutual love for each other that spills over into their love for those who believe 'into' Jesus."[19] It is this love that

---

14. Lincoln, *John*, 75.

15. See Lincoln, *John*, 75.

16. See Lincoln, *John*, 105–6.

17. Bultmann, *Theology*, 19.

18. Gorman, *Abide and Go*, 74. Gorman writes, "Thus we have a missional, mutually indwelling God who is forming a missional people who will be in a mutually indwelling relationship with that God. This is the fundamental missional theology and spirituality of the Fourth Gospel, and the two aspects (theology and spirituality) are inseparable in John. Accordingly, for John, there is also no spirituality without mission, and no mission without spirituality; that is, *there is no participation in God without mission, and no mission without participation in God*. If we use the language of theosis, then we must say that theosis is inherently missional" (emphasis his).

19. Johnson, *Holiness and the Missio Dei*, 91.

enables the mission of God to be carried out by Jesus's followers: "'Peace be with you. As the Father has sent me, so I send you.' When he had said this, he breathed on them and said to them, 'Receive the Holy Spirit. If you forgive the sins of any, they are forgiven them; if you retain the sins of any, they are retained'" (John 20:21–23).

Mark

When we come to the Gospel of Mark,[20] a curious phenomenon confronts us. On the one hand, Mark more than any other Gospel uses the title of "teacher" to describe Jesus. About twenty occurrences of "teacher" or references to teaching in Mark are not paralleled in the other Gospels. On the other hand, Mark has comparatively fewer actual teachings from Jesus, confining it to specific portions of the Gospel and leaving readers to surmise the precise words and content. The teaching *activity* of Jesus is important. Mark challenges readers, then and now, to reflect on Jesus as exemplar of faithful teaching who calls disciples to follow the master teacher. Mark's view of Jesus is often developed in a unique fashion through its narrative structure.[21] It starts with Mark's portrayal of Jesus's identity and his consequent authority.

The Authoritative Teacher

"He taught them as one having authority, and not as the scribes" (Mark 1:22).

How can this be? Mark's initial reference to Jesus as teacher occurs at the end of a series of vignettes presented in the programmatic chapter one. Here Mark establishes the identity of Jesus, which is the foundation for his authoritative action/teaching mission. In turn, the fulfilment of the mission depends upon the authority of Jesus.

Mark sets this mission up through his introductory statements: "this is the good news of Jesus Messiah, Son of God" (Mark 1:1), a clear notice for readers that encapsulates the entirety of the story that is about to unfold. Once this summary statement is finished, Mark earths the story firmly in the soil of the Isaianic hope of the new thing that God has promised to do.[22] Here we

20. Portions of the following discussion are indebted to Brower, *Mark*.

21. The genre of Mark is not unique—his writing fits into the category of ancient bios, even if there are unique features. See Burridge, *What are the Gospels?* See also Bauckham, *Gospel for All Christians*.

22. The importance of Isaiah to Mark is explored by Watts, *New Exodus*. See also

have clear return-from-exile language placed on the lips of the Baptist, whom Mark pictures as the restorer of all things, echoing the hopes of Malachi that fueled the popular imagination of Elijah *redivivus* (see Mal 3:1; 4:5–6; Mark 9:11–12).[23] In Mark's view, this new return from exile is indeed what is happening when "people from the whole Judean countryside and all the people of Jerusalem were going out to him, and were baptized by him in the river Jordan, confessing their sins" (Mark 1:5). "John's call is an invitation for the people to prepare themselves as a purified people ready for the coming of God and his reign and to participate in God's mission through Jesus Messiah, Son of God."[24] John's ministry is preparatory, in Mark's view, and is in fulfillment of the hope for this new day when Israel will "repent of its sins" and return to its corporate identity as God's holy people (see Exod 19:5–6).

The baptism of Jesus adds further strands to the identity of Jesus. He undergoes the same baptism of repentance as his fellow Jews. They are coming to be prepared for the mission. Modern squeamishness about the linking of this with any personal sinfulness seems not to have affected Mark. Rather, this is Jesus's full identification with the still-in-exile-but-ready-to-return people of God. Mark implies what Hebrews explicitly states: "he had to become like his brothers and sisters in every respect" (Heb 2:17). He is participating in their turning back to God's way and inaugurating his leading of them through the wilderness into renewal of their calling as a kingdom of priests and a holy nation.

But it is the descent of the Spirit and the Voice from heaven which are the crucial events in this episode.[25] As Jesus ascends from the water, he sees the rending of the heavens (εἶδεν σχιζομένους τοὺς οὐρανούς), a response to the plea of Isaiah 64:1. The identity of Jesus—the Son—is confirmed by the Voice; the descent of the empowering Spirit upon the Son, together with the Voice, inaugurates this incarnational and trinitarian mission. The echoes of both Psalm 2:7 and Isaiah 42:1 combined with Genesis 22:2 simply enhance the richness of this vignette.[26]

The Voice is for Jesus—"You are [σὺ εἶ] my Son, the Beloved; with you [ἐν σοὶ] I am well pleased" (Mark 1:11). Readers already know his identity from the opening and are privileged to hear the Voice. Other participants in the story gradually come to this identification. But his confirmation[27]

Hatina, *Scripture in Mark's Narrative*.

23. See Brower, "Elijah," 85–101.
24. Brower, *Mark*, 53.
25. See Brower, "Hearing Voices," forthcoming.
26. See Marshall, "Son of God or Servant of Yahweh?," 121–33.
27. Mark would find the view that this is when the human Jesus is somehow made

of identity forms the foundation for the inaugural teaching of Jesus. After Satan tests this identity, Jesus comes into Galilee announcing that "the time is fulfilled, and the kingdom of God has come near; repent, and believe in the good news" (Mark 1:15). It is Jesus's consciousness of his authority as the Servant of Yahweh and the beloved Son of God that enables him to make the bold and startling proclamation that God's rule is arriving and, implicitly, that he is the harbinger and instrument of this rule.

The next vignette is the call of four fishers, who respond to Jesus's terse call—no hint of what he said. The sequence is important: the mission of God which Jesus has just announced is for the people of God. Jesus is now accompanied by his disciples as he enters a synagogue in Capernaum. Mark shapes this episode by "bracketing." This literary tool enables two parts of a story to be mutually enhanced. Thus, Mark begins and ends with an emphasis on Jesus's authoritative teaching (Mark 1:21–22, 27–28). Into this story he inserts the exorcism of an unclean spirit (1:23–26).

Now with disciples, Mark has Jesus in the synagogue, teaching with authority (κατ' ἐξουσίαν—Mark 1: 22) based upon the fact that he is Spirit-possessed beloved Son (Mark 1:10–11). Like the people later in the story, the disciples are "amazed at his teaching" (see Mark 6:2; 7:37; 11:18). Mark does not tell us the content of his teaching, only its character, "as one who had authority." But a reasonable assumption is that he continues to proclaim the good news of the kingdom.

Interestingly enough, Mark does not seem to think of "proclamation" (κηρύσσω) as identical to teaching (διδάσκω). The disciples are able to proclaim the kingdom of God, but they do not graduate into teachers within the Markan narrative, gathering their own disciples.[28] There is only one authoritative, master teacher.[29] The "teachers of the law," who studied and interpreted Torah and gathered pupils, likely cited tradition to reach their conclusions, rather than offering fresh insight.[30] Jesus's teaching, however, unpacked the significance of his announcement that the good news of God's

---

into Son of God to be confusing and inadequate.

28. In Matthew, the risen Jesus sends his followers into the world to make disciples and to teach them (Matt 28:16). But they are to make disciples of Jesus, not of themselves.

29. See Mark 9:38–40, where Mark inserts a small story that firmly reminds the disciples that their authority on mission is as they are connected to Jesus.

30. Mark pictures Jesus at the authoritative interpreter of the Scriptures as well. This is seen clearly in the confrontation with the Sadducees in Mark 12:18–27 and the teaching on the great commandments (Mark 12:28–34). Mark's telling conclusion is this: "After that, no one dared ask him any questions."

deliverance was already taking place. "They represent the old régime, challenged by the fresh new teaching of Jesus."[31]

The appearance of a demoniac in the synagogue (ἦν ἐν τῇ συναγωγῇ αὐτῶν ἄνθρωπος ἐν πνεύματι ἀκαθάρτῳ), the inner core of the bracket, is tied directly to the teaching by the word "immediately." The demon seeks mastery over Jesus through his knowledge of him: "I know who you are—the Holy One of God!" (οἶδά σε τίς εἶ, ὁ ἅγιος τοῦ θεοῦ).[32] Jesus exorcises the demon (Mark 1:25–26), an act which elicits a startled, perhaps even alarmed, response from the onlookers. But "the key point for the disciples is that Jesus is identified by the unclean spirit as the Holy One of God. . . . The disciples are in the company of Jesus, the one with *exousia* who is the Holy One of God. They are part of God's holy people because they are with the Holy One."[33] Jesus's fame as a teacher spreads "over the whole region of Galilee." "But, significantly, his identity as the Holy One of God goes unremarked. Only gradually does the reality of Jesus's true identity dawn on the disciples, much less on the people in Capernaum (see Matt 11:23; Luke 10:15)."[34]

Our focus here is on Jesus's authoritative teaching. But by linking it directly to this exorcism, Mark shows that "the confrontation between good and evil is not merely a human conflict. . . . This story is a grim reminder that beneath the surface of this conflict lies systemic evil that feeds upon the wickedness of humankind but is greater than the sum of its parts. This story and the other exorcism accounts in Mark give notice that evil cannot ultimately rule in God's sphere."[35] The problem is cosmic in scope. So the solution must be cosmic in scope and significance. Jesus wins the first skirmish in the battle. But the war is not over.

Mark's sequence of call-teaching-exorcism-teaching is important at several levels. A teacher is not a teacher without students or disciples, so, first the call, then the teaching. But this event is far more than simply a rabbi gathering disciples. The narrative already hints that Jesus is renewing the people of God by transforming fishers into followers on mission.

For that mission, they will require the ἐξουσία that Jesus possesses. In a highly significant event, when Jesus ascends the mountain and calls "those whom he wanted, and they came to him" (Mark 3:13), Jesus acts as God acts.

---

31. France, *Mark*, 102.

32. For a helpful discussion of this title in Mark, see Ermakov, "Holy One of God," 159–84.

33. Brower, *Holiness*, 65–66.

34. Brower, *Mark*, 74.

35. Brower, *Mark*, 74.

He is recreating the holy people of God by gathering around himself the Twelve, the figural reconstitution of Israel echoing Yahweh on Sinai (Exod 24:1, 9–11). He names the Twelve, and, as the Holy One of God and Son of God, confers ἐξουσία on them (Mark 3:15). These are to be with him, to be sent to proclaim the message and to have authority over the demons. There can be no doubt that Mark intends us to understand that the disciples perform exorcisms with precisely the same ἐξουσία that characterizes Jesus's teaching. Just as his exorcisms are symbols of the cosmic conflict, so the authority wielded by the Twelve enabling them to perform exorcisms (Mark 6:7–29) is symbolic of the inbreaking presence of the kingdom of God.

Mark, however, is at pains to clarify the basis of this authority and does so by focusing upon the failure of the disciples. In Mark 9:14–29, the disciples are unable to exorcise a demon, much to their acute discomfort, and the anger of a crowd. Jesus performs the exorcism simply by a command (Mark 9:25), reminding the disciples of the totally derivative nature of their authority (Mark 9:29) in two ways: his own authority over the recalcitrant demon and the reminder of their own need for prayer. "That Jesus does not pray in the story has the same significance for Mark as it does in the calming of the sea episode. Jesus does not pray because he is acting as God."[36]

This reflection on the authority of Jesus has implications. First, the utter dependence upon God of Jesus's followers in their proclamation of the kingdom of God never ends. The proclamation of the gospel in word and deed is only authoritative in relationship to the one who has ἐξουσία in himself because of who he is: Messiah, the Holy One of God, the Son of God. Second, in contrast to the typical rabbi/talmid relationship of Ancient Judaism, followers of Jesus do not become masters on their own right. They always remain disciples, even when they become teachers. Both points are salutary reminders to Christian leaders to remain faithful to their identity and calling, and never to allow their heads to be turned by position or power or prestige.

The Compassionate Teacher

"He had compassion for them . . . and he began to teach" (Mark 6:34).

Again, a seemingly curious link is made, this time between compassion (σπλαγχνίζομαι) and teaching (διδάσκω), and again it is in a uniquely Markan context. The disciples have returned from their successful mission, and Jesus suggests a little rest (Mark 6:31). But crowds follow them, with Jesus responding to them in compassion with teaching. Immediately

---

36. Brower, *Mark*, 252. See also Brower, "Who Then Is This?," 291–305.

following this, we have the miraculous feeding of the five thousand (Mark 6:35–44). What are all these people doing here?

Great crowds often came to see Jesus.[37] But this seems different. In the context of violent opposition to Roman rule and the narrative sequence, this gathering would attract a few suspicions from attentive oppressors. The five thousand men in the wilderness, organized with military precision into hundreds and fifties; Jesus's wide-ranging mission, announcing and effecting the kingdom of God; and the disciples' successful mission, including their teaching about the kingdom, could have been a potent mix portending rebellion to throw off the Roman yoke. Inserted between the sending out (Mark 6:6b–13) and their return (Mark 6:30) is the story about the political confrontation between John and Antipas. The political overtones of proclaiming the arrival of the kingdom of God are difficult to miss. So is this the day that the revolution begins?[38]

Mark, however, diffuses this picture. After the miraculous feeding, Jesus dismisses the disciples and disperses the crowd himself. Could the disciples have been harboring ideas of a military intervention? (After all, if Jesus can multiply loaves, why could he not arm these men?) Mark doesn't tell us directly, but the narrative does not exclude the possibility of such a misunderstanding. But this does not seem to be Mark's emphasis.

Once again, Mark's intertextual echoes to Scripture may provide illumination. The miraculous feeding in the Elijah–Elisha cycle in 2 Kings 4:42–44 is fascinating but the Markan Jesus is not Elijah or Elisha, not one of the prophets, and not John *redivivus*. It may also evoke the wilderness tradition in which God provides food for the people (Exod 16:1–26; Num 11:4–9).

The description of the crowd as helpless and harassed sheep without a shepherd is even more significant. The metaphor of sheep and shepherd is used in the OT to describe the people of God and their leaders, whether Yahweh or the king. Sheep without a shepherd are people without leaders (see 1 Kings 22:17 where Micaiah ben Imlah describes Israel as "scattered on the mountains, like sheep that have no shepherd"). In Ezekiel 34:7–16 the "flock lacks a shepherd and so has been plundered and has become food for all the wild animals, and . . . [the] shepherds . . . cared for themselves rather than for [Yahweh's] flock" (v. 8, NIV). The irony is clear. Of course, the people have a titular leader, "King Herod," but despite Herod's ostentatious claim, his rule is mere parody. Juxtaposed to the story of Herod's extravagant and grotesque feast, this story tells of the hungry and helpless people of Israel.

---

37. The next paragraphs are an abridgment of Brower, *Mark*, 176–77.

38. The evocative title of Tom Wright's focus on Good Friday, *Day the Revolution Began*, answers "no" to this question—the feeding is not the day the revolution began!

But this problem is even deeper; the people of God are leaderless because the Jerusalem authorities have rejected Jesus (Mark 3:22–30). Significantly, in Ezekiel, Yahweh himself will gather and care for his people.

Several points of interest emerge. First, Jesus continually displays sensitivity to the needs of those around him. The use of σπλαγχνίζομαι, that marvelous word referring to the bowels of compassion, shows the response of Jesus to the perceived need. This word is virtually synonymous with "merciful," a prime characteristic of God (see Luke 6:36; Exod 34:6). Jesus cares for his people.

This second point is more challenging. The disciples' response to the need is that the people should be sent home. They do not know how to feed the multitude and so they simply want them to find their own food. On the deeper level, however, the disciples once again show their lack of perception. These people are being sent home because the disciples do not really grasp the character of Jesus's teaching and the leadership he gives. Despite the healings, exorcisms, his command of nature, they still fail to see. They have little sense of the significance of their appointment as the Twelve (Mark 3:13–15) and the authority they have just exercised (Mark 6:6b–13). But compassion at all levels is at the heart of proclaiming the good news. Indeed, compassion is intimately wrapped up in Jesus's redefinition of holiness. If Jesus's followers are to be the renewed holy people of God, they must participate in his mission of care. The disciples seem to think that teaching is enough; Jesus doesn't.

For Mark, the link between compassion and teaching is one of vital consequence. The people are leaderless—Jesus Messiah is their leader. They are like sheep without a shepherd—Jesus embodies Yahweh's shepherding of his flock. They are hungry—Jesus teaches them the good news of the kingdom and feeds them. The compassionate response of Jesus, the Master Teacher, penetrates to the very heart of the need and responds in compassion to it by his teaching and action. The kingdom is arriving in power.[39]

Prophetic Teaching

The prophetic stance of Jesus vis-à-vis his own generation, society, and religious establishment is set out in a double prophetic representative act in Mark 11:11–19.[40] Once again, Mark's narrative structure is important for understanding the full impact of this episode. The episode is introduced with a note which, at first glance, seems deceptively banal: Jesus "went into the temple;

---

39. Chilton, *God in Strength*.
40. See Brower, "Let the Reader Understand," 119–44.

and when he had looked around at everything, as it was already late, he went out to Bethany with the twelve" (Mark 11:11). But this casual observation, unique to Mark, is far from extraneous. It has a central phrase: Jesus "looked around at everything." That phrase echoes the language of Jeremiah 7:11, the passage which will feature prominently in the following temple scene. The passage reads: "Has this house, which is called by my name, become a den of robbers in your sight? You know, I too am watching, says the Lord." Jesus sees everything—and the judgement proleptically enacted through two linked prophetic representative acts has a context within Yahweh's words spoken through Jeremiah. Tim Geddert's perceptive question, "Does Mark suggest that Jesus was able to see from the divine perspective . . . and that readers are called to do the same?,"[41] expects the answer "yes."

This prophetic perspective sets up the central episode: the fig-tree/temple/fig-tree sequence. William Telford's conclusion still stands: "the cursing of the fig-tree signifies that the entry to Jerusalem and the temple story should not be understood as a Messianic purification but as a visitation in judgement upon the temple."[42] The intertextual link to Jeremiah 7 in Mark 11:15b–17 is augmented by other echoes that Mark might well have in mind. Jeremiah 8:13 has this telling language: "When I wanted to gather them, says the Lord, there are no grapes on the vine, nor figs on the fig tree; even the leaves are withered, and what I gave them has passed away from them." N. T. Wright notes the connection to "sorrowful Jeremianic demonstration that Israel, and the Temple, are under judgment."[43] This is "a prophetic representative act in which the Markan Jesus not only predicts but symbolically effects the prediction of judgement."[44] As Jesus returns to the temple after the night in Bethany, "seeing a fig tree in leaf, he went to see whether perhaps he would find anything on it. When he came to it, he found nothing but leaves, for it was not the season for figs" (Mark 11:13). Once again, Jesus sees. Unlike the intertext, this fig tree is in leaf. But, significantly, it is fruitless. Jesus curses the tree: "'May no one ever eat fruit from you again.' And his disciples heard it" (Mark 11:14).

The inner core of the bracket, the overturning of the money-changers' tables, is equally symbolic. The legitimate temple commerce was likely set up in the Court of the Gentiles, which was designed to be a place for the nations to worship. Jesus's action would scarcely have affected the functioning of the temple system. "He acts alone against a massive enterprise. This suggests that

---

41. Geddert, *Watchwords*, 129, cited in Brower, "Let the Reader Understand," 134.

42. Telford, *Barren Temple*, 261. It is not, however, judgement upon the common people *per se*.

43. Wright, *Jesus and the Victory of God*, 422, as cited in Brower, "Let the Reader Understand," 136.

44. Brower, "Let the Reader Understand," 136.

the problem is more than temple corruption. It is better to picture this as a prophetic-representative action, symbolizing and anticipating the destruction of the temple, which Jesus explicitly prophesies in Mark 13."⁴⁵

Confirmation of this is given in the closing bracket. When they again return to Jerusalem the next morning "they saw the fig tree withered away to its roots" (Mark 11:20). This whole episode—fig-tree/temple/fig-tree—then,

> is no mere cleansing of the Temple. Mark sees it as a judgement on the Temple whose leaders have distorted its intended purpose as the house of prayer for all nations. Instead of welcoming the foreigners, they have made it into "a den of λῃστῶν." Echoing Jeremiah's strident criticism of the Temple, through the juxtapositioning of the cursing of the fig-tree with the allusion to two highly charged OT texts and contexts, the Markan Jesus prophetically enacts the fate of the Temple. The message to the chief priests and the scribes was clear; their response was to seek a way to destroy him (11:18).⁴⁶

Jesus's action and teaching are akin to the strident criticisms of Amos and Jeremiah, who also perceived the abuse to which a close tie between commerce and the cult was prone. But Mark's prophetic representative actions are more than that. Together they proleptically enact the fate of the temple that has resisted the coming of the Messiah and has failed in its duty to be a place for the nations to come to Yahweh, instead concentrating on the separation that attention to code-defined purity expected.

Jesus's teaching, noted in Mark, is a fearless exposé of bankrupt modes of worship and a growing laxity in the commercial exploitation of the cult. This negative message is undoubtedly accompanied by the positive proclamation of the kingdom's actual presence in his own person which would universalize the good news of salvation, freeing it from the narrow confines of a legalistic, ritually pure, but in the end, heartless and ineffective religious system. Nevertheless, we simply are not told.

But what we do see is the fearless, revolutionary criticism with which Jesus castigated the religious establishment. He is ruthless with those whose piety is an external display of purity, and doubly severe with those who also are supposed to be the leaders of the people. Jesus called for righteousness wherever he saw wickedness and it was his eventual undoing. Jesus is condemned to death, according to Mark, by the religious establishment who has been out to do away with him from the very start: "Now the chief priests and the whole council were looking for testimony against Jesus" (Mark 14:55).

---

45. Brower, *Mark*, 298.
46. Brower, "Let the Reader Understand," 136.

Conclusion

The picture of Jesus as faithful teacher that has emerged from this brief study has highlighted the authoritative, compassionate, and prophetic dimensions of Jesus as the Master teacher. All four Gospels agree that Jesus's identity is the basis for his authority, compassion, and prophetic word/action. In turn, all of this is in service to this mission of God. Jesus's identity is set out in a constellation of images drawn from Scripture, none of which, on its own, is sufficient to encapsulate the profound phrase of Paul: "in him all the fullness of God was pleased to dwell" (Col 1:19); or of John: "And the Word became flesh" (John 1:14).

Those who are followers of Jesus are invited to participate in both the mutuality and the mission of the Triune God. We are called to be faithful to the same mission as Jesus. In the proclamation and enactment of the good news that God reigns, we do so in emulation of our Master Teacher, under, always, and only with his authority, in exercising compassion for the broken and bleeding and in calling out injustice and unrighteousness in prophetic enactment of the mission of God.

Bibliography

Allison, Dale C., Jr. *The New Moses: A Matthean Typology.* Philadelphia: Augsburg Fortress, 1994.

Bauckham, Richard, ed. *The Gospel for All Christians: Rethinking the Gospel Audiences.* London: T. & T. Clark, 1997.

Blomberg, Craig A. *Contagious Holiness: Jesus' Meals with Sinners.* New Studies in Biblical Theology 19. Downers Grove: InterVarsity, 2005.

Brower, Kent. "Elijah in the Markan Passion Narrative." *Journal for the Study of the New Testament* 18 (1983) 85–101.

———. "Hearing Voices: Identity and Mission in Mark." In *Listening Again to the Text: New Testament Studies in Honor of George Lyons*, edited by R. P. Thompson, 25–43. Claremont: Claremont, 2020.

———. *Holiness in the Gospels.* Kansas City: Beacon Hill, 2007.

———. "'Let the Reader Understand': Temple and Eschatology in Mark." In *Let the Reader Understand: Eschatology in Bible and Theology*, edited by Kent E. Brower and Mark W. Elliott, 119–44. Reprint, Eugene: Wipf & Stock, 2013.

———. *Mark: A Commentary in the Wesleyan Tradition.* New Beacon Bible Commentary. Kansas City: Beacon Hill, 2012.

———. "Who Then Is This?—Christological Questions in Mark 4:35—5:43." *Evangelical Quarterly* 81 (2009) 291–305.

Bruce, F. F. *Jesus and Christian Origins Outside the New Testament.* London: Hodder & Stoughton, 1984.

Bultmann, Rudolf. *Theology of the New Testament.* Introduction by Robert Morgan. 2nd ed. Waco: Baylor University Press, 2007.

Burridge, Richard A. *What are the Gospels: A Comparison with Graeco-Roman Biography.* 2nd ed. Grand Rapids: Eerdmans, 2004.

Chilton, Bruce D. *God in Strength: Jesus' Announcement of the Kingdom*. Freistadt: Plochl, 1979.

Davies, W. D. *The Settings of the Sermon on the Mount*. Cambridge: Cambridge University Press, 1966.

Ermakov, Arseny. "The Holy One of God in Markan Narrative." *Horizons in Biblical Theology* 36 (2014) 159–84.

France, R. T. *The Gospel of Mark: A Commentary on the Greek Text*. New International Greek Testament Commentary. Grand Rapids: Eerdmans, 2002.

Geddert, Timothy J. *Watchwords: Mark 13 in Markan Eschatology*. Journal for the Study of the New Testament Supplement Series 26. Sheffield: JSOT, 1989.

Goodacre, Mark. *The Case Against Q Studies in Markan Priority and the Synoptic Problem*. Harrisburg: Trinity, 2002.

Gorman, Michael J. *Abide and Go: Missional Theosis in the Gospel of John*. The Didsbury Lectures. Eugene: Cascade, 2018.

Guelich, Robert A. *The Sermon on the Mount: A Foundation for Understanding*. Waco: Word, 1991.

Hatina, Thomas R. *In Search of a Context: The Function of Scripture in Mark's Narrative*. Journal for the Study of the New Testament Supplement Series 232. Sheffield: Sheffield, 2002.

Hays, Richard B. *Reading Backwards: Figural Christology and the Fourfold Gospel Witness*. London: SPCK, 2015.

Johnson, Andy. *Holiness and the Missio Dei*. Eugene: Cascade, 2016.

Kupp, David C. *Matthew's Emmanuel: Divine Presence and God's People in the First Gospel*. Society for New Testament Studies Monograph Series 90. Cambridge: Cambridge University Press, 1997.

Lincoln, Andrew T. *The Gospel according to Saint John*. Black's New Testament Commentaries. Grand Rapids: Eerdmans, 2013.

Marshall, I. Howard. "Son of God or Servant of Yahweh? A Re-consideration of Mark 1:11." In *Jesus the Saviour: Studies in New Testament Theology*, 121–33. London: SPCK, 1990.

Mullen, J. Patrick. *Dining with Pharisees*. Minneapolis: Glazier, 2004.

Snow, Rob, and Arseny Ermakov. *Matthew: A Commentary in the Wesleyan Tradition*. New Beacon Bible Commentary. Kansas City: The Foundry, 2019.

Telford, William R. *The Barren Temple and the Withered Tree*. Journal for the Study of the New Testament Supplement Series 1. Sheffield: JSOT, 1980.

Thompson, Richard P. "Gathered at the Table: Holiness and Ecclesiology in the Gospel of Luke." In *Holiness and Ecclesiology in the New Testament*, edited by Kent Brower and Andy Johnson, 76–94. Grand Rapids: Eerdmans, 2007.

Van Voorst, Robert E. "Josephus." In *Jesus in History, Thought, and Culture: An Encyclopedia*, edited by Leslie Houlden, 1:509–11. Santa Barbara: ABC-CLIO, 2003.

Watts, Rikki E. *Isaiah's New Exodus and Mark*. Wissenschaftliche Untersuchungen zum Neuen Testament 2.88. Tübingen: Mohr Siebeck, 1997.

Wi, MiJa. *The Path to Salvation in Luke's Gospel: What Must We Do?* Library of New Testament Studies 607. London: T. & T. Clark, 2019.

Wright, N. T. *The Day the Revolution Began*. London: SPCK, 2014.

———. *Jesus and the Victory of God*. Christian Origins and the Question of God 2. London: SPCK, 1996.

3

Acts as a Faithful Source for Understanding Paul and His Christophanic Experience[1]

—Rob A. Fringer

Paul's revelation of Christ, or Christophanic experience, is arguably the most radical transformation story in the whole of Scripture. Nevertheless, to refer to this event as Paul's "Damascus Road Experience" (DRE) is not possible without the book of Acts (9:1–19; 22:3–21; 26:9–18), since Paul himself does not directly refer to the event in this way. Paul does, however, refer to receiving a revelation of Jesus Christ (Gal 1:12, 16), to having seen "Jesus our Lord" (1 Cor 9:1), and to having the resurrected Christ appear to him (1 Cor 15:8).[2] But are these the same event? And, if they are, is Luke's[3] narrative a faithful and reliable source for our understanding of Paul and his Christophanic experience? This chapter will evaluate the debate in scholarship concerning the reliability of using Acts as a faithful source for garnering information about Paul and his Christophanic experience.

---

1. I have known David McEwan for many years as both a colleague and a friend. His commitment to God, passion for education, and love for the church has been and continues to be an inspiration to many, myself included. This chapter is dedicated to him. To him I give the title: "David McEwan as a Faithful Source for Understanding John Wesley, His Life and Works."

2 These three accounts are the only direct references made by Paul about his Christophanic Experience. There are also two indirect references found in Philippians 3:4–14 and 2 Corinthians 3:1—4:6. This list, as with the whole of this chapter, only makes reference to the seven "undisputed" letters of Paul. For further information about these Christophanic references see Fringer, *Paul's Corporate Christophany*.

3. While there is some debate around the authorship of Acts, for the sake of this essay, we will refer to the author as Luke, who was also the writer of the Gospel that now bears his name.

A Tale of Two Pauls

The beginning of a dichotomy between the Paul of Acts and the Paul of the Pauline Epistles can be found in the nineteenth-century work of Ferdinand Christian Baur's, *Paul, the Apostle of Jesus*.[4] Baur argued that with regard to Paul, Acts was historically unreliable since it varied so greatly from the Pauline Epistles. Likening the argument to the difference between John and the Synoptic Gospels, Baur stated: "The comparison of both these sources must lead to the conclusion that, considering the great difference between the two statements, historical truth can only belong to one of them."[5] Such a bold declaration has garnered significant debate over the years, which in turn has produced additional arguments in favor of and against Baur's conclusion. In order to address the question of whether Acts and the Pauline Epistles give us a unified picture of Paul or two differing Pauls, we will divide our brief analysis into two sections. First, we will look at these sources with respect to what they tell us about the life and chronology of Paul. Second, we will evaluate these sources for understanding the theological perspectives of Paul that they present us.

Paul's Life and Chronology

In his book, *Paul's Early Period*, Rainer Riesner surveyed the status of scholarship between the seventeenth and twentieth century around the issue of Pauline Chronology.[6] His findings revealed a vast disagreement in dating in the early years moving toward some "relative consensus" after the discovery and publication of the Gallio-inscription in 1905. This growing continuity was also attributed to a greater reliance upon Acts and Galatians, a devaluing of other ancient sources (especially church tradition concerning Paul's conversion), and improved astronomical calculations for dating Jesus's death. Yet, as he moved beyond the 1970s, Riesner found that an increasing number of chronologies that deviated from this relative consensus were finding favor.[7] In his evaluation of more recent scholarship, Riesner divided chronological outlines into three categories which revolved around their treatment of Acts.[8]

---

4. Baur, *Paul, the Apostle of Jesus*.
5. Baur, *Paul, the Apostle of Jesus*, 5.
6. Riesner, *Paul's Early Period*.
7. Riesner, *Paul's Early Period*, 6.
8. See also Donfried, "Chronology: New Testament," 1:1011–22. Donfried states two major options: 1) those heavily dependent on the accuracy of Acts, and 2) those skeptical of Acts.

The first category was those who sought to preserve the framework of Acts. These scholars sought to harmonize Acts and Galatians and in so doing probably placed more stress on the former. The second category was those who sought to correct the framework of Acts and, therefore, who gave primacy to Paul's epistles. For this reason, most moved away from the five journeys to Jerusalem schema, as advanced in Acts, in favor of the three journeys specified in Paul's letters (Gal 1:18; 2:1; Rom 15:22–29).[9] The third and final category was those who ostensibly abandon Acts all together. This last category has produced the most diverse group of dating as each scholar within this group has latched on to different anchoring points.

John Knox's work, which followed in the footsteps of Baur, was a significant influence for those in this final category. Knox believed that too many scholars were relying almost exclusively on Acts for ascertaining details about the life of Paul. He sought to show the unreliability of Acts for such an endeavor and simultaneously to show that Paul's letters contained a great deal more details about his life, which would allow one to reconstruct a Pauline chronology.[10] For Knox, Acts had value only as a secondary source and where there were discrepancies Acts must be disregarded.[11]

Nevertheless, many of those in the third category, even Knox, evidence at least some reliance on Acts with the majority of scholars acknowledging the difficulties of producing a chronology of Paul without Acts. As Karl Donfried articulates, "Paul gives us not one specific date" and, therefore, "if one is to establish a possible chronology of this period, there will have to be some dependence on Acts."[12] Gerd Lüdemann, who falls within the third category, surprisingly concludes that the chronology produced strictly from

9. We should also note that it could be argued that Romans 15:22–29 and also 1 Corinthians 16:1–4 only *imply* a third visit. This is especially the case in the latter passage. For this reason, some scholars only work with the two visits mentioned in Galatians.

10. Knox, *Chapters in the Life of Paul*, 4–19.

11. Knox, "Pauline Chronology," 23. For another well-argued example of this third category, see Lüdemann, *Paul, Apostle to the Gentiles*. Lüdemann tried to show how an accurate exegetical understanding of Paul's letters and their forms enables a reconstruction of Pauline chronology that is not reliant upon Acts, and moreover, where Acts is unable to add to the discussion. Of particular interest is Lüdemann's multifaceted approach and particularly in his attempts at a form critical approach to Paul's letters in order to understand their chronology.

12. Donfried, "Chronology: New Testament," 1017. Donfried is very skeptical of Acts and favors many of Knox's and Lüdemann's conclusions. Similarly, Crossan and Reed, *In Search of Paul*, call Acts "a most ambiguous source for understanding Paul's life and work, mission and message" (16). Still, they do not totally disregard Acts. They rely significantly less on it and see archaeological discoveries of the first century as a more authentic gap-filler than Acts.

an evaluation of Paul's letters closely corresponds to Acts.[13] This discovery allows him to accept parts of Acts, and particularly Acts 18, in his timeline. Although, he does believe that on this point "Luke reworked traditions that derived from two different visits."[14] Such concessions by those in this third category appear to justify Riesner's conclusion that "A critical combination of Acts with the Pauline letters remains possible not just for individual Lukan traditions, but also for information regarding the larger framework."[15]

Ultimately, most of the tension boils down to whether one believes Acts to be a historically reliable source.[16] Craig Keener has done extensive work in arguing that the genre of Acts should be understood as ancient historiography, and he has shown the complexity and diversity of this genre by comparing it with other ancient historiographies.[17] Keener shows that, while there was more creative license afforded authors of ancient historiographies than we are accustomed to in modern historiographies, there was still a significant concern for historical accuracy.[18] "History was supposed to be truthful, and historians harshly criticized other historians whom they accused of promoting falsehood."[19] Authors of ancient historiography were also concerned with rhetorical presentation and wrote in narrative rather than chronicle style. Furthermore, like most writers (past and present), even

---

13. Lüdemann, *Paul, Apostle to the Gentiles*, 172.

14. Lüdemann, *Paul, Apostle to the Gentiles*, 200.

15. Riesner, *Paul's Early Period*, 413.

16. A significant bone of contention is the seemingly disparate accounts of Acts 15 and Galatians 2 with regard to the Jerusalem Council. Phillips builds a significant argument for the historical unreliability of Acts based on this issue and concludes, with others, that Acts is an attempt to "rehabilitate the Paul of the letters" (*Paul, His Letters, and Acts*, 196). However, many have argued that Galatians 2 actually corresponds with Acts 11:27—12:25 rather than with Acts 15. Some proponents of this view include: Bruce, "Galatians Problems," 292–309; Marshall, *Acts of the Apostles*; Longenecker, *Galatians*; Witherington, *Grace in Galatia*. There are also those like Schwartz who argue that these two accounts (Acts 11–12 and 15) refer to the same event/visit but are reporting on different aspects. Schwartz believes that the writer of Acts is not placing his material chronologically. Therefore, he also believes a reordering of Acts is a vital part of the exegetical process in our understanding of Luke's Paul and how it relates to the Paul of the letters ("Paul in Acts," 187–98).

17. Keener, *Acts: Volume 1*, 51–220.

18. Hengel and Schwemer, *Paul Between Damascus*, argue that those who see Acts as historically unreliable are "often relatively ignorant of ancient historiography" (p. 7). They also argue for an early date (c. 70 AD) for Acts and that Luke was a traveling companion of Paul.

19. Keener, *Acts: Volume 1*, 118.

historians, Luke had an agenda[20] and was seeking to persuade his audience toward particular ideas, truths, and actions.[21]

The same can be said of Paul. His epistles (a completely different genre) are written to specific audiences to address specific concerns. As such, Paul too had an agenda, one which was not explicitly focused on relaying historical data points that would allow us to reconstruct an accurate chronology. Still, Paul was not seeking to be ahistorical or to deceive anyone with regard to his comings and goings. Therefore, against Baur, we are not forced into an "all or nothing" approach in this debate. It is possible that some historical truths concerning the life and chronology of Paul could be (and are) found in both, and equally that some historical inaccuracies could be (and likely are) found in both.

Paul's Theological Perspective

While the above evaluation may give weight to the use of Acts in our understanding of Pauline chronology, it does not answer the question of whether we can justifiably view Acts as a faithful representative of the theology of the apostle Paul. Philipp Vielhauer, a contemporary of Knox, and Ernst Haenchen, provided significant foundational arguments against such an assertion. Vielhauer's analysis was primarily focused on the Lukan Pauline speeches, from where he believed a Lukan Pauline theology could be constructed. For Vielhauer, this Lukan Pauline theology differed considerably from the theology found in Paul's letters. Vielhauer concluded that "the author of Acts is in his Christology pre-Pauline, in his natural theology, concept of the law, and eschatology, post-Pauline. He presents no specifically Pauline idea."[22] Similarly, Haenchen writes: "[I]n Acts . . . we have no collaborator of Paul telling his story, but someone of a later generation trying in his own way to give an account of things that can no longer be viewed in their true perspective. . . . [I]t is no less evident that the real Paul, as known to his followers and opponents alike, has been replaced by a Paul seen through the eyes of a later age."[23]

20. E.g., Hengel and Schwemer argue that part of Luke's intent was "to mediate between [Paul] and the supporters of the earliest community" and how Luke also "*had to harmonize, to 'tone down' conflicts and pass over much that was unattractive*" because he didn't want to "put off Theophilus, for whom he was writing" (*Paul Between Damascus*, 10, italics theirs).

21. See Keener for the various agendas of ancient historiographies and Luke's possible agendas (*Acts: Volume 1*, 148–65).

22. Vielhauer, "On the 'Paulinism' of Acts," 48.

23. Haenchen, *Acts of the Apostles*, 116.

Many scholars[24] have addressed Vielhauer's and Haenchen's conclusions revealing multiple problems and shortcomings therein and arguing for more commonalities than differences between Acts and the Pauline Epistles, especially when taking genre and purpose into account.[25] In Mikeal Parsons words, "Given the strikingly different contexts, the similarities are more remarkable than the tensions."[26] Keener has also show that more recent developments in scholarship, such as New Perspective views on Jewish understanding of the law, have voided some of Vielhauer's conclusions; on issues concerning the law in Paul's epistles, Vielhauer is simply misreading Paul.[27] Equally, Haenchen's view of the epistolary Paul's diminishing commitment to Judaism can now be shown to be erroneous. "The Paul of the letters no less than the Paul of Acts is a good Jew who simply refuses to impose uniquely Jewish customs on the Gentiles."[28]

While Vielhauer, Haenchen, and others have overstated the tensions between Acts and the Pauline epistles with regard to Pauline theology, there are still differences that will continue to be debated and will not likely be resolved. The reality is that there are simply too many "gaps" in both of these sources for us to make definitive statements concerning which represents the "real" Paul and his thought. Too often, *argumentum ex silentio* has been among the strongest influence for divergence between these two Pauls. We should not assume that Luke included all the raw data at his disposal, nor that Paul tells us everything about himself and his theology.[29] Reidar Hvalvik's words are an important warning about overestimating or underestimating the value of either source. He writes, "The 'Pauline Paul' cannot be claimed to be more 'real' than the 'Lukan Paul.' . . . Paul's letters are

---

24. See also: Porter, *Paul of Acts*, 187–206; Keener, *Acts: Volume 1*, 250–57; Jervell, *Unknown Paul*, 68–76; Marshall, *Acts of the Apostles*, 42–44.

25. Porter, *Paul of Acts*, 199, 206. See also Donfried, *Paul, Thessalonica*, 90–96. Donfried argues that contradictions are also reduced when taking the full Pauline corpus into account and especially 1 Thessalonians.

26. Parsons, *Acts*, 258; cf. Jervell, *Unknown Paul*, 70.

27. Keener, *Acts: Volume 1*, 251–52 and n167. Interestingly, on this same point, Porter comes to similar conclusions with regard to New Perspective readings on this issue. Yet he, nevertheless, does not buy into these perspectives and instead sees other ways of lessening the tensions (*Paul of Acts*, 190–93).

28. Keener, *Acts: Volume 1*, 253 and n175. See also Hvalvik, "Paul as a Jewish Believer," 121–53.

29. Ladd refers to this practice as a "dangerous procedure," stating: "The fact that Paul's letters are *ad hoc* correspondence, usually called forth by specific situations in the Pauline churches, places certain limitations upon our study of his thought, the chief of which is that we do not have Paul's *complete* thought" (*Theology of the New Testament*, 415, italics his).

fundamental for the understanding of Paul, but they do not give us an unbiased presentation of the historical Paul. Paul had specific purposes when writing his letters, but none of them included a wish to give a complete picture of himself and his theology."[30]

While the assumption that we should prefer the Pauline Paul over and against the Lukan Paul has dominated for some time, it may be that we have been asking the wrong questions.[31] Could it be that both of these Pauls are equally "real" in one sense and at the same time equally "inauthentic" in another? They are real in that they paint an accurate picture of the diversity and complexity of the apostle and his thought while at the same time bearing the limitations of their literary contexts and purposes. They are inauthentic in that they are both primarily not trying to sketch a historical biography of Paul in the modern sense but rather are seeking to engage their intended audiences in the story of Christ and the implications of this story on the believing community and unbelieving world.

To summarize this section, the arguments posited by those who see the Paul of Acts as completely incongruent with the Paul of the letters, is unsubstantiated. There is still much work and discussion that must take place in this discipline and yet there is validity in a view which employs Acts to better understand the life and thought of the apostle Paul. We will now briefly compare the DRE references in Acts to Paul's Christophanic references in order to further substantiate the claims just made about the validity of Acts as a faithful source for understanding Paul.

Paul's Christophany in Acts and the Pauline Epistles

There are multiple similarities between the three DRE accounts in Acts (9:1–19; 22:3–21; 26:9–18), to the extent that we can confidently say they recount the same event. Nevertheless, scholars have long since recognized multiple differences between them. To illustrate, in 9:7 the men traveling with Paul hear the voice but see nothing, whereas in 22:9 they see the light but hear no voice; and in 22:14–15 Paul's commissioning is conveyed via Ananias, whereas in 26:16–18 the Lord imparts this commission directly

---

30. Hvalvik, "Paul as a Jewish Believer," 152.

31. See Thompson's excellent paper, which makes reference to this at several points. Thompson's desire is for us to start asking better questions that might shed more light on the argument at hand. He writes: "My purpose is to think again about the value of Acts as a source, and to ask, in light of recent Pauline study, whether the old reasons we give for distancing the Paul of Acts from the Paul of the letters are still as solid and convincing as they used to be. The goal here is not so much to answer questions but to ask for some better ones" ("Paul in Acts," 426).

to Paul. Some attempts to explain these variances include: Martin Dibelius, who believes different sources lie behind each account;[32] Charles Hedrick, who argues for varying literary methods/genres;[33] and Beverly Gaventa, who contends that Luke tailored the accounts according to their narrative functions.[34] Gaventa's proposal appears strongest and does not necessarily exclude either of the other possibilities. While Lukan inconsistencies is not the focus of this chapter, they do reveal that the author was quite comfortable recounting this story differently to meet his particular narrative agenda, and that he did not believe these changes detracted from either the account's historicity or his current argument.

Paul's accounts also evidence differences in their details. With regard to the way in which Christ was made known to Paul he says in Galatians 1:16 that Christ was revealed (ἀποκαλύψαι) in him (cf. Gal 1:12), in 1 Corinthians 15:8 that Christ appeared (ὤφθη) to him (cf. 1 Cor 9:1), in Philippians 3:12 that Christ apprehended (κατελήμφθην) him, and in 2 Corinthians 4:6 that God had shone (ἔλαμψεν) in his heart to give the "light of the knowledge of the glory of God in the face of Jesus Christ." These variances are less substantial than those found in Acts and would not necessarily be called contradictions. Nevertheless, when considering the larger pericopae in which these short references are couched, the differences are more substantial than those found in Acts.

In Galatians, Paul goes to great lengths to show that his gospel was not born of human origins (1:11–12; cf. 1:1). Instead, it came as a direct revelation from God. The radical shift from his past life in Judaism (Gal 1:13–14) to his new life in Christ (Gal 1:15–24) is proof of this reality. First Corinthians has two references to Paul's Christophany. In the first instance (1 Cor 9:1), Paul makes a passing reference to having seen the Lord, with no further details about the Christophany. In the second reference, Paul tacks his Christophany onto a list of multiple resurrection appearances (1 Cor 15:5–8), which are themselves part of a larger kerygmatic tradition (1 Cor 15:3–5) that bears evidence to the bodily resurrection of Christ. In Philippians, Paul's Christophanic reference is implicit, sitting in the background. While Paul does make mention of his former life in Judaism (Phil 3:5–6), the focus is on the surpassing greatness of knowing Christ, relying on his power, and pressing on toward the prize (Phil 3:7–14).

Second Corinthians 3:1—4:6 is perhaps the most controversial Christophanic reference, with some arguing that it has the most in common

---

32. Dibelius, *Studies in Acts*, esp. 1–25.
33. Hedrick, "Paul's Conversion/Call," 415–32.
34. Gaventa, *From Darkness to Light*, 52–95.

with the Acts accounts[35] and others arguing it is not a reference at all.[36] The biggest deterrent for viewing 2 Corinthians 3:1—4:6 as a Christophanic reference is Paul's continued use of the first-person plural ("we") to describe this experience. Seyoon Kim has argued that these "we-passages" are "stylistic plural[s] referring to Paul himself alone."[37] "Kim sees Paul as applying his own Christophany as a 'typical' model for believers' conversion, though not including a physical/outward seeing of Christ, and even adds that 2 Cor 4:6 is a 'typical' apostolic commission."[38] N. T. Wright, however, responds to Kim's claims, asking, "how could Paul have generalized from his experience—granted his placing of his seeing of Jesus at the end of a one-off sequence in 1 Cor. 15.8—to the experience he and the Corinthians all shared?"[39]

I have previously argued in favor of seeing 2 Corinthians 3:1—4:6 as a valid Christophanic reference and addressed the concerns of Wright and others about Paul's use of the first-person plural.[40] Therein, I showed that Paul's use of the first-person plural fit within the larger goal he had for this epistle, namely, to show the Corinthians that they were united together with Paul, the other ministers/apostles, and ultimately with all Christ-followers—to question Paul's authority was ultimately to question their own faith journey. The Christophanic reference, therefore, served to "provide a paradigm for believer conversion, call, and transformation, which would unite them together as the eschatological people of God. . . . [Paul sought] to lesson the gap between himself and the Corinthians. Rather than elevating his unique experience, Paul intentionally extrapolates the universal elements of his Christophany and re-particularizes the particulars for the benefit of his audience."[41]

Taking 2 Corinthians 3:1—4:6 as a valid Christophanic reference, let us compare the similarities between the various Pauline Christophanic references and the DRE accounts in Acts.

---

35. See esp. Kim, *Origin of Paul's Gospel*, 5–13, 193–99, 229–39; and Hafemann, *Suffering and Ministry*, 12–16.
36. See esp. Wright, *Resurrection of the Son*, 384–86.
37. Kim, *Origin of Paul's Gospel*, 235.
38. Fringer, *Corporate Christophany*, 31–32.
39. Wright, *Resurrection of the Son*, 384–85.
40. Fringer, *Corporate Christophany*, 31–33, 139–79.
41. Fringer, *Corporate Christophany*, 177.

	Similarity	Acts	Pauline Epistles
1	An appearance/revelation of Christ to Paul	9:3–5; 22:6–8; 26:13–15	Gal 1:12, 16; 1 Cor 9:1; 15:8
2	Paul's call to preach to the gentiles	9:15; 26:17–18; cf. 22:15	Gal 1:16; cf. 1 Cor 9:16–17
3	Evidence of a significant transformation in Paul's life and thought (including reference to previous life as a Pharisee)	9:18; 22:16; 26:19–20	Gal 1:23–24; 1 Cor 15:10; 2 Cor 3:17—4:6; Phil 3:7–12
4	Paul's reference to having persecuted the church	9:1–5; 22:4–8; 26:9–15	Gal 1:13; 1 Cor 15:9; Phil 3:6
5	Reference to Damascus	9:3; 22:6, 10–11; 26:12	Gal 1:17; cf. 2 Cor 11:32
6	This was an unsolicited event/by the grace of God	9:3–5; 22:6–7; 26:9–14	Gal 1:15; 1 Cor 15:8; cf. Phil 3:12
7	Reference to blindness/veiling	9:8–9; 22:11	2 Cor 3:14–15; cf. 2 Cor 4:3–4
8	Reference to having sight restored/veil removed	9:18; 22:13; cf. 26:17–18	2 Cor 3:16–18
9	Reference to light/glory	9:3; 22:6; 26:13; cf. 26:18	2 Cor 3:18; 4:6
10	Reference to being "set apart"	13:2	Gal 1:15; cf. Rom 1:1
11	Allusion to Isaianic servant's role as part of Paul's calling	26:18 (Isa 42:7, 16b; cf. Isa 49:6)	Gal 1:10–24 (Isa 49:1–6)

The first four similarities (1–4) are significant and make almost certain that these two authors are speaking about the same event. It could be argued that the similarities are so general that they would have been known to almost every first-century Christ-follower. Nevertheless, the other seven (5–11),[42] while less significant on their own, when taken together provide an even more significant case for viewing a closer connection between the various Acts and Pauline accounts. There are enough parallels to warrant deeper consideration of the sources utilized by Luke, making it appear more probable that Luke had personal access to Paul and/or his writings. Perhaps it is time to take more seriously the arguments for an earlier dating[43] of

42. Numbers 6 and 10 are taken from Keener, *Acts: Volume 1*, 241.

43. Jervell, *Unknown Paul*, 68–76. Jervell holds strongly to an early dating of Acts and to seeing Paul and Luke as having known each other and having traveled together.

Luke and for viewing the "we" passages of Acts as evidence that Luke was an eyewitness and traveling companion of Paul.[44]

As noted above, there are internal differences between the three Acts accounts, as also are with the various Pauline accounts. As such, it stands to reason that we will find multiple differences when comparing the Acts and Pauline accounts of the Christophany/DRE to each another. As with discussion concerning Paul's life, chronology, and theology, we have argued that these can be explained in terms of the differing genres and purposes between these various documents. In their various literary contexts, each account is seeking to accomplish something specific based on the authors' purposes and the needs of the various audiences; and these various contexts either allow for or necessitate said differences.

Furthermore, we must all admit that there is still much information and details we have not been given access to, gaps[45] in the text and in our understanding of the specific situations, which could easily account for the dissimilarities. It is true that Paul's recounting of his Christophany appears sparse. However, much of this sparsity is based on comparison with the Acts narrations. Paul's accounts assume, at least in part, prior knowledge of this event by his audiences (Gal 1:13; cf. 1 Cor 15:8), and he, therefore, has no reason to retell the story in the same way that Acts seems to necessitate. Instead, Paul recasts a known event within a particular epistolary context to carry out a specific agenda. Thus, we can say that they contain the necessary amount of material for said agenda, at least in Paul's estimation.

Conclusion

This chapter has highlighted the connections between Acts and the Pauline Epistles with regard to Paul's Christophany/DRE. It has also argued that there are enough connections between Acts and the Pauline Epistles, with regard to Paul's life and thought, that we cannot simply discard Acts. The onus still falls on those who would argue against such a claim as they have yet to make a strong enough case in their favor—Paul's Christophany in

---

Jervell writes: "I do not for a moment doubt that the author of Acts knew Paul well, if not personally" (73). For an extensive argument on a late dating for Acts, and, with Vielhauer, against an acquaintance between the writer of Acts and Paul, see Pervo, *Dating Acts*.

44. While this chapter does not have the space to address this issue, see: Porter, *Paul of Acts*, 199–206; Campbell, *"We" Passages*; Wedderburn, "'We'-Passages," 78–98; Gasque, *History of the Interpretation*, 283–91.

45. Matlock reminds us that "Paul's own 'conversion narrative' is almost all gaps!" ("Road to Damascus," 90).

correlation to Acts DRE being just another hurdle for them to overcome. At this point, Acts must still be seen as a faithful source for understanding Paul and his Christophanic experience.

Bibliography

Baur, Fredinand Christian. *Paul, the Apostle of Jesus: His Life and Work, His Epistles and His Doctrines: A Contribution to the Critical History of Primitive Christianity*. 2 vols. Reprint, Peabody: Hendrickson, 2003.

Bruce, F. F. "Galatians Problems: 1. Autobiographical Data." *Bulletin of the John Rylands Library of Manchester* 51 (1969) 292–309.

Campbell, William Sanger. *The "We" Passages in the Acts of the Apostles: The Narrator as Narrative Character*. Studies in Biblical Literature 14. Atlanta: Society of Biblical Literature, 2007.

Crossan, John Dominic, and Jonathan L. Reed. *In Search of Paul: How Jesus's Apostle Opposed Rome's Empire with God's Kingdom*. San Francisco: HarperSanFrancisco, 2004.

Dibelius, Martin. *Studies in the Acts of the Apostles*. London: SCM, 1956.

Donfried, Karl P. "Chronology: New Testament." In *The Anchor Bible Dictionary*, edited by David Noel Freedman, 1:1011–22. New York: Doubleday, 1992.

———. *Paul, Thessalonica, and Early Christianity*. London: T. & T. Clark, 2002.

Fringer, Rob A. *Paul's Corporate Christophany: An Evaluation of Paul's Christophanic References in Their Epistolary Contexts*. Eugene, OR: Pickwick, 2019.

Gasque, W. Ward. *A History of the Interpretation of the Acts of the Apostles*. Reprint, Peabody: Hendrickson, 1989.

Gaventa, Beverly R. *From Darkness to Light: Aspects of Conversion in the New Testament*. Philadelphia: Fortress, 1986.

Haenchen, Ernst. *The Acts of the Apostles: A Commentary*. Translated by Bernard Noble et al. Oxford: Blackwell, 1971.

Hafemann, Scott J. *Suffering and Ministry in the Spirit: Paul's Defence of His Ministry in II Corinthians: 2:14—3:3*. Carlisle: Paternoster, 2000.

Hedrick, Charles W. "Paul's Conversion/Call: A Comparative Analysis of the Three Reports in Acts." *Journal of Biblical Literature* 100.3 (1981) 415–32.

Hengel, Martin, and Anna Maria Schwemer. *Paul Between Damascus and Antioch: The Unknown Years*. Translated by John Bowden. Louisville: John Knox Westminster, 1997.

Hvalvik, Reidar. "Paul as a Jewish Believer—According to the Book of Acts." In *Jewish Believers in Jesus: The Early Centuries*, edited by Oskar Skarsaune and Reidar Hvalvik, 121–53. Peabody: Hendrickson, 2007.

Jervell, Jacob. *The Unknown Paul: Essays on Luke-Acts and Early Christian History*. Minneapolis: Augsburg, 1984.

Keener, Craig S. *Acts: An Exegetical Commentary: Volume 1: Introduction and 1:1—2:47*. Grand Rapids: Baker Academic, 2012.

Kim, Seyoon. *The Origin of Paul's Gospel*. Wissenschaftliche Untersuchungen zum Alten und Neuen Testament 4. Reprint, Eugene, OR: Wipf & Stock, 2007.

Knox, John. *Chapters in the Life of Paul*. New York: Abington-Cokesbury, 1950.

———. "The Pauline Chronology." *Journal of Biblical Literature* 58 (1939) 15–29.

Ladd, George Eldon. *A Theology of the New Testament*. Rev. ed. Grand Rapids: Eerdmans, 1993.
Longenecker, Richard N. *Galatians*. Word Biblical Commentary 41. Dallas: Word, 1990.
Lüdemann, Gerd. *Paul, Apostle to the Gentiles: Studies in Chronology*. Translated by F. Stanley Jones. Philadelphia: Fortress, 1984.
Marshall, I. Howard. *The Acts of the Apostles: An Introduction and Commentary*. Tyndale New Testament Commentaries. Grand Rapids: Eerdmans, 1980.
Matlock, R. Barry. "Does the Road to Damascus Run through the Letters of Paul?" In *Reading Acts Today: Essays in Honour of Loveday C. A. Alexander*, edited by Steve Walton et al., 81–97. London: T. & T. Clark, 2011.
Parsons, Mikeal C. *Acts*. Paideia Commentaries on the New Testament. Grand Rapids: Baker Academic, 2008.
Pervo, Richard I. *Dating Acts: Between the Evangelists and the Apologists*. Santa Rosa: Polebridge, 2006.
Phillips, Thomas E. *Paul, His Letters, and Acts*. Library of Pauline Studies. Peabody: Hendrickson, 2009.
Porter, Stanley E. *Paul in Acts*. Library of Pauline Studies. Peabody: Hendrickson, 2001.
Riesner, Rainer. *Paul's Early Period: Chronology, Mission Strategy, Theology*. Translated by Doug Stott. Grand Rapids: Eerdmans, 1998.
Schwartz, Daniel R. "Paul in the Canonical Book of Acts." In *The Writings of St. Paul*, edited by Wayne A. Meeks and John T. Fitzgerald, 187–98. 2nd ed. New York: Norton, 2007.
Thompson, Michael B. "Paul in the Book of Acts: Differences and Distance." *The Expository Times* 122.9 (2011) 425–36.
Vielhauer, Philipp. "On the 'Paulinism' in Acts." In *Studies in Luke–Acts*, edited by L. E. Keck and J. L. Martyn, 33–50. Nashville: Abingdon, 1966.
Wedderburn, A. J. M. "The 'We'-Passages in Acts: On the Horns of a Dilemma." *Zeitschrift für die neutestamentliche Wissenschaft* 93 (2002) 78–98.
Witherington, Ben, III. *Grace in Galatia: A Commentary on St Paul's Letter to the Galatians*. Grand Rapids: Eerdmans, 1998.
Wright, N. T. *The Resurrection of the Son of God*. Christian Origins and the Question of God 3. Minneapolis: Fortress, 2003.

4

You Have Been Called to Faithfully Follow Christ's Steps

A Missional Reading of 1 Peter

—Svetlana Khobnya

Preamble

The choice of 1 Peter[1] for tackling the question of Christian, faithful living is well-founded and deliberate for several reasons. Among many NT letters, this short letter manages to address Christians in different locations in Asia Minor, which underlines the world of plurality rather than singularity,[2] the world that reminds us of the one we live in today.[3] It acknowledges the personal significance of living by faith in Christ and the significance of living together as a community of holiness, giving practical instructions of faithful living in a society with its problems, suspicions, and hostility toward Christians. Perhaps for these reasons, 1 Peter is referred to as the "résumé of the Christian faith and of the conduct that it inspires"[4] and a guide for faithful living in a non-Christian world.[5]

Yet, 1 Peter is not an easy text to tackle in our contemporary society because it openly calls its readers to endure suffering as Christ did and insists that such suffering has God's approval (2:20). Moreover, the author appears to adopt a Roman perspective of life in the world when he advises readers to honor the emperor (2:17), asks slaves to accept the authority of their masters,

---

1. Authorship is not part of the discussion of this essay. For a helpful summary, see: Jobes, *1 Peter*, 5–19. I refer to the author as "First Peter" and "he" for convenience.
2. Smith, *Strangers to Family*, 15.
3. Christians are experiencing the power of "the empire" in different ways. Some live-in comparative freedom while others still live under tyranny and overt persecution.
4. Clowney, *1 Peter*, 15.
5. Davids, *First Epistle of Peter*, 3.

and teaches wives to submit to their husbands (2:18; 3:1). How can suffering be okay if it is not just? How can we interpret this text in modern Western societies where the subservience of women and the ownership of slaves is never acceptable? If we want to allow this scriptural text to influence new generations of Christians and to continue winning others with the liberating gospel of Christ, we need to find answers to these questions.

This essay takes on the challenge set up by a number of contemporary scholars about the importance of missional hermeneutic as one of the fundamental rubrics for biblical interpretation.[6] This reading focuses on understanding God's redeeming involvement in the world but also on his people's mission of proclaiming and living out their understanding of God's redeeming activity, which is fully revealed in Christ.[7] This second part of a missional hermeneutic and its openness to evaluate Christian call for new circumstances is of a particular interest here.

Such a reading of 1 Peter has been suggested before, usually as a part of the overall missional hermeneutic[8] or as an integral part of theological reflections on the relations between church and culture.[9] However, First Peter's specific picture of mission is less examined and deserves another look.[10] This essay will engage a search to answer the question: What does it mean to live as God's people in relation to the unbelieving world so that they "may be won without a word" (1 Pet 3:1-2)? More specifically: How is First Peter's social engagement in chapters 2 and 3 related to his call to follow Christ's steps?

First Peter's Framework

Two facets are absolutely crucial to identify before dealing with the question of Christian engagement in the world. They set forth 1 Peter's context. First, First Peter establishes the Christian identity as the people of God called through Christ. Structurally, he does this in two sets of affirmations (1:3–12 and 2:6–10) and exhortations (1:13—2:5 and 2:11—5:11).[11]

---

6. The issue is particularly articulated in one of the latest collections on reading the Bible missionally. See Goheen, *Reading the Bible Missionally*.

7. Wright, *Mission of God's People*, 24.

8. Wright, *Mission of God's People*; Flemming, *Recovering the Full Mission*, 209–30.

9. Volf, "Soft Difference."

10. Even in a recent volume on reading the Bible missionally, First Peter is only mentioned. See Goheen, *Reading the Bible Missionally*.

11. I tend to disagree with Davids who considers 2:1–5 as positive affirmation and 2:6–10 an exhortation, *1 Peter*, 50.

In the first set First Peter reminds his readers that they are united around and in Christ. They are aliens and exiles in Asia Minor (1:1), but united people of a living hope through the resurrection of Christ (1:3). Their belief in Christ eventually brings them salvation and, despite their present and immediate suffering in the surrounding world, their faithfulness and obedience to Christ will ultimately result in praise, honor, and glory (1:7, 9, 11). In these verses First Peter connects the revelations of Christ with what God has already been doing through Israel (1:10–11).[12] Now, the NT writers, and First Peter among them, confirm that the coming of Christ marks the fulfilment of the prophesies and the privileged position of the first-generation Christians. God's reason for hope and salvation has been announced to them and not even to the angels who wanted to know more (1:12).[13]

After framing the identity of Christians and after the value of the gospel of Christ is established, First Peter moves to the first set of exhortations (1:13—2:5). The appropriate response of the children of God is life in obedience to the Father (1:14). First Peter calls the audience to be holy in all their conduct as their Father is holy (1:14–16). This response is a proper witness to the action of God in Christ. These exhortations seem to be in place to shape Christian communities. Later, First Peter will instruct his audience on behavior in the world, but in these verses, he focuses on what Christian identity means and what it requires from them to be God's representatives in the first place. He asks them positively to prepare their minds for actions and hope in Christ (1:13), be holy in their conduct (1:14), love one another (1:22), and to get rid of all evil deeds (2:1).

In the second set of affirmations, First Peter writes his audience into the story of God and God's engagement in the history of Israel, ascribing multiple OT images to his audience.[14] For example, he reminds them, "Once you were not a people but now you are God's people" (2:10). These words are taken from Hosea 2:23a where the prophet pronounces God's call of reconciliation with Israel. The words reverse God's judgement of Hosea 1:9. God's reclaiming his people requires a reciprocal response and confession, "You are our God" (Hos

---

12. The prophets, he suggests, foretold the salvation that has come now in Christ. First Peter takes a known stand regarding the prophets' awareness: that they were serving not themselves but the present audience (1:12). That the prophets had spoken more for the upcoming generations than for their own has been known in Jewish tradition (1QpHab 7, 1): "And God told Habakkuk to write the things that would come upon the last generation; but he did not show him the final consummation."

13. Who these angelic figures are is not clear, but they are in submission to the resurrected Christ (3:22).

14. Boring counts at least seven, *1 Peter*, 98–100.

2:23b). First Peter uses Hosea's words for Christians of the diaspora (1:1) and those (whoever they are) in Babylon (5:13). In other words, God's mercy and love is not limited to Israel and Judah but extended to all new children born through participation in the death and resurrection of Christ. In these few verses, First Peter uses multiple images from Israel's past to place his audience in continuity with the people of Israel and their special relationship to God. They are God's chosen race, a royal priesthood, a holy nation, and God's own people (2:9, 10). The language that described Israel is applied to First Peter's readers. They are the people of God.

After reaffirming the identity of Christians as God's people in Christ, First Peter again moves to the exhortations in 2:11 that literally take over the rest of 1 Peter but are reinforced further by his appeal to the example of Christ in 2:21–24, the example of Sarah in 3:5–6, the example of Christ again in 3:18—4:1a, and his own example in 5:1. First Peter is convinced that Christian conduct in all aspects of life must be a direct consequence of their identity as God's people united by Christ. Moreover, this conduct, according to First Peter, must be proclaiming Christ as Lord and Savior and calling people to faith. It is clear in a way the author makes regular remarks as to why he asks them to behave in a certain way: "that you may proclaim the mighty acts of him who called out of darkness" (2:9); that "they may see your honorable deeds and glorify God" (2:12); that "they may be won over without a word" (3:2); that they "may be put to shame" by your conduct in Christ (3:16); "that God may be glorified" (4:11); "because you bear this [Christian] name" (4:16).

The second facet is the example of Christ that First Peter refers to extensively on two occasions (2:21–24; 3:18—4:1a) and mentions modelling the suffering of Christ several more times (e.g., 1:19–21; 4:13; 5:9). The position of Christ's example at key points in describing Christian behavior in the world is significant. Christ embodies suffering not only as an example to follow (2:21) but also as a saving act of God for all (2:24; 3:18). Through his suffering he is presented as a protector (2:25); and God's presence is active and glorified through him (4:11). Moreover, as Boring emphasizes, "the theological center of the section [2:18–25] affirms that the orientation 'for others' is at the heart of the universe, made know in Christ."[15] In the light of Christ's suffering Christian suffering also has a proclamation goal. The reality of suffering "manifests the reality of God's love that is oriented not to self . . . but to others."[16]

---

15. Boring, *1 Peter*, 123.
16. Boring, *1 Peter*, 123–24.

One more significant issue must be mentioned before we proceed with the investigation of First Peter's household codes. It is commonly recognized that Christian suffering as a consequence of persecution has a prominent place in this letter. There is a debate about the scope and precise nature of the persecution, but the modern consensus lies more and more in the conviction that the nature of persecution is the foundation for reading the entire letter.[17] My reading of First Peter will rest on this consensus.

First Peter's Mission Strategy in the Household Codes

If First Peter really thinks of proclaiming Christ's identity in his letter, then what is his strategy precisely? On the one hand, First Peter calls his audience to honor the emperor (2:17), asks slaves to accept the authority of their masters, and teaches wives to submit to their husbands (2:18; 3:1). On the other hand, First Peter's picture of believers as God's obedient children and followers of Christ suggests estrangement from society and a change of allegiance. Christians are aliens and exiles in the world they live in and are to conduct themselves accordingly (2:11–12; cf. 1:1). Does he discourage accommodation to the surrounding culture or encourage a level of adaptation to society? Or does First Peter provide a more sophisticated model of "differentiated acceptance and rejection of the surrounding culture"[18] as he seeks to say something more important to his audience? In other words, how does the author expect Christians to manifest their presence in the world?

First Peter recognizes the difference between Christians and the surrounding culture when he addresses the audience as "aliens and exiles"[19] (2:11) and reminds them that "you have already spent enough time in doing what the Gentile like to do" but "you no longer join them" (4:3–4). However, he emphasizes a positive process of establishing a Christian presence in the world: not breaking from the world but bringing Christ in by introducing and sustaining Christian values and, in this way, proclaiming Christ. To demonstrate First Peter's engagement with culture

---

17. A very helpful discussion of the nature of persecution in 1 Peter and its treatment in scholarship can be found in Williams's introductory chapter. See Williams, *Persecution in 1 Peter*, 3–14. Recently Smith offered an examination of how the epistle represents the earliest Christian construction of diaspora as a way of life. See Smith, *Strangers to Family*.

18. Volf, "Soft Difference," 22.

19. Literally, First Peter suggests that Christians are scattered in Asia Minor (1:1). How will their faith survive as they are spread around? But generally, Christians are aliens in Rome and anywhere, at home and in a new location in a world that is hostile to the gospel of Jesus Christ. See Jobes, *1 Peter*, 28–41.

let us examine his most debatable appeal to slaves, wives, and husbands (2:18—3:7), known as household codes.

First Peter's household order is part of his complicated instructions to his audience where he, on the one hand, urges believers to conduct themselves as godly and proper servants of God and differently from non-Christians (2:11–12, 15), and on the other, he asks them to accept the authority of every human being, including the emperor (2:13), and to accept hierarchy (2:18; 3:1). As such, First Peter's conversation here is not about ecclesiological structures and life within the Christian community but about Christian engagement with the non-Christian order of the world.

The household codes function to order society, a way of prescribed interaction between individuals and with the governing authorities. For Christians, to live according to the household codes must be a way of life in some sort of "commonality" with the empire.[20] The context openly suggests the instruction is given "to 'fit in' to the given social order."[21] But we need to remember that the interaction with the current culture is, as already established, preconditioned by their identity as God's people (2:10), by the behavior that in every case glorifies God (2:12), and by following the example of Christ (2:21).

In his household codes, First Peter addresses an audience that, in one way or another, is diminished in the eyes of the Roman hierarchical system: slaves, wives, and even husbands, because of their allegiance to the new religion. First Peter's households are written for the marginalized and, in a sense, outsiders of Roman high culture. By addressing them and assembling them around Christ, First Peter moves the marginalized Christians into a special category and brings them to the center of the universe.[22] He elevates them to some status of dignity and gives them a voice to speak and participate in the wider world. Christian slaves, wives, and husbands, who are now the kingdom of priests and holy nation, become "agents and participants in world-making, world-denying, and world-altering scenarios."[23]

It is interesting that First Peter does not address masters, an otherwise acceptable feature of the household codes in the NT (cf. Eph 6:9; Col 4:1) and elsewhere.[24] Usually, as Green reminds us, the household code "operates with a reciprocity of instructions, so that obligations appropriate to

---

20. Slater, *Ephesians*, 152.
21. Boring, *1 Peter*, 124.
22. Oakes, "Re-mapping the Universe," 322.
23. Lopez, "Minding the Gaps," 163.
24. Jewish and Stoic codes usually do not address slaves. See Balch, "Household Codes," 33.

their respective stations in life are outlined for both masters and slaves."[25] However, First Peter addresses only οἰκέται (household servants), which probably reflects the demographic reality of the churches being comprised more of servants than of masters.[26] But more importantly, the understanding of the household servants (οἰκέται) embody "the all but defenseless vulnerability of all" Christian aliens and exiles (2:11) in Asia Minor or perhaps even all Christians who are slaves of God (2:16).[27] The example of Christ that is placed in the middle of the household codes as a model to follow suggests that the vulnerable status of slaves refers to all Christians in the wider world.[28] If so, then the concept of "slaves" and their fate are exemplary, illustrative "both of the Christian situation in the Roman Empire and of the Christlike reaction they must adopt to it."[29] The apparent conformation to the societal norms here is not for the sake of integration with these norms but of living differently in submission to Christ, indeed, recognizing the existence of unjust suffering and following the example of Christ in such circumstances (2:21).

Christian women are called to behave exactly in a way that wins others over (3:1). I am sure that this challenging verse of submission to husbands has been used more than once to indicate women's overall subordination to men. But clearly a mission-oriented inclusion of "that they may be won without a word" by behavior must not be taken lightly to understand the thread of the passage. Christian women are to behave in a way that proclaims Christ without words, especially to their non-believing husbands. In Graeco-Roman society the wife must acknowledge the gods of her husband.[30] If First Peter addresses Christian wives who already turned away from their husbands' gods, then "maintaining a demeanor acceptable in all other areas to her non-Christian husband and his values not only lessens the tension within the household but may even contribute to the eventual conversion of the unbelieving husband."[31] In any case, a

---

25. Green, *1 Peter*, 77.

26. Although the precise number of slaves in the Graeco-Roman Empire is debated, their presence and usage in different spheres of society is undisputable. The centrality of slavery for reconstructing the demographic distribution in these emerging churches is recognized in scholarly publications. See Glancy, *Slavery in Early Christianity*.

27. Although other explanations are possible, the suggested option fits best the immediate context in 1 Peter. See Achtemeier, *1 Peter*, 192.

28. The idea is supported by many interpreters. See further discussion in Green, *1 Peter*, 78.

29. Green, *1 Peter*, 192.

30. Balch, *Let Wives be Submissive*, 83–86.

31. Achtemeier, *1 Peter*, 208.

great emphasis is given to the wife's behavior that may be acceptable to society without compromising her faith.

First Peter offers a model for such behavior from the past. He refers to Sarah in 3:6, indicating at least two exemplary actions from Sarah's behavior, namely her obedience to Abraham and her addressing him as lord (probably also to emphasize her obedience). Doing what is right and not being frightened are two further actions that are prescribed as the actions to follow for those who are truly her followers (3:6b). The relationship between Sarah and Abraham cannot always be described as her subordination to Abraham. Sarah, as it appears in Genesis 16:2 and 21:12, almost gives orders to Abraham and Abraham obeys her. But these episodes are hardly recalled in the history of interpretation. Overall, Sarah appears in Jewish and Christian literature as a woman of wisdom, virtue, and faith (1QapGen 20.2–8; Philo, Abr. 206; cf. Heb 11:11). Abraham and Sarah enjoyed a long and peaceful marriage together. Abraham mourned for Sarah deeply after her death and despite marrying another woman after her death, he was buried with Sarah. It is interesting that Sarah is described to be frightened when she lied to God (Gen 18:15) and not when she lied for her husband (Gen 12:10–12; Gen 22:2).

So, First Peter emphasizes the fact that Sarah obeys Abraham. Could First Peter allude to her obedience that extended to participating in Abraham's deceit of the Pharaoh and Abimelech? This allusion would certainly fit the context. Sarah's decision to suffer for her husband's sake and obedience to him exemplifies a certain marital behavior that stresses the importance of peace and harmony between husband and wife. It is possible that by providing a model of this virtuous woman from Israel's past, First Peter calls Christian women to create a positive atmosphere in the household, thus, accomplishing God's better way and providing a platform for turning to God, even if it means subjecting themselves to unjust treatment.[32]

But this must be clear: This statement does not mean that this model is just or liberating for women nor should it ever be seen as a pattern for perpetuating injustice towards women in a modern Christian household. A call to accept abusive behavior in our current social structure is never acceptable. At the most, First Peter calls Christian women to respond to their circumstances with a demonstration of service.

As a minority in the Roman world, Christians did not and could not change the societal structures. Probably, the reality of the situation in 1 Peter

---

32. Jobes, *1 Peter*, 206. Spenser adds another explanation comparing Sarah's decision to suffer for her husband's sake with the Christlike behavior while Abraham exemplifies a husband who disobeys the word. See Spencer, "Peter's Pedagogical Method," 113.

dictates the author's determination to ask his community to accept hierarchy in order to survive when the surrounding culture dominated the worldview and practices of all people, including those in the church.[33] However, what First Peter does is recognize the right for faith to play a role and for the allegiance of marginalized parties to be to Christ only. This is the alternative reality which is subversive to societal structures as people within them are transformed. In Christ's suffering he finds a model for his readers to survive their situation without losing hope and giving up in despair. Therefore, First Peter strategically places Christ's example (2:22–25) in the middle of his household codes so that these marginalized parties know their shepherd and protector (2:25) and even in submission should not be frightened (3:6b). Placing Christians solidly in the sphere of Christ, First Peter both challenges and encourages his readers to endure as Christ did. Perhaps, 1 Peter needs to be reread as "a response to dominion rather than as a template for it, bolstering contemporary claims that our cultural inheritance is not *for* empire but *against* it, that Christian can participate and always have participated in political processes, and that the imperial orientation of Christian churches is not a foregone conclusion."[34]

Husbands are to behave in a similar way (ὁμοίως), as First Peter insists in 3:7. The question is what parallel the author draws here. Should their behavior be analogous to Christian wives (3:1), to slaves (2:18), as appropriate for all God's people (2:17), and as genuine followers of Christ (2:21)? Most likely, he means all of these. This might explain the shortness of the instruction to husbands (only one verse). Since First Peter already explained what it means to live as Christians in the world for slaves and women, husbands are to follow a similar pattern, a pattern compatible with Christ and his suffering for humanity. They are to follow the same positive model of behavior; this time he specifies it more in terms of love and respect/honor. Their behavior must be winsome just as the behavior of slaves and wives is. First Peter uses a different word for "wives" here (in comparison to 3:1). The singular adjective "female" (γυναικεῖος) with a definite article refers to a class not necessarily to one woman.[35] Indeed, the model of genuine love and respect expected

---

33. The "staying alive" theme emphasized in Smith's monograph is a way this tricky passage can be successfully navigated. See Smith, *Strangers to Family*. It is a survival manual with the positive possible outcome that the unbelieving husband might somehow be won to Christ. But, in conversation with my colleague, K. Brower, he raises the issue of the text remaining a text of terror (and when as read as a template) in modern Western societies where the subservience of women and the ownership of slaves is never acceptable.

34. Lopez, "Minding the Gaps," 159.

35. Jobes, *1 Peter*, 207.

from Christian husbands in their households is expected to be given toward all women, whether they are Christians or not. If this notion of the conduct of a believing husband were to be extended to the empire that operates one large household, then First Peter's instruction to husbands has far-reaching consequences. If the attitude of men toward women in society is one of ruler and subject (Aristotle, *Pol.* 1.2), this is not how Peter views the Christian household. First Peter envisions transformation from within. Christian men are to demonstrate love and honor. "What is dishonored is to be honored," adds Green.[36] In fact, this model of love and respect toward women is the only way for Christian men to stand right in relationship to God. It is only then, First Peter writes at the end of 3:7, nothing may hinder their prayers. Achtemeier explains this bluntly, if any men "transfer cultural notions about the superiority of men over women into the Christian community," they "lose their ability to communicate with God."[37]

Finally, First Peter concludes the section on the household codes by giving instructions to all parties (πάντες) on their Christian conduct (3:8–22). Christians of any societal status and gender together are an alternative family in a sense that they are to live in unity, sympathy, love, compassion, and humility towards each other (3:8), and to respond nonviolently to and in a hostile society. This life is not only a proper conduct for God's people honoring Christ but also visible in relation to the world around (3:13–17) and beneficial in the eschatological sense (3:9). First Peter believes that a good life in Christ is enough for Christians to be visible in society, to subvert its structures, and to win non-Christians over.

Some Implications from a Missional Reading of 1 Peter

The question of how Christians are to fulfill the mission of spreading the gospel in the world has been continuously on the agenda among missiologists and practitioners alike. The methods can be different, but all used to rise from a tension between verbal witness and actions as a testimony of Christ. Recent scholars go beyond this old dichotomy between evangelism and social action admitting a complexity of mission in the world that has its roots in Scripture.[38] They recognize the significance of the identity of people called by God and sent in the world that is expressed in the ministry

---

36. Green, *1 Peter*, 100.

37. Achtemeier, *1 Peter*, 218.

38. Goheen, *Reading the Bible Missionally*; Volf, "Soft Difference"; Flemming, *Recovering the Full Mission*, 206–30; Wright, *Mission of God's People*.

of being, doing, and telling.[39] They refer to the missional hermeneutic as hermeneutic for the kingdom of God that emphasizes the movement from the particular to the universal.[40] This means that God's purpose moves from a choice of a particular person or a group towards others. Moreover, God's mission for the sake of all can be reached by way of the least. "The priority of the poor and the unimportant in God's mission is also for the sake of all, such that his saving purpose can reach the wealthy and the powerful only by the way of the least."[41] The mission of God is never oppressive and its scope is universal. It is both centripetal and centrifugal, but its center is always God.[42] The NT writers and First Peter among them point to this complexity in their writings.

Reading 1 Peter missionally adds to the picture of how the church mission in the world looks. By defining Christians as exiles and aliens, First Peter presupposes their counter-cultural character. As is evident above, First Peter establishes Christian identity as true and obedient children of God and followers of Christ, participants in his suffering, and as such, God's witnesses in the world. Having God in Christ as its center, Christians assume the position of social and cultural marginality. At the same time, assembling them around Christ, First Peter places them in a special category providing them with a voice and ability to participate in world-changing mission. This idea of having God in the center is the guiding principle for witnessing in the world. Bauckham believes that it needs to be taken seriously and reconsidered today in order to improve Christian witness of proclamation and compassion.[43]

The heart of First Peter's message is Christian good behavior that flows from their identity as God's people shaped by Christ and his suffering on the cross. Despite any hostile situations that Christians find themselves in (cf. 1:7–9), First Peter is adamant to embrace the diaspora in its totality and diversity[44] and participate in social structures by offering a testimony of good deeds. This model presupposes reexamining our personal stories in the light of the mission of the cross.

The question it raises though is how to keep the balance of the non-negotiable middle (centrality in Christ) with the possibility to adapt to the different and changing circumstances because the story of God's mission

---

39. Flemming, *Recovering the Full Mission*.
40. Bauckham, "Mission as Hermeneutic," 42–44.
41. Bauckham, "Mission as Hermeneutic," 43.
42. Bauckham, "Mission as Hermeneutic," 37.
43. Bauckham, "Mission as Hermeneutic," 37.
44. Smith, *Strangers to Family*, 26.

continues through his people in their engagement with the world.[45] A missional hermeneutic stresses openness to the new particularities and diversities, "narratives of other times and places, other groups and individuals, narratives with which the church's mission brings the biblical meta-narrative into relationship."[46] With this in mind, 1 Peter needs to be engaged and reread within the context of the twenty-first century.

Reading 1 Peter Today

First Peter is not an easy text to interpret for our contemporary society, with both an acute awareness of social justice and a sense of high integration with society.

What remains unchangeable for today's readers is First Peter's establishment of the Christian identity as the people of God. His claim is that the OT Scriptures provide a basis for the Christian understanding of what God really has accomplished for them and how he continues to direct them in Christ who fulfills the OT promises. Christ's followers are inheritors and successors of a rich antiquity and of the enabling power of God that breaks in the present and continues to shine through Christ. What an elevating and liberating idea to hold to and to pass on!

What changed? Culture, circumstances, and time! First Peter is not about ecclesiological structures but about Christian engagement with the non-Christian first-century Mediterranean world. It is about Christian survival and their soft mission[47] to be themselves that is to carry on Christian identity. It is about offering to society an alternative picture of life, values, and orientations. Studies and practice show that any model must be retested within new circumstances. This is the only way for an example to continue to work. Christians today are more aware of social justice, more vocal, and more empowered to challenge social structures. Christianity is not a minority in the world (certainly in the West) anymore but a community with a power of influence. And this power of influence must be Christlike.

What makes Christians Christians is not the submission to hierarchy but living for God and in Christ. Although First Peter gives the instructions of submission to slaves and women, he calls all (men and women of any status) for actions of genuine mutual love, hospitality, service, and humility

---

45. Wright, "Mission as Matrix," 103, 122.

46. Bauckham, "Mission as Hermeneutic," 41.

47. Volf's language of soft difference is appropriate here. It includes security in God and a life of making a difference in the world without fear but also without manipulation of "my way or no way." Christians "have no need either to subordinate or damn others but can allow others space to be themselves. For people who live the soft difference, mission fundamentally takes the form of witness and invitation" ("Soft Difference," 24).

(1:22; 4:7–11). Practically, there is no place for slavery, misuse, submission, or violence when there is love, hospitality, service to each other, and humility. First Peter is possibly less optimistic about changing society publicly, but he is hopeful about Christ working in Christians, transforming them and touching others through their good work. Maybe First Peter could even be said to encourage the subversion of hierarchical structures in those homes of Christians who still cling to the patriarchal model of antiquity. Contemporary Christians would not give offense by living lives of absolute rejection of slavery and hierarchical family structures!

Many Christians today are privileged to observe global cultural changes of accepting gender equality, concerns for social justice, and raising voices in solidarity and support of those who suffer. Is this time for the church to embrace these positive changes publicly, come out of survival mode and move further to deal with questions that still trouble us?

How do we make Christ visible even without words in the 21st century?[48] What do we do when we are CEOs in big companies or work as cleaners, have lived in a country long or asylum seekers? How do we entertain ourselves? Is Christ visible then? How can the language of submission be just and winsome? What is a missional model of a Christian woman/man today? How may we together proclaim Christ in our behavior? These and other practical questions are waiting responses from those who want to allow scriptural texts to come alive in their faithful and holy living that reflect convergence between the texts and our modern world.

Bibliography

Achtemeier, Paul J. *1 Peter: Hermeneia—A Critical and Historical Commentary on the Bible*. Minneapolis: Fortress, 1996.

Balch, D. L. *Let Wives Be Submissive: The Domestic Code in 1 Peter*. Society of Biblical Literature Dissertation Series 26. Atlanta: Scholars, 1981.

———. "Household Codes." In *Greco-Roman Literature and the New Testament: Selected Forms and Genres*, edited by D. E. Aune, 25–50. Atlanta: Scholars, 1988.

Bartlett, David L. "The First Letter of Peter: Introduction, Commentary, and Reflections." In *The New Interpreter's Bible: Hebrews–Revelation*, edited by Leander E. Keck et al., 12:229–319. Nashville: Abingdon, 1998.

Bauckham, Richard. "Mission as Hermeneutic for Scriptural Interpretation." In *Reading the Bible Missionally*, edited by Michael W. Goheen, 28–44. Grand Rapids: Eerdmans, 2016.

Boring, Eugene M. *1 Peter*. Abingdon New Testament Commentaries. Nashville: Abingdon, 1999.

---

48. In the world today, there are many places where women are still oppressed and where slavery is barely below the surface. This text is heard differently, for instance, in India or Pakistan or parts of Africa where the lives of many women are still hierarchical and abusive. We need to think how the gospel must have something to say to them, not in terms for feminism but in terms of the gospel.

Brownlee, William H. *The Midrash Pesher of Habakkuk*. Society of Biblical Literature Monograph Series 24. Missoula: Scholars, 1979.
Clowney, Edmund P. *The Message of 1 Peter*. Nottingham: InterVarsity, 1988.
Davids, Peter H. *The First Epistle of Peter*. New International Commentary on the New Testament. Grand Rapids: Eerdmans, 1990.
Flemming, Dean. *Recovering the Full Mission of God: A Biblical Perspective on Being, Doing and Telling*. Downers Grove: IVP Academic, 2013.
Glancy, Jennifer A. *Slavery in Early Christianity*. Oxford: Oxford University Press, 2002.
Goheen, Michael W., ed. *Reading the Bible Missionally*. Grand Rapids: Eerdmans, 2016.
Green, Joel B. *1 Peter*. The Two Horizons New Testament Commentary. Grand Rapids: Eerdmans, 2007.
———. "Living as Exiles: The Church in the Diaspora in 1 Peter." In *Holiness and Ecclesiology in the New Testament*, edited by Kent E. Brower and Andy Johnson, 311–25. Grand Rapids: Eerdmans, 2007.
Jobes, Karen H. *1 Peter*. Baker Exegetical Commentary on the New Testament. Grand Rapids: Baker Academic, 2005.
Le Roux, Elritia. *Ethics in 1 Peter: The Imitatio Christi and the Ethics of Suffering in 1 Peter and in the Gospel of Mark—A Comparative Study*. Eugene: Pickwick, 2018.
Lopez, Davina C. "Minding the Gaps." In *Bridges in New Testament Interpretation: Interdisciplinary Advances*, edited by Neil Elliott and Werner H. Kelber, 149–78. Minneapolis: Lexington, 2018.
Marshal, Howard. *New Testament Theology: Many Witnesses, One Gospel*. Downers Grove: InterVarsity, 2004.
Nienhuis, David R., and Robert W. Wall. *Reading the Epistles of James, Peter, John and Jude as Scripture: The Shaping and Shape of a Canonical Collection*. Grand Rapids; Eerdmans, 2013.
Oakes, Peter. "Re-mapping the Universe: Paul and the Emperor in 1 Thessalonians and Philippians." *Journal for the Study of the New Testament* 27.3 (2005) 301–22.
Slater, Thomas B. *Ephesians*. Macon: Smyth & Helwys, 2012.
Smith, Shively T. J. *Strangers to Family: Diaspora and 1 Peter's Invention of God's Household*. Waco: Baylor University Press, 2016.
Spencer, A. B. "Peter's Pedagogical Method in 1 Peter 3:6." *Bulletin for Biblical Research* 10 (2000) 107–19.
Volf, Miroslav. "Soft Difference: Theological Reflections on the Relation between Church and Culture in 1 Peter." *Ex Auditu* 10 (1994) 15–30.
Westfall, Cynthia Long. "Continue to Remember the Poor: Social Justice within the Poor and Powerless Jewish Christian Communities." In *The Bible and Social Justice: Old Testament and New Testament Foundations for the Church's Urgent Call*, edited by Cynthia Long Westfall and Bryan R. Dyer, 152–75. Eugene: Pickwick, 2015.
Williams, Travis B. *Persecution in 1 Peter: Differentiating and Contextualizing Early Christian Suffering*. Supplements to Novum Testamentum 145. Leiden: Brill, 2012.
Wright, Christopher J. H. "Mission as Matrix for Hermeneutics and Biblical Theology." In *Out of Egypt: Biblical Theology and Biblical Interpretation. Scripture and Hermeneutics Series*, edited by Craig Bartholomew et al., 5:102–44. Milton Kenyes: Paternoster, 2004.
———. *The Mission of God's People: A Biblical Theology of the Church's Mission*. Grand Rapids: Zondervan, 2010.
Wright, N. T. "Reading the New Testament Missionally." In *Reading the Bible Missionally*, edited by Michael W. Goheen, 175–93. Grand Rapids: Eerdmans, 2016.

Section 2

Theological and Historical Perspectives on Christian Faithfulness

5

The Faith of Christ

Theological Implications

—Thomas A. Noble

John Wesley's sermon "Salvation by Faith" was preached before the University of Oxford on 11th June, 1738, less than three weeks after his radical change of heart and mind at the meeting in Aldersgate Street on the 24th of May. Its significance is seen in that it was later published as the first in his *Sermons on Several Occasions*. It was a kind of manifesto of the preaching and theology of the eighteenth-century evangelical revival, and it has been published as the first sermon in the subsequent collections of Wesley's sermons. Starting from Ephesians 2:8, Wesley tries to define the faith "through which we are saved." First, he says, it is "a faith in Christ—Christ, and God through Christ, are the proper object of it." But he also goes on to say: "It is not barely a speculative, rational thing, a cold lifeless assent, a train of ideas in the head; but also a disposition of the heart."[1] And there, in those two statements, are what we might call the objective and subjective poles of faith. Subjectively, it is a "disposition of the heart": but the objective pole, that on which all relies, is Christ. The sermon thus truly reflects the balance in the account in his journal of the 24th of May. His reference later in the sermon to Martin Luther reflects the fact that it was while listening to the words of Luther in Aldersgate Street that he was moved to testify, "I felt my heart strangely warmed." But that subjective aspect (which has too often been regarded as the only key) was balanced by the objective aspect in the very next sentence: "I felt I did trust in Christ, Christ alone, for salvation."[2] There is the objective foundation for faith, the *solus Christus* of the Reformation!

---

1. Wesley, *Works*, 1:120.
2. Wesley, *Works*, 18:250.

Wesley's dependence on Luther is clear. His discovery of salvation by faith was in fact a rediscovery of the faith of the Reformation, and particularly, of Luther's understanding of the writings of the apostle Paul. But today, new developments in the understanding of the theology of Paul are raising questions about the whole trajectory of Protestant interpretation from Luther to Wesley and up to the recent past. Wesleyan theologians, therefore, need to take into account all the developments of recent decades which go under the general heading of "the new perspective on Paul."

Developments in Pauline Studies: Richard Hays

Krister Stendahl may be regarded as the forerunner of the "new perspective" with his critical essay of 1963, "The Apostle Paul and the Introspective Conscience of the West."[3] Paul did not suffer from a guilty conscience, he argued, before he met Christ on the road to Damascus, and we must not read the "conversion" experiences of Augustine, Luther, or Wesley into Paul's writings. But a wider "new perspective" arose with E. P. Sanders's criticism of the notion that the Judaism of Paul's day was a form of legalism akin to the Pelagianism attacked by Augustine, or what Luther regarded as the Pelagianism of the medieval church.[4] Judaism was not a form of legalism but was "covenantal nomism." James Dunn followed, reinterpreting Paul's phrase "the works of the law" as referring not to an attempt to achieve personal salvation through "good works," but as those particular "boundary markers" of Judaism—circumcision, sabbath-keeping, and the dietary laws. It was not legalism but exclusivism that Paul was attacking.[5] N. T. Wright argued that the overarching theme of covenant enabled us to see how Paul's gospel was in continuity with the faith of Israel. Jews in Paul's day were not focused on the salvation of their eternal souls in a transcendent heaven (like the later gnostics), but on the restoration of the kingdom to Israel and the return of Yahweh to Zion, thus ending the continuing state of "exile." Paul's zealous covenantal monotheism was revolutionized when he encountered the risen Messiah Jesus on the road to Damascus.[6] The weakness of the "new perspective" scholars may lie in their understanding of medieval and Reformation theology, but they have certainly stirred up healthy debate.

Perhaps the development in Pauline studies most directly relevant to the Lutheran and Wesleyan understanding of salvation by faith is found

---

3. Stendahl, "Apostle Paul," 199–215.
4. Sanders, *Paul and Palestinian Judaism.*
5. Dunn, *New Perspective on Paul.*
6. Wright, *Climax of the Covenant*; Wright, *Paul and the Faithfulness of God.*

in the writings of the Methodist Richard Hays. Of particular significance is Hays's contention in his book, *The Faith of Jesus Christ*, that the phrase *pistis Iēsou Christou*, traditionally translated as "faith in Jesus Christ," should be translated strictly according to the Greek genitive as "the faith *of* Jesus Christ."[7] The subtitle, *The Narrative Substructure of Galatians 3:1—41*, makes it clear that the book is about the wider matter of the narrative elements that undergird Paul's thought. The central thesis of his book is that "*a story about Jesus Christ is presupposed by Paul's argument in Galatians, and his theological reflection attempts to articulate the meaning of that story.*"[8] Originating as his doctoral thesis in the days when New Testament studies was dominated by Rudolf Bultmann, it was written to oppose Bultmann's attempt to "de-narrativize" Paul's thought world and understand the gospel as a message about human decision and self-understanding. Influenced by Barth and Frei, Hays presented the "diametrically opposed view," that "the story *is* the word of God, and we know God in no other way than as the God who has acted through the faithfulness of Jesus Christ to 'rescue us from the present evil age' (Gal 1:4)."[9]

Hays argues, following a line including Schweitzer, Dodd, Cullmann and Käsemann, that Paul's theology is rooted in the story of the gospel. In the letter to the Galatians, Paul recapitulates the gospel story he had preached to them in order to refute and dismiss the distortions of "another gospel." Employing the influential research on narrative structures developed by A. J. Griemas,[10] Hays analyzes two passages in the epistle with a similar structure. In Galatians 3:13–14, Paul writes that "Christ redeemed us from the curse of the law, having become a curse for us . . . in order that the blessing of Abraham may come in Christ Jesus upon the Gentiles." The sharp distinction between "the Gentiles" and "us" indicates that here Paul is viewing the event "from a clearly Jewish perspective."[11] In Galatians 4:4–5, Paul writes, "But when the time had fully come, God sent forth his Son, born of a woman, born under the law, to redeem those who were under the law so that we might receive the adoption of sons." Hays sees this as reflecting a "non-Jewish point of view." But both are versions of the same story of the gospel which is the "narrative sub-structure" for Paul's theological argument, and both lead to the reception of the Spirit. The first concludes: "that we might receive the promise of the Spirit through

---

7. Hays, *Faith of Jesus Christ*.
8. Hays, *Faith of Jesus Christ*, xxiv, his italics.
9. Hays, *Faith of Jesus Christ*, xxvi.
10. Hays, *Faith of Jesus Christ*, 82–117. Griemas is also influential for N. T. Wright.
11. Hays, *Faith of Jesus Christ*, 78.

faith" (3:14); and the second: "that we might receive adoption as sons. And because you are sons, God has sent the Spirit of his Son into our hearts, crying 'Abba! Father!' (4:6)."

The reception of the Spirit "through faith" brings Hays to the problem posed by the way in which Protestant theology since Luther has found in Galatians "classic proof texts for the doctrine that individuals are saved not by performing works but by believing in Jesus Christ." Hays notes the risk this always carries of turning faith into another kind of work, a human achievement. The response has been to argue that faith is not the product of human will but of divine agency. But Hays summarizes the problem:

> We must ask, however, whether this sort of explanation may be read into our texts in Galatians. Do these passages speak of *pistis* as a gift placed by God in the human soul? Is faith described here as an experience ("*Erlebnis*") that encounters us from above? What is the connection between faith and Christ? When Paul writes of *pistis Christou* does he mean to refer to a human act of "believing" (*das Glauben*) which has Christ for its object as well as its author?[12]

Hays notes that the starting point for discussion is often Galatians 2:16 in the traditional translation: "We ourselves . . . who know that one is justified not by works of the law but through faith in Jesus Christ (*dia pisteōs Iēsou Christou*) . . . even we have believed in Jesus Christ in order to be justified by faith in Christ (*ek pisteōs Christou*) and not by works of the law." The clause, "we have believed in Jesus Christ," is taken as determining the sense of *dia pisteōs Iēsou Christou* and *ek pisteōs Christou* as referring to our faith *in* Christ. Hays grants that this clause *does* refer to *our* faith *in* Christ, "an act of believing/trusting towards Christ as 'object.'" But the question is whether this determines the meaning of *pistis Christou* or whether it should not be translated as "the faith of Christ." "Is it possible," Hays asks, "that in Paul's thought the faith *of* Jesus Christ may play some role as well as our faith *in* Christ Jesus?"[13]

Hays's question should be carefully noted. He is not denying that our faith *in* Christ plays a role, but he is going to argue that *in addition to our faith*, Paul has in mind the faith *of* Christ himself. He undertakes a thorough exegesis of Galatians 3, and examines both the grammatical and theological issues to arrive at the conclusion that the grammatical evidence favors the view that *pistis Iēsou Christou* should be translated "the faith *of* Jesus

---

12. Hays, *Faith of Jesus Christ*, 122.
13. Hays, *Faith of Jesus Christ*, 123.

Christ" and that this is theologically intelligible.[14] Further examination of Galatians 2:20 and 26 and Romans 3:21–26 arrives at the same conclusion. He notes that this "should not be understood to abolish or preclude human faith directed toward Christ, which is also an important component of Paul's thought."[15] But, "in every case except Galatians 2:16 'the faith of Jesus Christ' provides a better and more satisfying sense than the traditional translation of 'faith in Jesus Christ.'" And even in Galatians 2:16 "it is justifiable to maintain that the text means 'we placed our trust in Christ Jesus in order that we might be justified on the basis of Christ's faithfulness.'"[16]

Hays goes on to analyze the logic of Paul's argumentation in Galatians 3:1 to 4:11 in order to establish the thesis that Paul's argument may be summed up thus:

> Christians are justified/redeemed not by virtue of their own faith but because they participate in Jesus Christ, who enacted the obedience of faith in their behalf. Abraham is understood by Paul not as an exemplar of faith in Christ but as a typological foreshadowing of Christ himself, a representative figure whose faithfulness secures blessing and salvation vicariously for others.[17]

Paul's argument does not follow "propositional logic" in which consequences follow necessarily from premises, but "narrative logic" in which each new event in a story is intelligible though not predictable, unexpected, and yet a consequence of previous events. "The constraints of narrative logic are thus determined by contingent and particular events rather than by 'the necessary truths of reason.'"[18] Hays's conclusion is "that Paul's argument in Gal 3:1—4:11 is a unified attempt to think through the implications of a gospel story in which salvation hinges upon the faithfulness of Jesus Christ."[19]

Theological Implications

Given the Reformation insistence on *sola scriptura*, fully endorsed by Wesley and all who are truly Wesleyan, this advance in our understanding of the thinking of Paul necessarily has implications for our theology. But as

---

14. Hays, *Faith of Jesus Christ*, 150, 153.
15. Hays, *Faith of Jesus Christ*, 161.
16. Hays, *Faith of Jesus Christ*, 162.
17. Hays, *Faith of Jesus Christ*, 166.
18. Hays, *Faith of Jesus Christ*, 195–96; with reference to Aristotle (*Poet.* 1452a) and Ricoeur.
19. Hays, *Faith of Jesus Christ*, 205.

David McEwan has emphasized, Wesley was a *pastoral* theologian and so Wesleyans must be clear that the implications are not merely abstract and cerebral.[20] All of our understanding of the Christian life, our relationship to God in Christ by the Spirit, our spiritual journey, and our preaching and pastoral practice, are shaped by our theology, informed as it is in turn by our reading of Holy Scripture. What then are the implications for our theology and so for our practice?

Implications for our Christology

The most obvious place to begin is with Christology. What are the implications for our understanding of our Lord Jesus Christ? The gospel we preach is "the gospel of God" (Rom 1:1) and is more specifically designated by Paul as "concerning his Son, descended from David according to the flesh, and designated Son of God in power according to the Spirit of holiness by his resurrection from the dead" (Rom 1:3-4). There is Christology in a nutshell, or rather, in the defining narrative of the gospel. The one who was humanly descended from David, and was crucified, was declared to be the Son of God by his resurrection. There is the narrative One-in-two structure of Christology which is embedded in the gospel. It is the one-in-two narrative of crucifixion and resurrection, resulting in the one-in-two confession of the One who is both fully human and yet worshiped as "Lord." This is the New Testament root of the Christology contextualized at the Council of Chalcedon (451 AD) in the Greek concepts of one "Person" in two "natures." The Christological significance then of speaking of "the faith *of* Christ" is clearly that it implies a deeper understanding of his true humanity and of its saving significance.

At this point, Wesleyan theologians will be aware that John Wesley has been charged with underplaying the humanity of Christ so seriously that he has been charged with the ancient heresies of monophysitism, Apollinarianism, or even docetism! It is doubtful whether monophysitism should be regarded as a heresy at all. It is the ancient position of the Coptic church in direct descent from the Alexandrian tradition of Athanasius and Cyril, which rejected the Chalcedonian terminology of two "natures" (*physeis*) but which still held to Christ's true deity and true humanity within an emphasis on the unity of the Person. On the other hand, Apollinarianism, the belief that in the Person of Christ, the Logos took the place of the human mind, was denounced as a heresy at the Council of Constantinople in 381. Docetism, that Christ was the Son of God but only appeared (*dokein*)

20. McEwan, *Wesley as a Pastoral Theologian*.

to be human, has always been regarded as a heresy since the writings of Ignatius of Antioch in the generation after the apostles, and indeed since the writing of First John.

The notion that Wesley was guilty of these heresies developed in the last few decades from a mere suspicion into an established assumption on the part of some, but can now be dismissed. Even the original suggestion of Albert Outler and John Deschner that Wesley had a tendency to underplay the humanity of Christ has been shown to depend on a misreading of the evidence.[21] But while Wesley was fully orthodox in his Christology, it is probably true to say that the *saving* significance of the humanity of Christ was not as fully understood in his era as it was among some of the Eastern Fathers. To explore that further, we need to focus on soteriology, particularly the doctrine of the Atonement.

Implications for the Doctrine of the Atonement

Soteriology, the doctrine of salvation, is generally regarded in the evangelical theology of the Reformation tradition as a matter of justification, regeneration, adoption, and sanctification. But these are matters of what we may call *subjective* soteriology. The concern is with how the believer enters into the salvation of Christ, and that was the focus of German pietism and of the eighteenth-century evangelical revival in Britain and her colonies. In continuity with the Lutheran Reformation, the focus of preaching and writing was upon justification by faith and the life of holiness in the life of *the individual believer*. The *ordo salutis* for the individual believer was the center of interest for Puritan and Pietist, Lutheran, Calvinist, and Arminian. Hence Wesley's sermon manifesto, "Salvation by Faith," was concerned to stress that the salvation of the individual did not come about by good works, but by faith in Christ.

But *subjective* soteriology (how one enters into salvation) is dependent upon *objective* soteriology. We have to ask: what is that salvation we receive when we believe? Where did it come from? How was it achieved? The answer is clear: it is that salvation completed by Christ on the cross, and all the Reformation traditions—Lutheran, Pietist, Puritan, Calvinist, Arminian (or at least *evangelical* Arminians)—viewed that primarily from the perspective of the Anselmic tradition. Indeed, it was not only understood from a generally Anselmic perspective, that Christ satisfied the Father by paying the price, suffering so that we need not do so, but in

21. See Vickers, "Christology," 555–58; and Van Kuiken, "Deschner's Wesley," 38–56; with reference to Deschner, *John Wesley's Christology*.

the more specific form of *penal* substitution, present in Luther's thought, but explicitly developed by Melanchthon and Calvin. In the "wondrous exchange," according to this view, Christ bore our sin in the sense that he bore our punishment in our place so that those who believe in him receive his righteousness and his eternal life.

It has to be said that the Anselmic tradition (both in the form of penal substitution and its other forms) lays great stress on the *humanity* of Christ. Anselm's treatise, *Cur Deus Homo*, argued that it was as "Man," that is, as *a human being*, that Christ represented us to God, paying the debt of honor that we could not pay and so giving "satisfaction." Ironically, the contrary perspective preferred by nineteenth-century "Liberal" theology, that Christ displayed the love of God in the cross so that *we* may respond in love, puts more focus on his deity! But although the Anselmic view of the atonement, which dominated the doctrine of Wesley and his evangelical contemporaries, focused on the *humanity* of Christ, it is arguable that it did not do so fully enough. True, they saw that in his "active obedience," Christ as "Man" fulfilled the law for us, and in his "passive obedience," he bore the wrath of God for us. But obeying the law and bearing a penalty are both rather external aspects of what it is to be human. Yes, indeed, Christ lived the perfect life of holiness, but was that merely a matter of the observation of the requirements of the law? Is that all that constitutes human holiness? And yes, indeed, Christ died on the cross suffering not only physical pain, but that agony of spirit which made him cry out in apparent despair, asking why God had forsaken him. But was his passion only passive? True, he was led "as a lamb to the slaughter," so there was a passive dimension. But was it *only* that he obediently but passively bore the physical and spiritual consequences of sin which should have been ours? Or is there more to this mystery? Is there something deeper here—something which goes beyond the physical suffering and death such as could be seen in the sacrificial death of an animal? And was there something which goes beyond the merely passive bearing of the spiritual anguish of a human being? Was the sacrifice not only passive, but also, in a sense, active? Was it only a matter of the suffering of his human body, or was there a deeper aspect in the active intention of his human mind and will? Was it merely a willing obedience to the penalties of the law, or was it in some sense a personal self-offering of faith and love to the loving and holy Father?

Implications for our Understanding of "the Faith of Jesus"

Those questions bring us to consider what it might mean that we are saved through "the faith *of* Jesus Christ," and here we need to consider the double meaning in the biblical use of the word "faith." The Hebrew word group ʾ*aman* comprehends the meaning of two words in English, "faith" and "faithfulness." In Genesis 15:6, it is said that Abram "believed the Lord": this is obviously belief or faith in the sense of trust. But in later Jewish literature it is more commonly said that Abram was faithful to God, and both meanings of the word, trust in another, and faithfulness to another, make sense within the context of personal relationships. In the New Testament, the epistle of James picks up this double meaning (Jas 2:21–23): genuine *faith* or trust in another will result in *faithfulness* to the other. Paul's complementary emphasis, given the unfaithfulness of Israel, is on the primacy of *faith* as trust in another. This is his interpretation of Habakkuk 2:4, "The just shall live by faith," in Romans 1:17, and he therefore establishes from Genesis 15:6 that Abram had "faith" in the sense of trust in God.

Given this double meaning, how then are we to understand the *faith* of Jesus Christ? Clearly it can be taken to mean the *faithfulness* of Christ: he remained faithful when all other human beings were unfaithful. That would therefore be another way of expressing the *obedience* of Christ, which Paul sees as so crucial in Philippians 2:8. We are saved through his faithful obedience to the will of the Father. But that surely does not exhaust the meaning. We also have to think of the faith of Christ as his *trust* in the Father. And it is at that point that we have to struggle to comprehend his true humanity. While we have come to understand that the charge that Wesley compromised the humanity of Christ cannot be supported, is it not the case that the whole Western evangelical tradition tends to underplay his true and full humanity? That may be a consequence of strongly insisting on the deity of Christ over against the perception that liberal theology compromises or even denies that. Perhaps this is not so much a problem with theologians, but at the popular level, is it not true that the emphasis on the deity of Christ has led to a widespread failure to grasp the reality of his humanity? Is there not in popular evangelical piety (including Wesleyan piety) an underlying Apollinarianism? Is there not an underlying tendency so to stress the omniscience and omnipotence of Christ in such a way as to underplay the limitations of his true humanity? And is there not, going along with that, a failure to understand that Jesus, as one who was fully human, walked the way of *faith*?

It is the epistle to the Hebrews which most fully develops this aspect of "the faith of Christ." No passage in the New Testament asserts the humanity of Christ more fully than Hebrews 2:5–18. This is where the writer introduces his title for Christ as the *archēgos* of our salvation—the pioneer, the one who goes first along the road. He participated in the same "flesh and blood," mortal human nature, in order that by dying he might bring us corporately through death to resurrection.[22] He had to be made like us "in every respect" (*kata panta*) in order that he might be our High Priest and expiate our sins. But the full enormity of what this means comes at 5:7—"In the days of his flesh, he offered up prayers and supplications, with loud cries and tears, to him who was able to save him from death, and he was heard for his godly fear." This must be one of the most staggering verses in the New Testament, and we must pause to reflect on what it says. It asserts that there was a sense in which the Savior was among the saved; he had to be "saved from death." And it asserts that he prayed to God to save him! This was by no means a perfunctory prayer; it was prayer and "supplication" (*hiketērias*), offered with "loud cries and tears." Jesus wept and cried out, deeply moved in imploring God to save him from death!

What are we to make of this? The particular setting for this in the narrative of the four Gospels is in the garden of Gethsemane, and Mark in particular records that Jesus was "greatly distressed and troubled" (Mark 14:33). His prayer, "Abba, Father, all things are possible to you: remove his cup from me," was evidently not answered positively. He was not to be spared the cross, its physical agony and its spiritual torture in the temptation to believe that God had abandoned him. And here surely is the measure of his faith, for if the prayer that moves mountains shows great faith, how much greater is the faith which continues to believe even when the mountains are not moved! If the faith which heals the sick is great faith, how much greater is the faith which continues to trust in God even when no healing comes, and the reality of death stares us in the face!

This surely was the faith which Jesus exercised in the weakness of his mortal humanity. In other words, we are not to think of Jesus going to the cross with the calm certainty that this was merely a passing episode. We are not to think that he went the way of the cross with a kind of Cartesian certainty that he would be raised from the dead. Rather, in his full humanity, he walked not by sight, but faith. He went to the cross *trusting* in the Father and *believing* that God would raise him from the dead. His declaration to his disciples that "after three days" he would "rise again" was, humanly speaking, a declaration of *faith*. Of course, in the end this prayer of faith was answered

---

22. The word "nature" should not be in the translation strictly speaking since it is not in the Greek text. Nevertheless, it is a valid interpretation of the text.

positively, not in the avoidance of the cross, but in that he passed through death to glorious resurrection, so opening the way for us.

Implications for Understanding the Holiness of Jesus

If this is the way in which we are to understand "the faith of Jesus," how then are we to understand his holiness *as a human being*? Quite clearly, we affirm the holiness of our Lord Jesus Christ as the Eternal Son, one of the Holy Trinity. But what constituted his holiness as a human being? If we still have a kind of Apollinarianism lurking in our minds, then it is not difficult to think of the holiness of the Son of God, infallibly and impeccably obeying the Father at every point. But if we truly grasp his humanity, we cannot be content with some notion of a sanitized or sterilized holiness, untouched by the dirt and disease of human life in the body. This boy was born in all the blood and messiness of a human birth, not even in the sterilized maternity ward of a modern hospital, but in the dirt and disease of a mucky stable. The genealogies (Matt 1:1–17; Luke 3:23–38) reveal he was the descendant of generations of sinners—cheats and murderers, liars and idolaters, and at least one prostitute. He was born into a family situation of scandal and gossip, in the midst of a tense political situation under the rule of a bloodthirsty tyrant, forcing his family to flee as refugees. He grew up in the poverty of a large family of brothers and sisters with all the tensions that are produced in a land that was harried by crime and festering revolution. The land was occupied by foreign conquerors and the Jewish people divided into warring sects—collaborating Sadducees and Herodians, nationalistic zealots, separatist Essenes, and the Pharisees, at least some of whom displayed a legalistic zeal to uphold the law of Moses. All of this family, cultural, and political context was rife with real temptations for the growing child and youth.

It is in this very human context of a deeply divided and sinful human society that the boy Jesus grew up, increasing "in wisdom and stature" (Luke 2:52), sanctifying human life (as Irenaeus so strikingly reminds us) at every stage of his development:

> He therefore passed through every age, becoming an infant for infants, thus sanctifying infants, a child for children, thus sanctifying those who are of this age . . . ; a youth for youths, becoming an example to youths, and thus sanctifying them for the Lord. So he was likewise an old man for old men that he might be a perfect master for all, not merely in the setting forth

of the truth but sanctifying the aged also.... Then at last he came on to death itself.[23]

But the secret of his human development in holiness is not his outward obedience: that is the consequence. The inner secret is his faith-relationship with the Father. In his prayer life, so carefully guarded (cf. Mark 1:35), he lives a life of gratitude to the Father in the Spirit (Luke 10:21–22). It was this faith-relationship with the Father in the Spirit which was the inner secret. This was what carried him through the temptations around him and even through the darkness and despair of Gethsemane and Golgotha and all that the powers of evil could throw at him. In his own Person throughout "the days of his flesh" (Heb 5:7), he sanctified the humanity which he had assumed from his mother, Mary, not only in the sense of the sanctification of his physical body, but the sanctification of his human heart and mind and will in the temptations and tensions of a fully human life and death. The sanctification of our human nature is thus completely worked out in the life of this human being through his unbroken faith-relationship with the Father in the Spirit coming to its culmination in the cross. That is surely the realistic picture we must have of the *pistis Iēsou Christou*—the faith of Jesus Christ.

Implications for Understanding Corporate and Personal Salvation

The consequence then of this faith *of* Jesus Christ's is the salvation of the world. It is through *his* faith that he is "the Lamb of God who takes away the sin *of the world.*" Wesleyan theology, standing in the Arminian tradition, has always stood with the central tradition of the church catholic in asserting that Christ died *for all*. Along with Christians across the spectrum, Wesley rejected passionately the unbiblical innovation of Calvinism (though not of Calvin himself) that Christ died only for the elect, along with the unthinkable and horrific notion that God had created a portion of the human race in order to damn them. The Wesleyan tradition embraces the biblical doctrine held across the church through all the Christian centuries that Christ died *for all*. That is the doctrine of universal atonement, but it is not (as Calvinists sometimes allege) universal*ism*—the teaching that in the end all will be saved. Both universalism and the Calvinist doctrine of limited atonement result from illegitimately misapplying deductive logic. But the great church's biblical affirmation of universal atonement might be

---

23. Irenaeus, *Haer.* 2, 32, 4: Irenaeus argued from John 8:57 that Jesus was almost fifty years old, a good age when the life expectancy was much lower than in many countries today. But this does not affect the main point.

better expressed as "*corporate* atonement." Both Calvinism and Arminianism operate with the individualistic perspective of modernity; but to think about this biblically, we must think about it *corporately*. To say that we are saved by the faith *of* Christ is to say that we are saved by *participation in Christ*, that is, as members of his body. Hays states this in the positive thesis we have already quoted: "Christians are justified/redeemed not by virtue of their own faith but because they *participate* in Jesus Christ, who enacted the obedience of faith in their behalf."[24]

In admitting that Arminians have thought too individualistically about this, we can think for example of the assertion sometimes made that Christ's atonement only brought about the *possibility* of salvation whereas it is the believer's act of faith which makes that salvation *actual*. One can understand the motivation for such a statement; it is trying to ensure that the doctrine of universal atonement does not slip into a doctrine of universal salvation ("universalism"). But this is surely not the way to do it! What this implies is that the center of our faith is not the cross, but the moment of my conversion. It results in conversion-centered rather than Christ-centered theology. It makes my personal testimony and not the gospel of Christ the central narrative of the faith. It makes Christ merely the forerunner and the believer his or her own savior. Christ merely provides the *possibility* of salvation, but I save myself by my own faith or "decision"!

Certainly, we must guard against the universalism that is so fatal to the mission of the church, but we can do so without falling into the rampant individualism of this way of thinking. By speaking of *corporate* atonement rather than universal atonement, what we are saying is that since in his incarnation the Son of God united himself to the human race understood corporately ("all flesh"), his death on the cross was the death of the old corporate Adamic humanity (Rom 6:3–10). He was not only passive in suffering pain and death: but as our representative, the last Adam, he *actively* carried through his *faithful* obedience to the will of his Father (which was also his will as God) in fully human *faith* and *trust* that he would be raised from the dead. This supreme action of *faith* reconciled *humankind as such* to God. The human race as such is now reconciled *in Christ* to God. Such a corporate understanding of the atonement is the basis on which we may affirm that infants who have not yet come to understanding (and indeed perhaps others who have no opportunity to respond individually) are "covered by the blood" of Christ. What other basis could we have for such an assertion? But it does not mean that every human being will automatically be saved in the end. The call to "repent and believe" still must go out to the

---

24. Hays, *Faith of Jesus Christ*, 166, italics added.

ends of the earth, and in the end God in his righteousness, grace and mercy will determine who shall be saved. We must not presume to pronounce the last judgement in advance. But what we can and must say is that it is only by believing, by being baptized "into" Christ, that we may be confident of our salvation at the last day. Only those who have put their faith in Christ have the assurance of eternal life.

How then are we to preach this gospel?

What difference does this perspective make to the preaching of the gospel? Richard Hays quotes T. F. Torrance as one of those who preceded him in advocating that *pistis Iēsou Christou* should be understood and translated as "the faith *of* Christ."[25] For Torrance, this is an aspect of Christology, understood as a two-way movement in the one Christ. Christ not only represents God to us in his true deity, but also represents us to God in his true humanity. This is what it means to say that he is our High Priest. In Christ, not only is the God-humanward movement of grace completed, but also the human-Godward movement of faith. As human, Jesus exercised perfect faith in God, made perfect acknowledgement on our behalf of our sin, and made the only perfect self-consecration of himself to God, thus completing the at-one-ment between God and corporate humanity *from both sides*.[26] In his Didsbury Lectures, *The Mediation of Christ*, Torrance develops this in a chapter on "The Mediation of Christ in our Human Response." He writes:

> We are accustomed to think of faith as something we have or as an act in which we engage, and of believing as our activity. *And that of course would be right*, not least in view of the summons of the gospel to repent and believe . . . but we would be misconstruing that if we thought of faith or belief as an autonomous, independent act which we do from a base in ourselves.[27]

Even in the Old Testament, Torrance writes, Israel is called to have faith, but within the covenant relationship, "The covenant faithfulness of God surrounds and upholds the faltering response of his people." So then in the New Testament: "Jesus steps into the actual situation where we are summoned to have faith in God, to believe and trust in him, and he acts in our place and in

---

25. Hays, *Faith of Jesus Christ*, 145–47, referring to an early article by Torrance, "Biblical Conception of Faith," 111–14.
26. See the development of this in chapter 3 of Torrance, *Atonement*, 88–96.
27. Torrance, *Mediation of Christ*, 81, italics added.

our stead from within the depths of our unfaithfulness and provides us freely with a faithfulness *in which we may share*."[28]

We are not therefore "thrown back on ourselves" to work up our faith or belief. We certainly must repent. But we are not called to work ourselves up to a certain meritorious level of repentance before we are acceptable to God. Both faith and its concomitant, repentance, are the gift of God. It is therefore not by focusing our attention upon our sin that we find faith, but by having our attention drawn in the preaching of the gospel to God's gracious canceling of the guilt of the world in the self-offering of the Lamb. God's act of forgiveness in the cross of Christ *precedes* our repentance, and the proclamation of that free and universal forgiveness in the power of the Spirit is what *releases* us to believe. There is a sense therefore in which we may speak (as Wesley does) of faith as the "condition" of salvation.[29] But it is not a condition we have to fulfil in our strength. True, we can resist and reject the grace of God and cut ourselves out of the salvation he has won for us; but when we believe, we come to realize that that trust in Christ has been given to us. Torrance proposes the beautiful illustration of teaching his infant daughter to walk: "I can still feel her tiny fingers gripping my hand as tightly as she could. She did not rely upon her feeble grasp of my hand but upon my strong grasp of her hand which enfolded her grasp of mine within it."[30]

The implication for our preaching then is that while we must not fail to speak of God's law and God's justice and so of God's coming judgement, yet the focus of our preaching should not be on law and judgment, but upon grace and forgiveness. The cry for justice (including "social justice") is real and must not be neglected in the proclamation and ministry of the church. But God's justice is revealed in the gospel of grace. That was the focus of Luther and Wesley and must be the focus of our ministry and our preaching today. And at its heart is this "new perspective" on the unchanging gospel: that our salvation is not based on the strength of our faltering faith, but that the faith which saves us is the faith *of* Jesus Christ.

Bibliography

Deschner, John. *John Wesley's Christology: An Interpretation*. Dallas: Southern Methodist University Press, 1960.

Dunn, James D. G. *The New Perspective on Paul*. Rev. ed. Grand Rapids: Eerdmans, 2008.

---

28. Torrance, *Mediation of Christ*, 82, italics added.

29. See for example Sermon 43, "The Scripture Way of Salvation," in Wesley, *Works*, 2:153–69, and esp. 162.

30. Torrance, *Mediation of Christ*, 83.

Hays, Richard B. *The Faith of Jesus Christ: The Narrative Substructure of Galatians 3:1—4:11*. 2nd ed. Grand Rapids: Eerdmans, 2002.

McEwan, David B. *Wesley as a Pastoral Theologian*. Milton Keynes: Paternoster, 2011.

Sanders, E. P. *Paul and Palestinian Judaism: A Comparison of Patterns of Religion*. Philadelphia: Fortress, 1977.

Stendahl, Krister. "The Apostle Paul and the Introspective Conscience of the West." *Harvard Theological Review* 56.3 (1963) 199–215.

Torrance, Thomas F. *Atonement*. Milton Keynes: Paternoster, 2009.

———. *The Mediation of Christ*. 2nd ed. Edinburgh: T. & T. Clark, 1992.

———. "One Aspect of the Biblical Conception of Faith." *Expository Times* 68 (1957) 111–14.

Van Kuiken, Jerome. "Deschner's Wesley and the Monophysite Meme." *Wesleyan Theological Journal* 54.2 (2019) 38–56.

Vickers, Jason. "Christology." In *The Oxford Handbook of Methodist Studies*, edited by William J. Abraham and James E. Kirby, 555–58. Oxford: Oxford University Press, 2009.

Wesley, John. *The Works of John Wesley*. Vol. 1, *Sermons I (1–33)*. Edited by Albert C. Outler. Nashville: Abingdon, 1984.

———. *The Works of John Wesley*. Vol. 2, *Sermons II (34–70)*. Edited by Albert C. Outler. Nashville: Abingdon, 1985.

———. *The Works of John Wesley*. Vol. 18, *Journal and Diaries I (1735–1738)*. Edited by W. Reginald Ward and Richard P. Heitzenrater. Nashville: Abingdon, 1988.

Wright, N. T. *The Climax of the Covenant: Christ and the Law in Pauline Theology*. Edinburgh: T. & T. Clark, 1991.

———. *Paul and the Faithfulness of God*. Christian Origins and the Question of God 4. London: SPCK, 2013.

6

The Sacramental Life

Towards a more Holistic and Faithful
Understanding of Holiness[1]

—DEAN G. SMITH

Introduction

Modernity has bequeathed to the West a world largely divested of the sacred.[2] With the rise of science and technology humankind has found itself in less and less need of a God "out there." Even for the faithful living against the grain, religion has largely been marginalized and privatized with many Christians living their lives between two worlds, the sacred and the secular, the world of the body and the world of the spirit.

As Grace Jantzen highlighted a generation ago now,[3] Western theological discourse has for the most part been stuck supporting a destructive binary logic that sets God over against the world and the material over against the spiritual. At the end of one era and the beginning of another,[4] I, like a growing number of Christians, are caught on the horns of a dilemma; on the one hand wanting to reject a reductive materialism, but to do so find ourselves reinforcing its binary opposite—a supernaturalism that has little currency in a twenty-first-century scientific Western world. This has left us at odds with the very reality that does have currency in the twenty-first

---

1. This chapter is a revision of a previously published article: Smith, "Sacramental Life," 186–201.
2. Taylor, *Secular Age*.
3. Jantzen, "Healing our Brokenness," 131–42.
4. According to John B Cobb Jr., we are living at the end of an era. If you agree with Cobb, then we stand at the beginning of a new era. If Cobb and others are right, then we are the inbetweeners. Having been formed in one particular era yet at the same seeking new possibilities for the present and the future.

century scientific Western world—the material world and our lived life in a physical universe.

This is none more evident than in mainline holiness traditions where the doctrine of holiness is almost always framed in terms of the ongoing sanctifying work of the Holy Spirit within the believer's life.[5] The problem here is not with the doctrine as such but with the loss of the centrality of the doctrine of the Trinity and the binary alternative that in the modern period has set up a choice between the metaphysical frameworks of reductive materialism, as in much of modern science, and supernaturalism, as reflected in the language of holiness traditions. This has only served to reinforce the God-world, spirit-matter, and/or soul-body dualism that has characterized much of Western theology and is an indication that reductive materialism and reductive super-nationalism are really the two sides of the same metaphysical coin.[6]

Now while it is certainly not my intention in this paper to jettison the language of spirit from a discourse on holiness, a criticism that no doubt will be leveled at me, I do want to disrupt the traditional discourse around holiness by exploring the implications of an alternative and complimentary model informing our understanding of the same. What is the traditional way of understanding that I wish to disrupt? Teilhard de Chardin spells it out much more clearly than I could in the following quote:

> Speaking in general terms we may say that until quite recent times, and in the West, mysticism has never doubted but that God must be looked for only 'in heaven', that is to say in more or less direct and profound discontinuity with 'here below'. To be spiritualised = to be de-materialised. Such was (and such, in a static Cosmos, had to be) the basic equation that expresses Holiness.[7]

---

5. I grew up in Australia during the seventies as a member of the Salvation Army, and while in recent years there has been a recovery of the Wesleyan emphases within our movement, it was other theological ideas dominant at the time that would inform my youthful mind. On the one hand there was a strong reformed theological strand that emphasized our sinful nature and the gulf that exists between us and God prior to conversion, while on the other hand the charismatic movement was exerting its own influence on our movement, highlighting the baptism of the spirit and reinforcing a view common to the holiness movements—the need of a second work of grace. The net effect of these ideas was a reinforcement of the notion of an interventionist God and a relative valuing of the spiritual over material reality.

6. This may have more to do with a failure of modern Christianity to maintain a central focus on the doctrine of the Trinity. See Lacugna, *God for Us*, 21–181.

7. Teilhard de Chardin, *Heart of Matter*, 45.

My hope then is to explore a more holistic and faithful vision of what it means to live the holy life. A more holistic vision, in that holiness considered as the sacramental life, is grounded in embodied life, rather than an escape from it. A more faithful vision, in that it is more faithful to our embodied experience, to our reason that seeks for coherence in our system of belief, according to a significant number to Scripture and to a somewhat lost Christian tradition. If holiness is to regain the ability to capture the imagination and intellect of western Christians then the model informing our practice needs to take the material world seriously and the substantial dualism of a model that pits body against spirit needs to be overcome/transcended.

In recent times there have been creative and productive attempts by theologians to go beyond the well-worn theological paths and in the process expand our theological vision. Joel Green has presented his kaleidoscopic view of the atonement[8] as a way of broadening the debate beyond any one single model of the atonement. Sallie McFague and other feminist writers have encouraged Christians to move beyond the traditional theological patterns of thinking and speaking about God[9] in the hope that we might break free of the dominant paternalism tied to traditional theological models. In turning to the topic of holiness I too hope to encourage Christians within holiness traditions to break free of the well-worn theological paths in the hope that revisiting alternative ways of thinking about holiness might breathe new life into Christian faith and practice.

I might best describe the position taken in this paper as a Christocentric approach to holiness rather than a Spirit-centered one. Now one should not read this as an attempt on my part to replace the later with the former. Rather, in a quite legitimate Wesleyan move I will engage with the broader Catholic tradition with a particular emphasis on metaphysics and cosmology in order to disrupt the traditional holiness discourse and to shift the emphasis toward a discourse on holiness informed by the notions of incarnation and sacramentality.

In particular, I will seek to reorient the discussion on holiness around a more generalized sacramentality with particular reference to the evolutionary Christology of the type outlined by Karl Rahner and Pierre Teilhard de Chardin. In this evolutionary model the divine is at the very center of material reality and does not enter our reality from outside. Within this framework, awareness of the unfolding of the divine at the center of life becomes the practical work of the Christian. Life itself takes on a sacramental quality. Holiness then is understood in terms of living the sacramental life.

---

8. Beilby and Eddy, *Nature of the Atonement*.
9. McFague, *Models of God*.

A Pastoral Context

Just as Paul Tillich was critical of much of the theology of his day because it seemingly addressed the questions nobody was asking, we who call ourselves theologians need to be constantly on our guard lest the same criticism is leveled at us. This was a vital concern for the Catholic theologian Karl Rahner who believed that theology should develop in response to the questions people are asking. Theology, that is always and at the same time pastoral theology, has the task of bringing theology down to earth.[10]

I have to acknowledge at this point something of the autobiographical nature of this paper. It in fact represents a response to my existential questioning as a result of my experience of alienation throughout my life within the context of the church. My experience as a child and then as a teenager was one of living a fundamentally divided life. I lived my life between two realities—the world of church and family and the world of school and work. I valued the world that nurtured my "spiritual" needs and was completely ambivalent about the other areas of my life.

Quite early on in my Christian experience I recognized that the traditional language of holiness, of the infilling and sanctifying work of the spirit within my soul, did not help to overcome my sense of alienation but rather actually reinforced it. At this stage in my experience I had no conceptual tools to deal with my cognitive and existential dissonance. This would come much later.

In his book *Small is Beautiful*,[11] E. F. Schumacher argues that much of our contemporary problems are related to the failure of metaphysics. These are the big ideas that guide our reasoning and our praxis. These are literally the ideas through which we think and by which we live. What I have come to be convinced of is that the problem needing to be addressed is the alienating metaphysics that has until recently informed my conceptual world, the lens through which I interpreted my life in the world.

It was in the deep world and life affirming sacramental theology of Karl Rahner and Pierre Teilhard de Chardin that I would eventually find a metaphysics and a language that was able, to a much greater degree than ever before, to overcome my alienation both conceptually and existentially. This for me is a significant point given that my own tradition was not well

10. Banks, *Business of Life*.
11. Schumacher, *Small is Beautiful*, 60–80.

equipped to respond to my quest. The sacramental thinking in my own tradition had been a source of division and disagreement with the emphasis being on why we did not practice the sacraments rather than on developing an adequate sacramentality based on sound theological principles.

The question that has exercised me for some time now and the one that I am endeavoring to respond to is this: "Could it be that a recovery of a deep sacramental theology might help us in the holiness traditions to overcome the tendency we have to compartmentalize our lives and to challenge our commitment to an unhealthy binary system in which one binary symbol is emphasized at the expense of the other?" For example, transcendence over against immanence, God over against the world, soul over against body, and the divine over against the human in Christ. John Macquarrie certainly thinks that the sacramental principle is one very important way of maintaining a balance.[12] Dare I suggest that a deep sacramental theology may aid in healing our alienation and help us in living out an integrated Christian vision? Further, could a rethinking of our sacramental theology actually precipitate the rehabilitation of our doctrine of holiness?

The Sacramental Life—Where to Begin?

In a not particularly move, I will begin my explication of the sacramental life with the notion of our being part of a sacramental universe. Macquarrie certainly follows this pattern in his *Guide to the Sacraments*.[13] He begins his exposition of the sacraments with a chapter entitled "A Sacramental Universe," and here he identifies that "perhaps the goal of all sacramentality and sacramental theology is to make the things of this world so transparent that in them and through them we know God's presence and activity in our very midst, and so experience his grace."[14]

To speak of the world as a sacrament counters all the views that at worst, treat the world as evil, and at best, treat it as an encumbrance to all things spiritual. The Psalms in particular witness to the fact that nature is a reliable source of God's revelation. While in the early part of the twentieth century Karl Barth's stress on the transcendence of God and his rejection of natural theology is to be understood as a corrective to the excesses of the liberal theologians' stress on the immanence of God, we find ourselves again in need of recovering the depth dimension or immanence of God in the world. Evangelicals in particular need to recover the notion of a sacramental universe.

12. Macquarrie, *Guide to the Sacraments*, 4.
13. Macquarrie, *Guide to the Sacraments*.
14. Macquarrie, *Guide to the Sacraments*, 1.

Unpacking the Definition of the Term "Sacrament"

Duns Scotus defined a sacrament as "a physical sign, instituted by God, which efficaciously signifies the grace of God, or the gracious action of God."[15] The definition of sacrament as outlined in the *Book of Common Prayer* is this: "an outward and visible sign of an inward and spiritual grace given unto us, ordained by Christ himself, as a means whereby we receive the same, and a pledge to assure us thereof." According to these definitions a sacrament links the two worlds in which we have to live, or the dualities under which the one world keeps appearing.[16] The sacrament links outward and inward, physical and spiritual. Macquarrie makes the important point that these dual aspects while distinguishable, and sometimes even at variance, are not separable.[17]

This is a particularly important point to consider given that in some Christian contexts, my own included, "sign" has often been interpreted as merely "a pointer to." When we interpret sacrament in this way the outward sign then becomes unnecessary to the mediation and experience of Grace. However, as Macquarrie emphasizes, the sacrament is that which unites (links) the outward sign and inward grace. As we will see below this is particularly important if the incarnation is to be central to a generalized sacramentality. According to Christian teaching the incarnation provides us with the clearest model of sacramentality. It is in the humanity of Christ that we have the outward and visible sign of the inward divine life of grace. In Christ we have a profound sacramental reality.

Now the church has always been careful to protect the real connection (union) between the humanity and the divinity of Christ, between the outward and visible sign and the inner divine reality. The technical term for this connection is the hypostatic union. What this means in the case of Christ is that the outward and visible sign (the humanity of Christ) not only stands for or points beyond itself to another (divine) reality, but it is united with or linked to that reality in such a way that it actually *is* the mediator of grace to the world.

Karl Rahner provides a beautiful analogy from everyday experience to explain the importance of a real connection between a sign (the outward manifestation) and that which is signified (the inward reality). Rahner offers the kiss or the handshake as examples of the outward signs of love. It would make very little sense for us to think of love without its physical or "outward" manifestations or signs. We show love (an inner

---

15. As quoted in McGrath, *Reformation Thought*, 163.
16. Macquarrie, *Guide to the Sacraments*, 5.
17. Macquarrie, *Guide to the Sacraments*, 5.

disposition) by way of physical signs (outer manifestation). Psychologists have conclusively shown that without human touch infants simply do not develop properly and may even die. It would be no defense for a parent up on a charge of neglect to say that although they offered no physical signs to their child, they nevertheless really loved them. It would also be a most unsatisfactory situation if one of the partners in a marriage were to suggest to their spouse that henceforth the marriage would be conducted on a purely "platonic" or "spiritual" plain without the diversions of physical signs. Here I am not just referring to the sexual union of husband and wife, but rather the entire range of physical signs of love and affection. Few would seriously consider this to be an acceptable course of action, yet it is sometimes imagined that when it comes to divine reality the outward sign is unnecessary for the mediation of this reality. It is only when we lose sight of the incarnation as our model for sacramentality that we can fall into the trap of thinking that a real connection between the outward and visible sign of inward divine grace is not important. To do so, however, is to sever the connection between the human and divine in Christ and to call into question the very act of incarnation itself.

In the debate over the sacraments there are those who do reject the notion of a real connection between the outward and visible sign and the inner grace that is signified in the Lord's Supper. This in fact was the position of the Reformer Huldrych Zwingli who believed that sacraments were nothing more than memorials and so no real means of grace. He did not believe that the Real Presence of Christ was in the sacrament. The other Reformers rejected this view and retained the more traditional understanding of Christ being in some sense "really present" in the act of communion. Those come close to the view of Zwingli who make the claim that outward signs are no more than pointers to grace. Indeed, this distinction has sometimes been emphasized to the point where one is encouraged to focus on some purely "inward" or "spiritual" experience of grace without the outward sign or symbol being necessary.

But Christians of an orthodox stripe simply cannot make such a claim without falling into the not-so-uncommon dualistic heresy of docetism. Docetism was an early belief that Jesus was purely spiritual in his manifestation and only appeared to be a real human being. Some Christians, and dare I here include my own tradition, have at times come close to this view when it is imagined that spirituality is some reality divorced from its historical and physical instantiation. This has for some become the rationale for not practicing the traditional sacramental rites. We can experience the inner grace, so the logic goes, without the need of any outward sign. Again, to reach such a conclusion is to lose sight of the incarnation as the basis of our deep sacramental view. If we accept the truth of the incarnation, then we cannot but be a sacramental people in the very deep sense of the term. That is, grace is mediated through its outward manifestations or signs.

Within orthodox Christianity we get a glimpse of how certain physical signs can be mediators of grace. But what if our entire universe of signs was being directed toward a sacramental end? What if it were true that human endeavor could be seen to cooperate to complete the world in Christ Jesus? What if not only our passivities but also our activities could be seen as being part of the divinization of the world?

The Organic Sacramentality of Karl Rahner and Pierre Teilhard de Chardin

In the evolutionary Christology of Karl Rahner and Pierre Teilhard de Chardin the incarnation is central to understanding a more generalized sacramentality in which creation and incarnation are seen as moments in the one process of the coming to be of the world in Jesus Christ. The term given to this process by Teilhard is Christogenesis. This understanding of incarnation and creation is particularly significant given that during the twentieth century a good many theologians were at best ambivalent to the view that creation is in any sense a true sacrament. McKinlay highlights the fact that while Karl Barth affirmed baptism and Eucharist, he was skeptical of a generalized sacramentality.[18] Consider the following quote from Barth:

> And was it a wise action on the part of the church when it ceased to recognise in the incarnation . . . the one and only sacrament, fulfilled once and for all, by whose actuality it lives as the one form of the one body of its Head, as the earthly-historical form of the existence of Jesus Christ in the time between His ascension and return?[19]

By correlating Christology with an evolutionary worldview, Rahner and Teilhard place the incarnation at the center of God's creative impulse. Incarnation is then to be understood not as a unique supernatural event in the history of the world but is both precursor and goal of all creation—the divinization of the world. With this approach the world takes on a much more important status. It is not just a stop on our journey to heaven; it is not a place to be escaped. Rather it is our home and with us is destined to become the icon of God.

18. McKinlay, "Meaning of Sacrament."
19. Barth, *Church Dogmatics*, 55.

Quite early in his reflections Teilhard settled on a term to describe the way he had come to see reality. He speaks of the *Divine Milieu* by which he means both the divine center that animates and has the power to unite all things *and* an environment of transformation. "God revels himself everywhere, beneath our groping efforts, as a *universal milieu*, only because he is the *ultimate point* upon which all realities converge."[20] According to Ursula King, one can think of it (the divine milieu) as a field of divine energy that has one central focus—God—from which everything flows, is animated and is directed.[21] King goes on to explain:

> For Teilhard the idea of the "divine milieu" was particularly important in capturing the universal influence of Christ through God's incarnation in the world, in its matter, life and energy—an extended, cosmic understanding of the incarnations that far transcended the historical limitations of time and place associated with the person of Jesus.[22]

Of course, Teilhard was concerned about the pastoral implications of his mystic vision of the world as a divine milieu. Teilhard wanted to help Christians see that their action in the world can indeed be sanctified and that human endeavor is important in relation to God. He was unhappy with the traditional solutions to holiness and perfection that led people in the direction of seeking an escape from the material world and the denying of the importance of anything other than "spiritual" endeavors. In a divine milieu the divinization of our activities and the divinization of our passivities "represent a continuous process of transformation whereby we can find communion with God in the world."[23]

Is it then possible to believe that our entire lived reality can be the site or locus of God's overflowing grace? Paul refers to believers as being "in Christ"[24] and Peter speaks of our participation in the divine life.[25] Our embodied life "in Christ" *is* the sign of God's grace by virtue of our union with Christ our living sacrament. We, as the corporate body of Christ, the church, and we, as members of that body, are the outward sign of the divine life and energies within us. We are a sacrament! The Real Presence of Christ is lived in and through us in both our activities and our passivities.

20. Teilhard de Chardin, *Divine Milieu*, 85.
21. King, *Spirit of Fire*, 110.
22. King, *Spirit of Fire*, 110.
23. King, *Spirit of Fire*, 113.
24. Paul uses this phrase twenty-seven times.
25. 2 Pet 1:4.

Participating in the Sacramental Life

Now that I have outlined what I mean by "the sacramental life," I now need to say something about what this looks like in practical terms. For my purposes I would like to explore the contours of the sacramental life under the following headings.

Seeing

Living the sacramental life is as much about learning to see rightly. While it may be true according to Rahner and Teilhard that the world is destined for completion in Christ, this truth alone is not a sufficient condition for living the sacramental life or Life with a capital L. There needs to be a conscious participation in the divine reality at the corporate and individual level. Living the sacramental life does not happen automatically. As the Wesleyan scholar Randy Maddox has captured in the title of his book *Responsible Grace*, our relationship with God is to be thought of in terms of both grace and responsibility. In our ongoing experience of redemption there is God's part and there is our part. Our part is corporately and individually to appropriate the grace that informs our life. Without corporate and individual discipline, the sacramental remains only at the level of potential and we live life with a small "l." It is discipline that helps train our vision so that we can learn to "see" the sacramental reality before us. Our life, our activities, our multifarious being in the world can be truly sacramental but only to the degree that we learn to "see" things in a sacramental way. The poet Elizabeth Barrett Browning had learned to see things this way. She expressed it beautifully in the following lines:

> Earth's crammed with heaven,
> And every common bush afire with God;
> But only he who sees takes off his shoes,
> The rest sit round and pluck blackberries.[26]

Consider also the vision of Pierre Teilhard de Chardin:

> Throughout my whole life, during every moment I have lived, the world has gradually been taking on light and fire for me, until it has come to envelop me in one mass of luminosity, glowing from within.... The purple flush of matter fading imperceptibly into the gold of spirit, to be lost finally in the incandescence of a personal universe.... This is what I have learnt from my

---

26. Barrett Browning, *Aurora Leigh*, book 7.

contact with the earth—the diaphony of the divine at the heart of a glowing universe, the divine radiating from the depths of matter a-flame.[27]

This profound vision, this way of seeing must be cultivated and we must train ourselves and our people to see the presence of God in the world and in the people around us. I believe that the term "mindfulness" best captures the discipline by which we train our vision so that we can truly live and experience the sacramental life. I am well aware that this is a term traditionally used in Buddhist philosophy and practice; however, I see no reason why as Christians we should not appropriate it for our own purposes. I could just as easily have used the term awareness. Whatever language we choose to use we certainly need to become more intentional, more mindful, as we train our vision as Sacramental people.

Let me reiterate, we live the sacramental life when we come to *see* that everything we do is a potential sign of God's inward grace. Notice the way I have qualified the statement through the use of "potential." As stated earlier there is nothing automatic about the sacramental life and without intention much of what we do remains in the realm of possibility and does not live up to the idea of being sacramental in any real sense.

If the various outward signs, words, and actions are the channels through which we access grace, intention must be the key. Without intention signs at best are dead signs. Without intention words are mere sounds, actions—activity without significance. Intention is what helps us to awaken openness to transcendence-in-immanence.

The sharing of a meal at the family table can be a true sacrament, a true "breaking of bread" or it can be simply individuals meeting their basest needs. Our work can be a sacrament if it is seen in the right way or else it becomes nothing more than an encumbrance to our more "spiritual" pursuits. It is important to realize that there is nothing automatic about living a sacramental life. Without intention there can only be for us an unrealized or impoverished existence.

Doing and Acting

However, for the person trained to see their life as a sign of God's grace, there is no limit to what can become a sacrament and means of grace for us. As a faithful Anglican, Wesley encouraged his people to seek God's grace through the various outward signs, words, and actions that God had

---

27. Teilhard de Chardin, *Divine Millieu*, xiii–xiv.

ordained as "ordinary" channels for conveying saving grace to humanity.[28] These included both corporate and individual practices like the Lord's Supper, corporate worship, prayer, communal support, mutual accountability, private exercises, and works of mercy. There is a certain preeminence given to traditional means of grace that have sustained the church throughout the centuries, and this is only right and proper. However, there is nothing stopping us from moving beyond these traditional means to incorporate other outward signs, words or actions.

If, as I have been arguing, our entire life can become the locus of God's gracious unfolding activity in our lives, I see no reason why, in addition to the traditional means of grace, we should exclude any practice as a possible means of grace. That is, if we have trained ourselves to see our actions in such a way. Given my rejection of our tendency to dualize, I pose the following question. What would it be like if not just our "spiritual" life but our entire bodied life was included in our sacramental vision and our so-called "ordinary" actions became the means of grace?

Let me suggest a number of very "ordinary" activities that may become sacramental when approached in the appropriate way. Take the common activity of walking. I have no doubt that Henry David Thoreau understood walking to be a sacramental activity. He wrote much about this activity and if you read his accounts you get the impression that he was very aware of informing grace as he went for his many long walks. I too can testify that I also find the act of walking a sacramental activity. Here is a quote from Thoreau about walking:

> I think I cannot preserve my health and spirits, unless I spend four hours a day at least,—and it is commonly more than that,—sauntering through the woods and over the hills and fields, absolutely free from all worldly engagements. You may safely say, A penny for your thoughts, or a thousand pounds. When sometimes I am reminded that the mechanics and shopkeepers stay in their shops not only all the forenoon, but all the afternoon too, sitting with crossed legs, so many of them,—as if the legs were made to sit upon, and not to stand or walk upon,—I think that they deserve some credit for not having all committed suicide long ago.[29]

Consider the following list of everyday activities that may also become sacramental activities if seen in the right light:

---

28. Maddox, *Responsible Grace*, 193.
29. Thoreau, *Walden and Other Writings*, 629.

- Walking[30]
- Taking Tea
- Reading
- Gardening
- Driving
- Listening to Music
- Shopping
- Working
- Making Love
- Sleeping[31]

Being

I represent a tradition of activists and so probably do not have difficulty conceiving of our actions as means of grace and therefore as having sacramental significance. However, we should also consider the possibility that being is also a means of grace and therefore has the potential to have great sacramental significance. Let it be said though that Being is always qualified being. We are embodied beings, so it is always being-with, or being-for, or even being-there for another. There may be no words spoken or any obvious actions performed. It may simply be the case that we are present for another person. You may have heard the story of the little girl who was expressing her fear of the dark to her father and her desire that he stay with her while she fell asleep. Don't be afraid, said the father to his little girl, God is with you. I know that, said the little girl, but I need someone with skin on. Most of us know that God is with us but like the little girl found comfort in the presence of someone "with skin on."

In the context of a discussion on the practices of the church in the book *Virtues and Practices in the Christian Tradition*, Nancey Murphy identifies witness as an enduring practice of the church and identifies the virtue of "presence" as being necessary for the practice of witness.[32] Our being present for the other can, I believe, be a means of grace. By being

30. See the book by retired Australian Anglican priest Adam Ford, *Art of Mindful Walking*.

31. See what Robert Banks has to say about our need for a theology of sleep in *Business of Life*, 9–10, 72–73.

32. Murphey et al., *Virtues & Practices*, 36.

present for another, we can be the sacrament given for and on behalf of Christ who is living in and through us. Consider the following quote from James McClendon:

> Presence is being one's self for someone else; it is refusing the temptation to withdraw mentally and emotionally, but it is also on occasion putting our own body's weight and shape, alongside the neighbor, the friend, the lover in need.
>
> But is presence, even in this extended sense, really a virtue, or is it like left-handedness or curiosity, merely somebody's quality or distinguishing feature? Earlier in this chapter [of ethics] the black church was set forth as displaying the quality of presence. When black slaves had no other earthly resource, they knew how to be present to and for one another, and knew that Another was present for them as well. . . . To characterize this presence as a virtue is to say that it is a strength or skill, developed by training and practice, which is a substantive part of (the Christian) life.[33]

Conclusion

Might it be possible that by reorienting the discussion on holiness around a more generalized sacramentality, a new generation of Christians unmoved by the traditional language of holiness might find a new way of understanding and experiencing what the traditional notions of holiness have always set out to help the believer know and experience—a deeper communion with God. The deep sacramental theology of Karl Rahner and Pierre Teilhard de Chardin provide resources for understanding our sacramental reality and potential life in God. Our lives are tied to the unfolding life of Christ at the center of the universe. In this vision the spiritual and material aspects of our life work together in the process of Christogenesis—the rise within us of the forces of communion leading to the completion of the world in Christ.

Within this framework, awareness of the unfolding of the divine at the center of life becomes the practical work of the Christian. Life itself takes on a sacramental quality. Holiness then is understood in terms of living the sacramental life. Integration at the conceptual as well as the practical level becomes possible with profound implications for living our life in the world. Let me finish with a quote from a homily given by Greek Orthodox Ecumenical Patriarch Bartholomew in 1997:

---

33. McClendon, *Ethics*, 116.

[E]verything that lives and breathes is sacred and beautiful in the eyes of God. The whole world is a sacrament. The entire created cosmos is a burning bush of God's uncreated energies. And humankind stands as a priest before the altar of creation, as microcosm and mediator.... All things are sacramental when seen in the light of God. Such is the true nature of things; or, as an Orthodox hymn describes it, "the truth of things," if only we have the eyes of faith to see it.

Bibliography

Banks, Robert. *All the Business of Life: Bringing Theology Down to Earth*. Sydney: Albatross, 1987.
Barrett Browning, Elizabeth. *Aurora Leigh*. Reissued edition. Oxford: Oxford University Press, 2008.
Barth, Karl. *Church Dogmatics*. Vol 4, *The Doctrine of Reconciliation—Part 2*. Edinburgh: T. & T. Clark, 1958.
Beilby, James, and Paul R. Eddy, eds. *The Nature of the Atonement: Four Views*. Downers Grove: IVP Academic, 2006.
Ford, Adam. *The Art of Mindful Walking*. Sydney: Ivy, 2011.
Jantzen, Grace M. "Healing our Brokenness: The Spirit and Creation." *The Ecumenical Review* 42 (1990) 131–42.
King, Ursula. *Spirit of Fire: The Life and Vision of Teilhard de Chardin*. New York: Orbis, 1996.
Lacugna, Catherine Mowry. *God for Us: The Trinity and Christian Life*. New York: HarperCollins, 1993.
Macquarrie, John. *A Guide to the Sacraments*. London: SCM, 1997.
Maddox, Randy L. *Responsible Grace: John Wesley's Practical Theology*. Nashville: Kingswood, 1994.
McClendon, James W. *Systematic Theology*. Vol. 1, *Ethics*. 2nd ed. Nashville: Abingdon, 2002.
McFague, Sallie. *Models of God: Theology for an Ecological, Nuclear Age*. Minneapolis: Fortress, 1987.
McGrath, Alister E. *Reformation Thought: An Introduction*. 4th ed. Oxford: Wiley, 2012.
McKinlay, Brian. "The Meaning of Sacrament and Its Links with Creation and Incarnation." Unpublished, 2017. http://nottoomuch.com/essays/e2123.pdf.
Murphey, Nancey, et al., eds. *Virtues & Practices in the Christian Tradition*. Notre Dame: University of Notre Dame Press, 1997.
Schumacher, E. F. *Small is Beautiful*. London: Vintage, 2011.
Smith, Dean. "The Sacramental Life: Towards an Integrated Christian Vision." *Wesleyan Theological Journal* 50.2 (2015) 186–201.
Taylor, Charles. *A Secular Age*. Cambridge: Belknap, 2018.
Teilhard de Chardin, Pierre. *The Heart of Matter*. London: Collins, 1978.
———. *The Divine Milieu*. New York: Perennial, 2001.
Thoreau, Henry David. *Walden and Other Writings*. New York: The Modern Library, 2000.

7

Wynkoop

On the Presuppositions of Christian Faithfulness[1]

—JOHAN TREDOUX

Introduction

I had the privilege of meeting Wynkoop in 1980 during the Nazarene General Assembly which was held in Kansas City that year. I recall a gracious and humble lady who was very present in the moment. Little did I know that Wynkoop had become a key figure in effecting a major paradigm shift in the holiness movement to a relational way of thinking about sin and holiness. Wynkoop's influence was especially felt in her observation that a "credibility gap" existed between the doctrines held in the Wesleyan-Holiness Movement and the way these doctrines were lived out in real life. It was Wynkoop's introduction to critical thinking and the idea of basic presuppositions in her university philosophy classes that made possible new insights into her intellectual and spiritual life. Through her doctoral

---

1. It was the spring of 2015. I was sitting across a small coffee table in the Roasterie Cafe with Dr. David McEwan in Brookside, MO, a few miles from the Nazarene Theological Seminary in Kansas City. David had flown all the way from Australia for education meetings, and this was our time to get together. My anticipation for this meeting was loaded since David was my second supervisor for my Ph.D. work on Mildred Wynkoop and John Wesley. Our meeting was like old friends who had known each other for a long time, all because we both loved Mildred Wynkoop and John Wesley. We talked about her influence on our lives and her faithfulness in serving the church as a pastor, theologian, missionary, evangelist and seminary president. Given the purpose of our meeting, it didn't take long for our conversation to zero-in on the presuppositions of Wynkoop's theology of love, especially her emphasis on the credibility gap and what that represented. We talked about her theological anthropology and her understanding of *agapē*. As I think back about our time together, David's self-awareness and his ability to be present were very prevalent. Now, three years later, it was an easy decision to accept the invitation to write a theological essay on the presuppositions of faithfulness that formed the backdrop of Wynkoop's theological outlook.

work in biblical interpretation and her master's work in theological anthropology, she concluded that the problems causing the credibility gap were present at a presuppositional level and that the solutions would have to be addressed at that level as well.²

For Wynkoop presuppositions were the ideas taken for granted when human beings talk to each other. It was "deeper down and farther back" than the words used and became for her the real test of truth. She said: "Presuppositions need to have their feet held to the fire, so to speak, and in the case of the feet of Christian teachers and pastors, held to the cleansing fire of Scripture and the collegiality of the church."³ With these thoughts as a backdrop, we propose that for Wynkoop, Christian faithfulness is a dynamic journey of "real people" following Christ in his "this-world" kingdom, whose walk can be described as an existential and relational journey of Christ-like love. As we pay attention to these terms, we hope to reveal their essential relatedness at a level below the surface, and by their light, gain a deeper understanding of the underlying presuppositions that shaped Wynkoop's theology of faithfulness.

Faithfulness is Existential

To be true to Wynkoop and to reflect on her assumptions for a theology of faithfulness, will require us to explore her existential, "on the street" grasp of theology. She said: "Christian life is not as simple as Christian theology. The moment clean-cut theological conformations are laid against warm, flesh-and-blood human situations, the lack of simplicity begins to show. Theology is much like a signpost pointing the way into and through the very rugged country over which a Christian must travel—on foot."⁴ Wynkoop's street theology was all about recovering the dynamic life out of which our theological words came. Even though Wynkoop used "existential"⁵ in a very broad and general sense, this term became useful for her, as it enabled her to give voice to the credibility gap she observed. In short, the credibility gap was the dualism she saw between doctrine and life. She said: "Words may be bridges from God's truth to life. But a bridge must touch two shores, not end up in the air somewhere. We need our words, but we need them, too,

   2. Wynkoop, "Some Implications," 1.
   3. Wynkoop, "Look Out," 2.
   4. Wynkoop, "Theology of Depth," 5.
   5. By the word "existential," Wynkoop seeks to emphasize the essential, vital involvement of a person in his or her theological affirmations. It is Christian truth incarnate in the dynamic flow of everyday, ordinary, human life. Wynkoop strongly rejects the stereotypical abstract ideas that ignore the unique situated-ness of human life.

baptized with the dynamics of life; and may I say, the vibrant life of the Holy Spirit."[6] She observed that theological concepts and terms had been abstracted from dynamic living situations which were caught up in the words. Some of the theological concepts Wynkoop inherited as a "second-generation" evangelist in the American Holiness Movement were reflected in terms like "sanctification," "the blessing," "entire sanctification," "cleansing," and "baptism with the Holy Spirit." These terms were emotionally loaded as they described the religious experiences, values and sacred memories of the previous generations. Out of loyalty to the first generation, along with her peers, Wynkoop began to preach doctrinal messages with the invitation to seek "it." Wynkoop wrote:

> In my early preaching life the exquisite logical beauty of theology, its almost mathematical perfection, intoxicated me. I recall often baiting my intellectual trap and at the psychological point of climax in a sermon clinching my holiness argument by "some absolutistic" conclusion that I felt settled forever the opposition. I sat on a high, remote, and glorious mountain peak of self-assurance. In mercy and desperation, I presume, the Holy Spirit often moved on the audience, and there were frequent great moves to the altar. But I did not know what to do with those who came. I began to observe that most of the people were seeking the "absolutes" in order to be released from the debilitating humanness of their daily lives. They were seeking "blessings" (mathematically differentiated) and "it" and "something I will know about" and abstracts such as "sanctification" and "cleansing."[7]

This self-awareness on the frontline of her evangelistic campaigns helped her to see that theological terminology un-translated into vibrant life, tended to isolate people from life. She wrote, "If I could count the number of times I have poured tears on some worn altar rail seeking for holiness, I would be ashamed of it. Excellent early training plus the thrilling early Nazarene services in which the 'glory came down' conspired to set a 'norm' in my thinking of what religion ought to be and could be, and kept me everlastingly trying to abolish the vast chasm between my own experience and that norm."[8] Time and time again she placed what was known as the "unknown bundle" on the altar. Her journey to the altar went on for several years, every time seeking that which she already professed, that she was saved and

6. Wynkoop, "Some Implications," 3.
7. Wynkoop, "Some Implications," 4.
8. Wynkoop, "What Holiness Means," 3.

sanctified and going all the way. She had a page in her Bible on which she entered the dates and the places that she went to the altar to seek entire sanctification. She wanted to be able to testify the day she was sanctified, but she had so many entries that she could never decide which one of them to use at any given time. At last count, she had forty entries in her Bible when, one day in humiliation, she tore that page out of her Bible and destroyed it. This preoccupation with the when and the how—essentially ceremonial holiness—did not deal with the content of holiness in her heart.[9]

This action signaled a real turning point in her life. She met some Episcopalians who were in the grip of a spiritual awakening through the Oxford Group. She attended the group meetings and heard doctors and bricklayers and housewives share with complete frankness and the complete absence of any stereotypical expressions the problems they were facing and the change that Christ wrought. This period in her life was the beginning of a new quality of Christian experience for Wynkoop. It was this dynamic immersion into real-life experiences that helped her to make sense of what holiness was all about. The new was not only measured in terms of emotions and sentiment but in genuineness and depth.[10]

It was these very personal experiences and her exposure to basic presuppositions that opened her eyes to the undercurrents at work in the preaching and pastoral experiences in which she participated. The basic problem she saw was that, rightly or wrongly, she had acquired very static and therefore passive concepts of Christian truth. These static concepts of Christian truth were more at home in the world of ideas than being expressed in real life. The need Wynkoop saw was for the Christian words to be baptized with the dynamics of life as well as the vibrant life of the Holy Spirit. This involvement is what Wynkoop means by "dynamic." What Wynkoop realized was that one of the sources for the static concepts of Christian truth was the Greek Platonist philosophy that characterized her Christian theology. It had a way of placing truth just outside the reach of human experience and isolating people from life. She wrote: "It is my conviction that in the lives of some of our people our 'holy words' have become escapes from thinking and action, substitutes for the vital Christian freedom and holy aggression which belong to the Spirit-filled life and to the holiness message. This escape is a response to a real area of misunderstanding. The Hebrew connotation of 'Word' as personal must in our tradition prevail over the more static and formalized and abstract Hellenistic concepts."[11] What Wynkoop realized was that she

9. Wynkoop, "What Holiness Means," 3.
10. Wynkoop, "What Holiness Means," 3.
11. Wynkoop, "Word Became Flesh," 3.

was swimming upstream in a Hellenistic world where the universal ideas or "numina" were considered to be more real than the down-to-earth "phenomena" of people's everyday experience.

One of the ways Wynkoop sought to overcome this credibility gap was through her existential reading of Scripture. This particular way of reading Scripture came about when she decided to go back to school at the age of forty-five to learn Greek and Hebrew. The date of a revolution in her own thinking happened when she put her newly learned Greek to use in re-polishing an old sermon on Romans 12:1–2. She said: "I found that 'presentation' to God was an aorist action but that 'transformation' was not aorist at all but a present indicative indicating a very long and arduous process. I saw that the rest of Romans 12 and 13 was an exhortation for man to put into life the things I had said God did."[12] It began to dawn on her that one of the ways to overcome the credibility gap was to stay with the language of Scripture. By this, she meant that it was the recovery of the existential meaning of the scriptural words, not just the theological use of the words. From her own life experience and through the recognition of her own underlying presuppositions, Wynkoop realized that the Bible, properly used, could become a bridge to life, to involvement, to relevance, and to holiness. This was a critical factor in her desire to respond to the static presuppositions of her tradition who presented holiness as the arrival at a state of grace.

Wynkoop wrote:

> There were those who thought statically and others who thought dynamically. . . . In each case, the explanations were very different though the basic Christian experience was the same. The difference was reflected in quality and effectiveness in the lives of Christians. Some measured Christian life in terms of mathematics, terminology, psychological reactions, and such like, all curling back in oneself. Others were free and released and less inclined to obsession with the superficial and more involvement with outreach, love and the unity of the Spirit in the bonds of peace.[13]

This revelation opened a brand-new world for Wynkoop in the classroom and on the road as an evangelist. She would encourage preachers to take a text and look behind the words to find the human situation to which the words were addressed.[14] In other words, for her, history is important,

---

12. Wynkoop, "Some Implications," 4.
13. Wynkoop, "Look Out," 5.
14. Wynkoop, "Theology of Depth," 48.

and the context is as important to the message as are the words.[15] Wynkoop wrote, "The human element in the Bible to which the divine speaks is the common life-blood that keeps the divine meaningful to all who partake of life. The story is the flesh around the idea. It preserves the idea from becoming so detached and irrelevant and intellectualized that it loses all contact with reality. It saves justification and sanctification from abstraction."[16] In her encounters with Fundamentalism, Wynkoop was able to assert her position that the living Word (Christ himself) can never become mere doctrine or end up as an idea only. She wrote: "Fundamentalism reemphasized the objective authority of a book but failed to come to terms with any experiential dimension. It supposes that the Bible is an end in itself, and is itself revelation. In this scenario, revelation is propositional and hence, intellectual only."[17] Here we can see that for Wynkoop, the Bible's relevancy is directly related to principles of interpretation that will do justice to its spiritual nature. The Bible can then only be a means to an end—that of introducing to us a living Christ to be vitally experienced—not an end in itself.[18] One can then see that for Wynkoop an existential reading of Scripture presupposes an encounter with the living Christ.

Wynkoop's existential interpretation of faithfulness then brings two recommendations for us: first, she recommends that we pay attention to the verbal expression of theological ideas to make sure that they are biblically and contextually anchored; and second, she encourages us to make sure that an adequate life expression of that doctrine in terms of a personal moral transformation plays out in real life situations.[19] Faithfulness for Wynkoop is to be seen as a theological idea fully immersed in real life. Being set apart to faithfully follow the Lord brings Wynkoop to this conclusion: "It is a doctrine but it is a doctrine in shoe leather, as well as on the books. Its beauty is not mainly in words, for words apart from vital living condemn it. Its loveliness and power are in a life lived out by the grace of God."[20]

Faithfulness is Relational

Throughout Wynkoop's existential interpretation of holiness, it is clear that she gave great priority to the study of the doctrine of humanity. She realized

---

15. Wynkoop, "Theology of Depth," 48.
16. Wynkoop, "Theology of Depth," 51.
17. Wynkoop, "Authority of Christian Scriptures," 19.
18. Wynkoop, "Authority of Christian Scriptures," 22.
19. Wynkoop, *John Wesley*, 30.
20. Wynkoop, *John Wesley*, 30.

that the role she gave to humanity would determine, to a large extent, the nature of the theology she confessed. From early in life, Wynkoop showed interest in the practical matter of understanding how sanctification can be faithfully lived out in real life, especially since Wesleyan theology presented sanctification as a "possibility in this life."[21] She felt that when human nature was viewed as an enemy to be conquered, this idea had a profound impact on the expectation for existential holiness for everyday life.[22] The fact that humans are made from dust but also in God's image prompted her to use both a soteriological and psychological filter in her theological anthropology. In reference to Adam, she said, "He is a creature of the earth with a 'natural history.' His body is shared with the natural order. He is in history, a part of it. This must never be forgotten."[23] As such, she saw Adam as a dynamic being who can communicate with God, who, in partnership with Eve, is not to be viewed through Western individualistic lenses but, rather, as a corporate personality. She wrote:

> The Hebrew man found his dynamism, not in static beingness, but in his social relatedness. His "living" self, his totality, stood in relation to a larger unity, the social entity. . . . Hebrew man was in an essential way one with "his fathers" and his family, his tribe and his nation. This was not a crude metaphysical or genetic unity, but a spiritual interconnectedness that penetrates to the core of what mankind is.[24]

Wynkoop's relational filter is a strong presupposition in her theology of faithfulness. This is evident in the way she carefully protected the unity of the person in contrast with Platonist views that was prone to uphold a speculative dichotomy, dividing body and soul as separate parts of a person. It was important to Wynkoop to describe a person in terms of what he or she is as a whole. In other words, heart, mind, soul, spirit, conscience, flesh, and body are not distinguishable parts that a person *has* but, rather, a description of what a person *is*.[25] In Wynkoop's world, the trichotomous view of a human being as body, soul, and spirit has to give way to the more biblical view of a human being as a unified personality. She wrote, "Any multiple views of personality makes the Christian life a source of conflict, not of peace. It makes salvation destructive of wholeness and integrity in that grace sets the

---

21. Wynkoop, "Holiness Theology," 1.
22. Wynkoop, "Protestant Theology," 1.
23. Wynkoop, *Theology of Love*, 114.
24. Wynkoop, *Theology of Love*, 123.
25. Wynkoop, *Theology of Love*, 122.

soul against the body. It impugns the grace of God. A disturbed personality becomes the badge of Christianity, and death a savior."[26]

It dawned on Wynkoop that in her pursuit of holiness she was still working within a narrative, which colluded with Gnosticism. This collusion happened when Christians went beyond Platonism and embraced Gnosticism, which portrayed humans as a combination of a divine soul and an evil body. Under this philosophy, all matter is evil, including human nature, and with it comes the misconception that salvation consists in an escape from this body and from this world. In this Platonic world, the soul is understood as a separate aspect of a person, somehow distinct and imprisoned in the body.

This collusion with the Platonic world was not far removed from Wynkoop's holiness circle. One example can be seen in the theological presuppositions of Keswick holiness teaching. As a way to preserve holiness teaching, they conceived of the human person as consisting of several parts, each with a different value and different relation to the self and sanctification. Wynkoop wrote:

> From the Greek philosophies, they derived the notion that a union of body, soul, and spirit constitute human nature; the spirit was god-like, and the body was its prison. This paradigm was borrowed from Greek philosophy and became a way to preserve the perfection of sanctification by the Holy Spirit, from the imperfectability of the body. Under Christian holiness absolutes, then, only the spirit of human beings surrendered to the Holy Spirit is sanctifiable and the body can operate under less stringent rules. The challenge in this is to determine how human nature as such comes under the rules of sanctification. From the Keswick theory has come the two-nature theory, which puts spirit and body into ever-greater conflict as the Christian grows in grace. So, in Keswick theology the challenge is to curb the demands of nature—suppressionism—rather than honing human nature to its highest expression under the Lordship of Christ.[27]

This example of the holiness/human nature binary points directly to deep presuppositions. Wynkoop shows that this second-century problem with Gnosticism has never really gone away and becomes a direct threat to the gospel. When the physical body is seen as a hindrance to the spiritual life, it does not take much to arrive at the conclusion that an escape from

26. Wynkoop, *Theology of Love*, 200.

27. Wynkoop, "Look Out," 6. Also, see a very helpful and readable book on the source of the Greek theory of the composite nature of man in contrast to the biblical Hebrew view in Ladd, *Pattern of New Testament Truth*, esp. chapter 1 (pp. 9–40), "The Background of the Pattern—Greek or Hebrew."

the body becomes the essence of salvation. These pagan ways of thinking had a way to distort the Christian truth, not by badness but by wrong presuppositions that in turn produced wrong theology. What the Keswick tradition called the "two nature theology" set the conflict between nature and grace and body and spirit as the sign of increasing spirituality. The "death of self" meant the suppression of human nature, rather than presenting the whole of human nature to God as the essence of a faithful holiness relationship.[28] Wynkoop brought attention to this factor since Keswick teaching influenced large sections of the Nazarene church. Much of this influence came via J. O. McClurkan in the South, who found the simplicity of Keswick literature useful, and indeed, of the enormous amounts of literature published for his people, probably half was from Keswick pens and almost nothing of Wesley. The Keswick theme inoculated a whole area of the United States reinforcing itself over and over again.[29] With it came a shift in emphasis from the *historical* to the *apocalyptic* interpretation of existence. The historical interpretation emphasized the continuity of events to provide meaning of the present. The apocalyptic stressed the discontinuity of events, the breaking in on history of new, unrelated forces and events. In this view, crisis experience "happens" but cannot be made to mesh with life prior to experience.[30] Wynkoop wrote:

> The Keswick terms, *surrender* and *possessed by* are favored over the very active terms, "present your bodies," "yield your members" and, "put off and put on." In the apocalyptic view, the human nature is not considered a real asset to the life of Christian grace, in stark contrast to the Biblical and Wesleyan understanding of the full need of the whole human person to be the bearer of grace to the world. . . . The call to holiness, in this context, is to begin the search for a specific kind of experience. It is not the pilgrimage toward love which engages the whole of a person's moral relations, but a disattachment to these relations—a moving inward toward oneself—a kind of separation discouraged by Jesus and Paul.[31]

This subtle shift away from Wesley's teaching was experientially elevated but relationally disconnected from real life on the ground. Wynkoop wrote a thirty-page booklet called *John Wesley: Christian Revolutionary*, with a major portion of this booklet dedicated to an exploration of Romans

---

28. Wynkoop, "Look Out," 6.
29. Wynkoop, "Unity of Personality," 5.
30. Wynkoop, "Whole Wesley in a Broken World," 8.
31. Wynkoop, "Whole Wesley in a Broken World," 10.

12:1. Paul's exhortation that we are to "present [our] bodies as a living sacrifice" in her mind confirms this holistic perspective. She said, "When one commits his body to something, the rest of what man is tags along pretty faithfully. . . . The body is the locus of 'me'—you."[32] In response to Gnosticism Wynkoop here affirms the apostle Paul's high view of the human body. She wrote: "The highest offering we can make is the very body that the pagan philosophies considered to be the least valuable and the least object of God's interest and the least capable of the sanctification that Paul is talking about."[33] This presuppositional stance in her theological anthropology is a key anchor point in her understanding of the relational nature of faithfulness. When a human being acts, he or she acts as a unity. It is the whole person who acts. From Romans 12:3 to 15:9 Paul shows how faithfulness shows up in the rough and tumble of life in various relationships of social involvement. All the complexities and practical reality of the human person is fully taken into consideration. There is nothing in the text about conquering one part of the person by another but about the whole person relating as a self to the many relationships in life, in love and what love is.[34]

The Holy Spirit was front and center in her relational understanding of faithfulness. For her, the dynamic of the Holy Spirit is not an abstract doctrine that only shows up in intellectual conversation, but rather someone that is to be experienced personally. She wrote: "The heart of the Wesleyan theology is precisely the personal relationship of the Holy Spirit to human beings in actual human experience. . . . He is the personal presence of Christ in men. He cannot operate externally to men."[35] The importance of the total person, totally and actually committed to God, fully indwelt by the Holy Spirit cannot be overstressed. For Wynkoop, faithfulness was not to be found "in principle" but in real experience. For her the self is dynamic, ever-expanding and searching for fulfilment. And it is precisely this kind of being that God designed who is able to relate to the Holy Spirit and to whom the Holy Spirit seeks to relate himself. If we then circle back to Paul's "altar call" in Roman's 12:1–2, we hear the clarion call to "present our bodies as a living sacrifice." This whole dynamic self is to be centered in God of which the outflow into real life brings love to self and neighbor into focus. Here we see not only how to treat others, but how to regard ourselves.

32. Wynkoop, *John Wesley*, 16.
33. Wynkoop, "Look Out," 10.
34. Wynkoop, "Look Out," 10.
35. Wynkoop, *John Wesley*, 10.

Faithfulness as the Reordering of *Agapē*

What is unique in Wynkoop's theological anthropology is that she did not align herself with the West in its tendency to think Adam was created in an already-perfect state. Wynkoop, rather, sided with the Irenaean view that Adam was created with room for development and growth. In agreement with the Greek fathers, she made a distinction between "image" and "likeness" and did not consider these concepts to be a Hebrew parallelism. Whereas the "image" denotes the human potential for life in God, for her "likeness" opened the door for the progressive realization of that potentiality. Hence, Wynkoop's emphasis on Adam being endowed with the "capacity for faithfulness" should be read with an Eastern lens. The capacity for development and perfection was embedded in the concept "likeness" and was, according to Wynkoop, an essential part of the way God created Adam. Even the fall did not change this basic disposition. Since, in her mind, likeness is found in the realm of human personhood where moral probation operates, the potentiality for likeness remained, even in fallen humanity. It is then important to note that, for Wynkoop, the potential for Christian faithfulness is anchored in creation, not in the fall. This is so since in her mind grace does not have to recreate or restore the moral disposition of humanity after the fall but, rather, operates to renew or redirect the disposition or faculties that remained intact. This pre-suppositional stance in Wynkoop's theological anthropology has a direct bearing on how she defined faithfulness.

Wynkoop did not see faith as something given to human beings but as an inherent disposition that remained intact after the fall. This is a key presupposition in her understanding of faithfulness. She said, "The exhortations to exercise the faculty of faith were addressed mainly to unbelievers, obviously, and hence, to those who were in sin."[36] For Wynkoop, this is not a "partially restored faculty" but a faculty that remained fully intact after the fall, now expressed as rebellion or unbelief. The antithesis to saving faith for her, then, is not no faith but full, active rejection.[37] Wynkoop wrote, "The concept of the whole-man psychology in which all aspects of personality are seen to work as a unit—faith and will, heart and mind, love and obedience—preserves the integrity of personality without losing the idea of dependence on God's grace."[38]

According to Wynkoop, this is especially true when viewed from the perspective of human beings' relationship to God. In this relationship, faith

---

36. Wynkoop, "Biblical Study of Man," 126.
37. Wynkoop, *Theology of Love*, 232.
38. Wynkoop, *Theology of Love*, 225.

seems to be an essential element in personality.[39] However, she was cautious in describing this elusive faculty called faith. She wrote, "We ought not to be obsessed by the act of our faith. Faith in the New Testament sense describes the very reaching out of our most inner selves toward Christ, not conscious of faith as such, but conscious of the grasp of mutual love, a deep, profound resting and trusting and love in and for Christ. Faith is by definition obedience and love from the heart. Faith never appears unclothed and abstract. Faith is dynamic."[40] It is then the activity of "someone" (the Holy Spirit) who helps human beings to change the direction of their affection. It is not the initiation of a new power. An "implanted" saving faith rising apart from human participation was not exactly what she had in mind when she reflected on Christian integrity in this divine-human interaction.

Likewise, she came to realize that love, in the biblical sense, is not something added to our lives, but a change in the direction of life's deepest commitment. In the evangelical world, *agapē* as "divine love" is generally described as something given to us by the Holy Spirit. However, Wynkoop had a totally different understanding of this Christian word for love. It was Wynkoop's assessment that *agapē* is basic to all human beings. No one is free not to love. She wrote, "The deviant person loves, the Christian loves, the non-Christian loves. At the point of loving there is no difference among human beings. All people engage in what the Bible calls agapē. By translating agapē by the English word 'love,' the meaning of the term is totally lost."[41] Wynkoop's basic position was that *agapē* is defined by its object. It can describe either holiness or moral disintegration. She wrote:

> Agapē is man's operational commitment to a center which determines his lifestyle. By agapē man erects his God and establishes the lordship under which he serves, consciously and responsibly, or blindly, almost by default. The startling fact emerges from the biblical usage that one may agapē God and make him Lord, or he may agapē "the present world" as Paul said Demas did, and forfeit God. Agapē toward God opens up the whole person to the whole rich potential of existence as a human being that God intends for man—to discover his desirable will (Romans 12:2).[42]

Wynkoop is saying that the same heart that loves God can also be the heart of unbelief. It is to the self that God appeals. "The legitimate—essential

---

39. Wynkoop, *Theology of Love*, 227.
40. Wynkoop, "Problem of the Relationship," 3.
41. Wynkoop, "Quality, the Price of Love," 7.
42. Wynkoop, "Quality, the Price of Love," 8.

relationship of life, never to be eliminated but brought into harmony with the self, is to 'aim at God.'"[43] For Wynkoop, the dedication and total self-giving aimed at God describe the essence of Christian faithfulness. This *agapē* set on God will then also affect all other relationships, whether *erōs*, *philia*, or *storgē*, and find the fulfilment intended for each of them.[44] With this background we come to understand Wynkoop's position that sin is love, but "love gone astray."[45] She wrote, "Sin is love locked into a false center, the self. . . . Holiness is love locked into the true center, Jesus Christ our Lord."[46] Basically, Wynkoop believes that holiness is *agapē* to God and sin is *agapē* to self. By placing sin in juxtaposition to love, Wynkoop opened the door to grasp what freedom from sin requires. It is the object that reacts back on and defines the quality of love. *Agapē* is not a higher kind of love but the basic faculty necessary to make relationships possible. Perfect love, or holiness, becomes possible when *agapē* is redirected to Christ by the enabling grace of the Holy Spirit, but *agapē* set on the self throws all human relationships into chaos and destruction. Both Peter and John affirm this position. In 2 Peter 2:15, Peter describes those who loved (*agapē*) the wages of unrighteousness, and in 1 John 2:15, John is emphatic that "if anyone loves (*agapē*) the world, the love for the Father is not in them."

Her succinct description of the state of human beings after the fall says it all: "The apparatus is intact in fallen man, but the light is out." In other words, for Wynkoop, the moral mold is cast, but only through the prevenient ministry of the Holy Spirit can humans reach their God-given potential. Only in fellowship with the Holy Spirit can human beings experience true self-realization and assurance by aligning their love to Christ. Self-awareness and personal identification, then, are all wrapped in the ministry of the Holy Spirit. Only through the Holy Spirit are human beings truly brought face-to-face with their real selves.[47]

Faithfulness is Christocentric

Christ as the "living Word" and Christ as the "image" became important building blocks in the way Wynkoop constructed her existential theology of faithfulness. The practical significance of the "living Word" becoming flesh and living among us, calling for humanity's renewal in the image of Christ,

43. Wynkoop, "To Dr. Darrell Moore."
44. Wynkoop, *Theology of Love*, 37.
45. Wynkoop, *Theology of Love*, 157.
46. Wynkoop, *Theology of Love*, 158.
47. Wynkoop, *Theology of Love*, 203.

was at the heart of Wynkoop's exploration. One of the key markers in her theology is that love is revealed in Christ. Jesus not only showed humanity how to be human, but he also demonstrated what it looks like to *agapē* the Father by living a life totally dedicated and surrendered to his will.

For Wynkoop, legitimate faith experiences were seen to be teleological. The idea of growth and development was more important than just a specific episode. It was to be caught up in the kingdom of God (the reign of Christ) as a partner with Christ in the recreation and renewal of this broken world. Wynkoop described her faith as directed to the person of Christ, describing this relationship as personal, rather than on an impersonal level. For her, faith was through and through personal. She was interested in the "lawgiver back of the law."[48] She wanted to protect the integrity of both parties, the personhood of Christ as well as the personhood of the one responding to the overtures of God's grace. "It is putting dishonesty in God," she said, "to say that a man is objectively righteous and subjectively unrighteous even by means of Christ's atonement."[49]

Given her holistic approach, the idea of "accepting Christ" as a way of appropriating faith was to her a far cry from biblical teaching. She wrote, "Interesting enough, no New Testament passage gives the slightest hint that we are to 'accept' Christ or 'what he has done for us.' We are exhorted 'to believe in him.' In the occasions where 'accept' refers to a relationship of men and Christ (or God), it is man who is to make himself *acceptable*. The tremendous exhortation of Romans 12:1 is to the effect that we present ourselves 'holy and acceptable' to God."[50] This outward focus towards Christ's kingdom indicates that Wynkoop did not see human beings as the subject of the gospel. For her it was not about Jesus coming into our small world, but rather us coming out of our small world to join the big world of Christ's mission. She is basically saying that when it comes to faithfulness in Christ's kingdom, the focus is not primarily on us. We do not invite Christ into our kingdom, but we are exhorted to enter his kingdom. In this scenario, Christ is the subject of the gospel. It is about his reign and mission to restore our broken world and our enabled response to his invitation to join his kingdom. She wrote:

> He is the Lord of the kingdom of God. In Him is the reversal of all that the old man has done. By His death and resurrection, He established His headship and ends the alienation of the race from God. He is God with us, Emmanuel. In Christ, the true

---

48. Wynkoop, *Theology of Love*, 238.
49. Wynkoop, "Theology of Depth," 170.
50. Wynkoop, "Theology of Depth," 176, emphasis added.

Head of the Church, men become one with the new Corporate Personality. In each believer is incarnated the total life of the new race; and Christ, the Head, incorporates into himself, as the New Man, every believer. This is the kingdom of God . . . Christ is Lord, constituted so by God independent of our acknowledgment of the fact. We do not make Him Lord; we enter the Kingdom where He is Lord. This basically is the "law of the land."[51]

Wynkoop's kingdom outlook is a key-integrating factor in her assumptions about faithfulness. Here the focus is not just about our hearts being renewed but joining Christ's kingdom society. This is as she said, "the new law of the land." In Wynkoop's tradition seekers had to first accept Jesus as their Savior and then later make him Lord of their lives. Here Wynkoop takes issue with this way of describing the gospel. For her it was not primarily what happens to you when you die, but what happens while you are alive. And as such, it is not about making him Lord of our lives but entering the kingdom where he already is Lord. This is then what Wynkoop has in mind when she reads Romans 12:1–2: "Present your bodies as a living sacrifice holy and pleasing to God." Gnosticism had a tendency to privatize and look for secret knowledge within as well as pushing salvation to the future and "out there" in a platonic heaven after we die. This is what Wynkoop saw as a distortion of the gospel and a stumbling block to the call to faithfully follow Christ in this world and to become like him.

Conclusion

This short study has brought us to the place where we can reflect on the implications of Wynkoop's perspectives of *agapē* holiness as a foundation for Christian faithfulness. As we have seen, Paul's perspectives in Romans 12:1–2 resonated with Wynkoop's theological anthropology. In her world, persons are dynamic beings—not static—and are constantly reaching out for fulfilment. She is convinced that in so doing, all human beings exercise *agapē* as an *ipso facto* mindset native to their basic humanity. She considered each person as unique and believed that every human entity derives identity by its prevailing priority selection. This to her meant that when something other than God served as a person's central priority, it had a way of determining the whole value system of the person.

For Wynkoop, God's call to human beings is to present their bodies (entire responsible self) as a living sacrifice to him, undergirded by the promise that what God requires he also makes possible. She anticipated

---

51. Wynkoop, *Theology of Love*, 332.

that a response to this call would be of the whole self—not of parts of the self. She was convinced that what God created remained intact but should be under the lordship of Christ. When we postulate that for Wynkoop faithfulness is Christocentric, we are saying that for her Christ is Lord and must be enthroned in the heart and life without a rival for that central place. For Wynkoop, faithfully following Christ is relational, personal, and life-transforming. Sin is not an impersonal thing residing in us causing us to sin. We sin because the whole self is rooted in a love contrary to Christ's Lordship. Holiness as a faithful expression of following Christ results when Christ is made the true center. To be "in Christ" is to be in the body of Christ, in the fellowship of the Holy Spirit "knitting" every individual into every other by love until we all come to the fullness of the stature of Christ. For her, participation in Christ's kingdom reign was a "this-world" reality fully lived out on the ground as an existential relationship where loving God, yourself, and your neighbor is at the heart of what it means to be a faithful follower of Christ.

Bibliography

Ladd, George Eldon. *The Pattern of New Testament Truth*. Grand Rapids: Eerdmans, 1968.
Wynkoop, Mildred Bangs. *A Theology of Love*. Kansas City: Beacon Hill, 1972.
———. "The Authority of Christian Scriptures." File 2227-3. Unpublished, undated.
———. "The Biblical Study of Man in His Relationship to the Image of God." Master of Theology Dissertation. Western Evangelical Seminary. File 1432-3. Unpublished, 1952.
———. *John Wesley: Christian Revolutionary*. Kansas City: Beacon Hill, 1970.
———. "Holiness Theology and Moral Development." File 1425-21. Unpublished, 1978.
———. "Look Out, Our Presuppositions Do Show." File 1426-2. Unpublished, undated.
———. "The Problem of the Relationship between the First and Second Works of Grace." File 1434-13. Unpublished, undated.
———. "Protestant Theology and the Imago Dei." File 1432-7. Unpublished, undated.
———. "Quality, the Price of Love." File 1432.7. Unpublished, undated.
———. "Some Implications of the Existential Doctrine of Holiness." File 1432-7. Unpublished, undated.
———. "Theology of Depth." File 1431-15. Unpublished, 1958.
———. "Unity of Personality." File 1425-21. Unpublished, undated.
———. "What Holiness Means to Me." File 2227-14. Unpublished, undated.
———. "The Whole Wesley in a Broken World." File 1432-5. Unpublished, undated.
———. "The Word Became Flesh." File 1425-21. Unpublished, undated.
———. "Wynkoop to Dr. Darrell Moore." File 1427-17. Unpublished, 1981.

8

Faithfulness to the Gospel
An Interpretation from the Early Church Fathers

—DAVID RAINEY

Christian theology, from its beginning, had a missional direction. Right from the start, in the first century and leading into the second century, communicating to culture would create a level of conflict in synthesizing culture, or Greek philosophy, to the gospel. Greek culture found its direction in Platonic categories but, by the first century CE, there developed the integration of other philosophical models of thought in what would be called "middle Platonism." Christianity, as a missionary movement, would be caught up in the world of middle Platonism.

The formulation of Christian doctrine which was essential for the progress of Christianity must first speak the language of the Christian community, but when that language is inadequate to explain God in relation to life and creation within culture, the language will be reinvented until it becomes the norm of communication. For instance, it is apparent that the apostle Paul did not use the language of Jesus in the missionary work to the Greco-Roman world. Evidently, the church will be in the perpetual task of speaking the gospel when pagan, or secular, or religious cultural norms are not in agreement with Christian speech.

The early church fathers become a useful model for the analysis of the gospel, language, and culture. The language of culture outside of Christianity was dominated by the Greco-Roman worldview of Platonic thought, though there was a mixture of other philosophical traditions. We find that within the earliest attempts to communicate the gospel there were diverse ways to communicate. The method used to assess the challenge of speaking to culture, in this chapter, will be to use selected primary sources along with secondary sources that attempt to analyze Christianity's success at speaking to a culture unfamiliar with Christian language and the understanding of

Christianity's distinctive form of reality. Speaking of a crucified savior who rose bodily from the dead, once and for all, could not be aligned with any pagan philosophy although points of contact may be found.

The point that this chapter will develop is the awareness that the Platonic language became inadequate for theological development and so theological language had to be created. The challenge that this created left its lasting mark on the church. We will begin in the second century and finish with the Council of Chalcedon in 451 CE, remembering that Emperor Theodosius declared that Christianity had become the official religion of the Roman Empire in 381 CE.

Keith Ward discussed the future of Christianity in *A Vision to Pursue: Beyond the Crisis in Christianity*.[1] Importantly he saw Christianity as constantly revising itself in light of the surrounding culture. In the history of the early church he assumed that the encounter with philosophy, that is, the cultured Greco-Roman world, met with a required revision of Christian thought according to the culture. This effected the way Christian theology defined Christology. Apparently, Christianity did not have the means to articulate Christology, so it borrowed from the Greco-Roman world. Ward stated, "the concepts of Hellenistic philosophy were introduced to give shape to classical doctrines of Jesus as the 'second person of the Trinity.'"[2] It appeared that Keith Ward believed Christian doctrine was dependent on Hellenistic philosophy for its key conceptual framework. But there is a possibility of oversimplifying the relation of the so-called "Christ and culture" debate when, in fact, the relation was quite complex. G. R. Evans wrote:

> The Greek philosophical heritage was already very complex when Christianity began. The Middle Platonism of the first Christian centuries combines elements of Stoicism, parts of Aristotle's teaching, scraps from a number of philosophical systems. However certain governing principles had a common currency as a result of Plato's teaching and these gave the thought of the day a predominantly Platonic character.[3]

When approaching Plato's concept of the divine he dealt with the division of the world we know by our senses, and, the world of the intellect or ideas. Above this intellect and sense is God and as G. R. Evans stated, God is "so remote from the worlds we know, that he cannot properly be said even to 'be.'"[4] There was no commonality with Christianity at

1. Ward, *Vision to Pursue*.
2. Ward, *Vision to Pursue*, 8.
3. Evans et al., *Science of Theology*, 11.
4. Evans et al., *Science of Theology*, 12.

this point and it is an important non-intersection. Yet within this whole philosophical tradition the emerging Christianity had to work with culture, language, and communication.

Still, we are required to pay attention to language. On the first page on the inside of the cover page of *Philosophy in Christian Antiquity*, Christopher Stead stated, "In the ancient world 'philosophy' included all branches of higher learning except mathematics and medicine."[5] A person should be careful with the use of the word since today it appears as a department in a university education program as distinct from other academic disciplines.

So, from the second to the fifth centuries two dynamic and fluid systems existed: 1) Platonic philosophy was dominant but constantly changing; and 2) Christianity began to capture the civilized world and culture. At the end of the fourth century Emperor Theodosius declared Christianity to be the true religion of the Roman Empire. This effected both the Eastern (Greek speaking) and Western (Latin speaking) realms of the empire. Stead's useful summary of Christian theology was that Christian theologians were more faithful to the Scriptures than Platonic philosophers had been faithful to Plato.[6]

The language and terms of the Greco-Roman world were constructed by ancient philosophy and there is no doubt that Christian theology was indebted to this ancient tradition. Yet as Christopher Stead emphasized, the early Church Fathers were not committed to any philosophical system or methodology. His conclusion was, "Our point is rather that their allegiance to biblical and Church tradition left little room, in most cases, for dispassionate critical study that philosophy requires."[7] Then he added, "Thus what has been called Christian philosophy generally proves to be Christian theology, systematically stated with the aid of elements borrowed from philosophy."[8] Christopher Stead concluded that by the fifth century, Cyril of Alexandria and Gregory the Great had studied philosophical texts but had "absorbed little in the way of philosophical discipline."[9] This included the important conclusion that the monastic way of life, as the cornerstone of mission for the church, was "untouched by philosophy."[10] One of Christian theology's standard assertions was the resurrection. While this could be understood within the Hebrew mind, "It proved something of an embarrassment; the

---

5. Stead, *Philosophy in Christian Antiquity*.
6. Stead, *Philosophy in Christian Antiquity*, 79.
7. Stead, *Philosophy in Christian Antiquity*, 80.
8. Stead, *Philosophy in Christian Antiquity*, 81.
9. Stead, *Philosophy in Christian Antiquity*, 83.
10. Stead, *Philosophy in Christian Antiquity*, 85.

notion was ridiculed by many Platonists, for whom the body was necessarily the source of sensuality and corruption and ought to disappear forever."[11] Primarily the earliest Christian writers were not interested in the philosophy of religion. Again, Stead emphasized, "in the early Church it is clear that the main items of Christian belief were seldom, if ever, argued out in this way; they are the product of Christian reflection upon the Scriptures, accepted by faith as the word of God in the context of a common life of devotion to Christ, accepted by faith as Lord, Illuminator and Redeemer."[12] Basil of Caesarea could not be listed as a supporter of ancient philosophy in the sense that it could clarify Christian faith.[13] In line with this, Christopher Stead was adamant, "there are relatively few points at which philosophical work was incorporated into the accepted structure of Christian teaching."[14]

Yet, John Rist described the situation in this way: "Platonism has two basic principles which proved overwhelmingly attractive to early Christians and put other philosophical systems in the shade . . . its belief—in contrast to Stoicism—in a transcendent world peopled with immanent beings (though in the second century, for fear of Gnosticism, Christians preferred initially not to speak of Forms), and, its theory of *eros*, that power—its full capacity was debatable—by which man expresses his desire for the beauty of divine things."[15] Now we know, from reading Christopher Stead and John Rist, that the relation between Greco-Roman philosophy and Christian theology was complex.

Rist further elaborated on the inevitable dilemma of the integration of pagan culture to Christian thought, "As Christianity developed, Christian thinkers found themselves ever torn between the desire to exploit the riches of their pagan philosophical inheritance and a growing awareness of where the limits of assimilation must be set: Is there a difference between Platonic likeness to God and a Christian imitation of Christ?"[16] Pertinent to this point is the analysis by the utilitarian consequential ethicist, Peter Singer. In 1993 he published his ethical analysis and supported the contentious issue that Christianity triumphant over pagan philosophy with the Christian "image of God" for human creation. Singer was negatively critical of Christianity over the protection of newborn infants. He wrote, "it may be worth

---

11. Stead, *Philosophy in Christian Antiquity*, 87.
12. Stead, *Philosophy in Christian Antiquity*, 90.
13. Stead, *Philosophy in Christian Antiquity*, 91.
14. Stead, *Philosophy in Christian Antiquity*, 93.
15. Rist, "Christian Theology," 108.
16. Rist, "Christian Theology," 108.

remembering that our present absolute protection of the lives of infants is a distinctively Christian attitude rather than a universal value."[17]

There is one further controversy in developing an understanding of "Christ and culture" in the early history of the church. This involves current secondary interpretations. John Rist wrote, "For scholars have been tempted to argue ideologically of each specific Christian figure some will insist that his thought is, though extremely Christian, in fact heavily dependent on, or even subservient to contemporary philosophical trends. Or, if not that, the other extreme: on the surface we shall read, though he may be Platonic, everything important in his thought is purely biblical."[18] So, the questions that this chapter deal with are: how did Christian theologians use Greek philosophy, and to what extent did philosophical concepts outside Christian theology control Christian thought?

Now we can look at a select number of Christian theologians with their varying methodologies in relation to "Christ and culture." A basic chronological order will be given rather than a topical order. The early second century Apologists tended to use the scientific philosophical language of the day and wrote that Christ fulfilled the search for truth in philosophy. The Apologists moved the functional subordination of the New Testament relation of the Father and the Son to essential subordination of the Son to the Father and assumed the dualism of the physical and spiritual world. The Logos had now become a type of inferior divine person to the Father. This was written with clarity in Justin Martyr.

Justin Martyr and Clement of Alexandria

Justin Martyr (ca. 100–165) was a Middle Platonist philosopher who encountered an elderly man while walking along the seashore. Through the encounter he became a Christian and with his Middle Platonist views he constructed his belief that Christianity was the best philosophy. Importantly he did not reject his former philosophy but became a critic by adding Christianity as the true philosophy. Justin is still considered to be a creative Christian philosopher since he had no precedent to work with. His most famous writings are his *First Apology*, then his *Second Apology*, followed by his *Dialogue with Trypho*. There is evidence that he sounds like creating two Gods as a result of trying to combine Middle Platonism with biblical Christological thought.

17. Singer, *Practical Ethics*, 172.
18. Rist, "Christian Theology," 109.

Like Justin Martyr, Clement of Alexandria (ca. 150–215) had an education in Middle Platonism and was a convert to Christianity. After becoming a Christian his goal was to bring Christianity, as growth in Christian perfection, into the Greco-Roman culture. In order to bring people to faith it was important to work within culture and demonstrate Christianity's adaptability while remaining distinctive. He wrote *Paidagogos* which dealt with the life of holiness and then *Miscellany* or *Stromateis* which was a call for the reader to growth in the truth of the Christian gospel. As with Justin Martyr, Clement believed the OT formed the basis for Greek philosophy.

The true gnostic, countering the philosophical system of Gnosticism, was the person who lived the life of perfection. This life was given by God and a person must make the effort to attain its reality. For Clement the Logos tended to be the principle of wisdom rather than the person of Christ and here he gave strong evidence of the Greek philosophical influence. At this point he used Gnostic language to communicate Christian truth to the educated culture.

Irenaeus of Lyons

A second-century alternative to Justin Martyr and Clement of Alexandria was Irenaeus of Lyons (ca. 120/140–200/203). Dominic J. Unger, in his translation of Irenaeus's *Against the Heresies*, established a key evaluation of the importance of Irenaeus. Unger stated, in relation to Irenaeus's theological writing, that it "establishes Irenaeus as the most important of the theologians of the second century and merits him the title of founder of Christian theology."[19] He is in agreement with earlier evaluations.[20] In the light of studies in gnostic thought, it has been established that Irenaeus gave an accurate portrayal of the philosophical systems he would critique.[21]

Added to the accuracy of Irenaeus's description of Gnosticism, he was also a defender of the existing church tradition grounded in Scripture. Tradition did not stifle Irenaeus's theological creativity, in fact, it enhanced his creative genius.[22] Irenaeus could do more than repeat Scripture and tradition, he could move tradition forward into a relevancy for the church

19. Unger, *St. Irenaeus of Lyons*, 1.

20. Gunton, *Yesterday and Today*, 225: "He is a model of a theological integration of incarnation, saving death, resurrection and ascension, all embraced within a trinitarian framework according to which the creating and redeeming work of God the Father is mediated by the Son and the Holy Spirit."

21. Unger, *St. Irenaeus of Lyons*, 1: "Studies thus far, however, substantiate the centuries-old belief in the reliability of Irenaeus as a source."

22. Unger, *St. Irenaeus of Lyons*, 2.

in the second century. "For Irenaeus, the main witnesses to the Truth are Scripture and tradition."[23]

Irenaeus recognized that tradition could be developed in other ways than what was true to the gospel and philosophical intrusion was capable of creating another tradition. For Irenaeus, though, the authentic gospel developed in direct line from the apostles. The authentic gospel had spread throughout the world and the tradition that preserved the gospel was the truly Catholic tradition.[24]

In *Against the Heresies* 1.10, Irenaeus asserted the openness of the gospel to humanity that cannot be altered regardless of cultural setting. A few quotes from chapter 10 will clarify his position. After he explained the gospel, Irenaeus continued:

> The Church as we have said before, though disseminated throughout the whole world, carefully guards this preaching and this faith which she has received as if she dwelt in one house. She likewise believes these things as if she had but one soul and one and the same heart; she preaches, teaches, and hands them down harmoniously, as if she possessed one mouth. For, though the languages throughout the world are dissimilar, nevertheless the meaning of the tradition is one and the same. To explain, the churches which have been founded in Germany do not believe or hand down anything else; neither do the those founded in Spain or Gaul or Libya or in the central regions of the world . . . the preaching of the Truth, shines everywhere and enlightens all men who wish to come to the knowledge of the Truth.[25]

Irenaeus re-enforced this at the end of chapter 10. "The reason is that, as was said previously, the entire Church has one and the same faith throughout the whole world."[26] For Irenaeus the world of Platonic thought and the multi-various philosophical traditions added nothing to theology and the revelation of the one gospel.

Origen

We will turn to an extended discussion regarding Origen (ca. 184–253). The third century contained a number of theological controversies for the church, but the dominant figure was Origen. In his own lifetime he was

23. Unger, *St. Irenaeus of Lyons*, 8.
24. Unger, *St. Irenaeus of Lyons*, 11.
25. Irenaeus, *Against the Heresies* 1.10.1.
26. Irenaeus, *Against the Heresies* 1.10.3.

controversial. He was born at a time in the Roman Empire when there was political chaos, instability, and violence, and eventually he died as a martyr. His intellectual ability was recognized early in his life and he was made a master at the Christian school in Alexandria at the age of seventeen. He was educated in Christian theology and pagan literature and made ample use of Middle Platonism but did it as a critic and as well as an admirer. Students of Origen recognized him as a scholar in biblical exegesis, the use of allegory, a preacher, a moral ascetic, all in the context of Platonic philosophy. His particular use of pagan philosophy created key critics and eventually his writings were condemned at the Fifth Ecumenical Council in 553 CE, long after he died.

Origen was innovative in making Christian thought distinct from pagan philosophy, but he could also incorporate pagan philosophy in order to win over pagan intellectuals. At this point the Bible was a key point of discovery for Origen because he believed that Christ was revealed in the Bible and Christ is the Scriptures' interpreter, and the controversial use of allegory was under the control of Christological hermeneutics. By this method the Bible is a unity and becomes a model of progressive revelation. As in the incarnation, God descended to speak the language of humans at the level of the understanding of humans. So, there were multiple ways to use progressive revelation according to the various levels of understanding of human ability.

Rowan Greer wrote, "His theology was an attempt to translate the Gospel into a language intelligible to the pagan, especially the thoughtful and educated."[27] His skill was demonstrated, controversially, in the interpretation of philosophy and the church's theology. As Greer further commented, he shows with his contemporary Plotinus a concern "to move beyond skeptical and dualistic forms of Platonism, as well as a speculative and open approach to philosophical issues worthy of Plato himself."[28]

Origen was important in initiating appropriate language for the Trinity in that *hypostasis* meant "person" while *ousia* meant "essence." Normally, the two words had been synonyms. Later Basil of Caesarea would make maximum use of Origen's language. Still his doctrine of the Trinity bore evidence of distance within God, as well as to humanity, and it would create problems for an effective understanding of the Trinity. Later, Athanasius in his trinitarian proposal would close the gap in the relationship of the Father, Son, and Holy Spirit. Origen's language was so complex that Colin Gunton would call into question that Origen actually had a conceptual Trinity.

27. Greer, "Introduction," 2.
28. Greer, "Introduction," 5.

Gunton explained, "For Origen, God the Son was a second God derivatively divine, we might say, and the Spirit was the highest of the creatures, sent by God to sanctify the believer."[29] To Gunton's credit, he referenced an alternative reading of Origen.[30]

There was also clear philosophical evidence in Origen's doctrine of creation. He believed that human beings had a heavenly existence as minds which required a physical body for earthly existence. Rowan Greer explained this in the following words,

> For Origen God is essential goodness and consequently He wills to have beings to whom He may convey His goodness by giving them life and knowledge of Himself. To this end He creates apparently without reference to time, the rational creatures. They are minds, all immortal, equal and eternal. We can imagine them as pupils in a heavenly schoolroom, directing their attention to the Word, who reveals the Father to them.[31]

Now we can add Origen's own words,

> Therefore why do we hang back and hesitate to put off the perishable body, the earthly tent that hinders us, weighs down the soul, and burdens the thoughtful mind (Wis 9:15)? Why do we hesitate to burst our bonds and to depart from the stormy billows of life with flesh and blood (cf. Phil 1:23; I Cor 15:50)? Let our purpose be to enjoy with Christ Jesus the rest proper to blessedness, contemplating him, the Word, wholly living ... By the true and unceasing Light of knowledge our minds will be enlightened to gaze upon what is by nature to be seen in that Light with eyes illumined by the Lord's commandment (cf. Ps 19:8; Eph 1:18).[32]

It is evident, clearly, that the mind is prior over the material body, an idea still evident in many areas of popular Christian theology. It was an idea developed in Platonism and continued in Origen.

Now we can turn to the critically important fourth century. The perpetual discussion on God, creation, and time and, consequently, the relation of the Father to the Son took a new turn at the beginning of the fourth century. Christianity created a firm identity at the Council of Nicaea in 325

---

29. Gunton, *Father, Son & Holy Spirit*, 78.
30. See Rainey, *Argument for the Deity*, 11–13; see *First Principles* I.3.7, for the source of Origen's trinitarian theology.
31. Greer, "Introduction," 10.
32. Origen, *Exhortation to Martyrdom* XLVII.

CE. Still, the Platonic worldview by now took more than one form and was still a predominate force. Rowan Williams quoted Richard Sorabji's comment that, "[Plato's] influence was . . . due to his very unclarity and suggestiveness which left room for so many subsequent interpretations."[33] Though Aristotle made his own contribution against Plato on time and creation, Williams still concluded, "Up to about 200 AD, then, the consensus among philosophers was that God and matter were co-eternal . . . God is not responsible for the existence of the eternal pre-cosmic chaos, but only for its organization into a rational world."[34]

Arius

From this brief discussion on creation and time in pagan philosophy we arrive at Arius (*ca.* 250/256–336 CE) in the early fourth century, a presbyter, in the city of Alexandria. His bishop Alexander was not happy with the theology that Arius promoted. As shall be pointed out, Arius had been influenced by the cultural norms of neo-Platonism and was challenged by Bishop Alexander regarding Christian identity. Arius understood the simplicity of God, which had been well developed, against his bishop's understanding of plurality in essence, in a trinitarian form, which still lacked a defined clarity. To state this in the understanding of Arius, "The Logos as condition of plurality must exist in some sense 'between' God's eternity and the *chronos* of the universe."[35] In other words, the Logos or Son could not be co-eternal with the Father.

A background to Arius is required. Plotinus was a contemporary of Origen and, like Origen, had a great influence on Christian thought. With Plotinus we are interested, particularly, in the mind, or *nous*, and the One. Our major source for Plotinus is his *Enneads*. For Plotinus, the One is beyond knowledge and experience, but from the One comes the mind. Plotinus established a complex understanding of the One and the *nous* and here we will summarize the philosophical presentation of Plotinus from Rowan Williams's magisterial but controversial study on Arius. Through the philosophical influence of Greek or pagan philosophy we can arrive at an understanding of Arius. Williams wrote of Plotinus, "the paradox of understanding is that, as pure need or openness, *nous* is truly in contact with the One; but in its seeking to realize itself actively as understanding it produces the multiplicity of the world of ideas, which separates it from the

33. Williams, *Arius*, 181.
34. Williams, *Arius*, 184.
35. Williams, *Arius*, 191.

One."[36] "The One cannot be known, nor can it know, 'Knowing' suggests that movement rising out of need which constitutes the activity of *nous*; and the One can have neither need nor motion."[37] This is complicated by the *nous* which becomes a conundrum since "*Nous* exists as it does because of its fundamental hunger for the One; and what it seeks in all its activities is the contemplation of the One."[38] We can hear Williams's conclusion: "Arius' entire effort consisted precisely in acclimatizing Plotinic logic within 'biblical creationism.'"[39]

We are required to acknowledge that material on Arius's writings is sparse because his work was not well preserved and our sources are largely from his opponents so as Rowan Williams admitted, "All that has been said about Arius' relation with the philosophical developments of the third Christian century is inevitably speculative,"[40] so we move ahead with some caution but not in complete ignorance. Arius proposed that the Son is not in communion with the Father in the Athanasian (*ca.* 296/298–373) understanding of the Trinity,[41] but as Williams asserted, "a sufficiently distinctive point in Arius' theology to lend some seriousness to the conjecture of Neoplatonic influence in this matter; and it is hard to see anywhere other than the fifth *Enneads* from which Arius might have derived the dual assertion of the Son's ignorance of the Father *and of himself.*"[42] Williams reached this conclusion regarding Arius's effort at defining theology and Christology which created the Nicene crisis in 325 CE: "the question of how it was that Arius came to express his theory in such idiosyncratic, novel and 'sharp-edged' terms we cannot wholly ignore those philosophers of his age with whose distinctive positions he exhibits so many parallels."[43]

In this brief analysis it is important to recognize that for Arius, God is beyond experience and so the Logos, a creature, is our source of spiritual life. Still, Arius was committed to the theology that there is no mixture of substances between the Father and the Son and the corollary that the Son became human was not possible. Arius was then required to develop an intricate theology within his preferred philosophical sources and having accepted

36. Williams, *Arius*, 201.

37. Williams, *Arius*, 201–2.

38. Williams, *Arius*, 202.

39. Williams, *Arius*, 209.

40. Williams, *Arius*, 230.

41. Athanasius, *Ep. Serap.* These letters describe an approach to the doctrine of the Holy Spirit that will be used by Basil of Caesarea and accepted at the Council of Constantinople in 381 CE that will form the orthodox doctrine of the Trinity.

42. Williams, *Arius*, 209.

43. Williams, *Arius*, 213.

a form of a doctrine of revelation, God created the perfect creature to enable humanity to grasp salvation through a mediator between God and humanity. In Arius's theology the mediator was neither God nor human.

To the contrary, Athanasius provided the beginnings of the understanding of the Trinity which were later developed more fully by the Cappadocian Fathers. There all three persons of the Trinity share in the same essence and communicate to humanity a fully grounded salvation by grace given to the human condition. When Rowan Williams stated that Athanasius was not a philosopher[44] he meant that Athanasius did not depend on philosophical categories to develop his thought. But when Williams repeated a similar phrase for Arius[45] he meant that Arius was not a technical philosopher but borrowed categories to construct his theology. The distinction is quite important. Arius saw himself, primarily as a biblical interpreter[46] but he required an access point, in philosophy, to communicate to culture.

I will use Williams's summary points to conclude the analysis of Arius, theology, and culture.

i. God alone is self-sufficient, *agennētos*, he is immaterial, and thus without any kind of plurality or composition; he is subject to no natural processes, no emanation or diffusion of his substance.

ii. He is entirely free, rational, and purposive.

iii. He initiates the creative process by freely bringing the Son into being, as a subsistent individual truly (*alēthōs*) distinct from himself; he does this "before all ages," yet there is a sense in which the Father exists prior to the Son, since the Son is not eternal, that is, not timelessly self-subsistent.

iv. By the will of God, the Son is stably and unalterably what he is, a perfect creature, not just "one among others"; he is the "inheritor" of all the gifts and glories God can give him, but, since this the effect of God's sovereign will, the Father's glory and dignity is in no way lessened by such a gift.[47]

Arius believed he was following Origen, but the complicated manner of Origen's theology developed into a variety of interpretations. In the fourth century one group known as the Cappadocian Fathers appreciated Origen's theological efforts at gospel assimilation to culture within a missionary

---

44. Williams, *Arius*, 225.
45. Williams, *Arius*, 236.
46. Williams, *Arius*, 107.
47. Williams, *Arius*, 98.

theology. Morwenna Ludow analyzed the Cappadocian contribution in this manner, "The Cappadocian use of contemporary Hellenistic philosophy is an extremely complicated issue.... First while the Cappadocians clearly use philosophical vocabulary, this does not always mean that they used it in the same way as philosophers did.... Thus, although it is often helpful to know the previous philosophical uses of a word like *hypostasis,* the more important question must be what did the Cappadocians mean by the word?"[48] We will take a brief look at the more clearly Platonic use of philosophy in Gregory of Nyssa (*ca.* 330–95) which was distinct from his older brother, Basil of Caesarea, and colleague, Gregory of Nazianzus.

Gregory of Nyssa

Gregory of Nyssa has been recognized as the theologian of the ascent into the life of God. He was able to incorporate Platonism into his theology without losing sight of the gospel; he also remained within the Nicaean theological orientation. Though Gregory of Nyssa was not a Platonist who expressed Christian thought, he was a Christian who redefined Platonic language to clarify theology.

Catherine Roth discussed the way to interpret Gregory of Nyssa and she sided with the group that concluded that Gregory was a Christian who expressed his views in the contemporary categories of the prevailing worldview.[49] Hans Boersma put it this way, "It seems to me that this (creator-creature distinction) is essentially a correct assessment.... I too believe that for St. Gregory the most basic ontological distinction is that between creator and creature and that this is a Christian metaphysical 'novelty'. The presence of Platonic and Stoic elements in his thinking notwithstanding, Gregory is first and foremost a Christian thinker."[50] While traditional Platonic thought places the priority on the soul to the neglect of the material world, and distinct from Origen, Gregory was not prepared to turn the material world or embodiment into the category of evil.

A Doctrinal Interlude: The Doctrine of the Trinity

We shall now turn to the second key theological doctrine developed in the fourth century; the doctrine of the Trinity was not constructed or

---

48. Ludow, "Cappadocians," 182.
49. Gregory of Nyssa, *On the Soul,* 11–12.
50. Boersma, *Embodiment and Virtue,* 6.

influenced by any attempt of association with non-Christian triadic theologies or philosophies. The basis for the Trinity came out of the Christology of the humanity of Christ and Paul's identity of Christ with God's preexistent Wisdom.[51] In this sense we can identify the Christian Platonist style from Justin Martyr to Eusebius as weak in trinitarian thought but Athanasius and the Cappadocian Fathers, influenced little by any type of philosophical conceptual ideas, were strong in trinitarian constructive theology. The less ancient philosophy influenced Christian identity, the stronger this distinctive Christian identity was.

This can be analyzed from the previous position of Irenaeus who used ancient philosophy to attack the philosophy of the gnostic Christians. Interestingly, he used their system against them in matters of defining the gospel that spread throughout the empire. But when Irenaeus constructed Christian theology, the ancient philosophical multi-varied system was not a source.[52] In like manner Athanasius regarded himself as upholding the earlier tradition of the church through Irenaeus. He was "far less open to suggestions from the philosophers."[53] The Nicene language of *ousia* and *homoousios* did not have a bearing in Aristotle as some have suggested. Stead commented, "Christian writers took little notice of Aristotle's *Categories* and its distinctive treatment of substance until at least the late 350s, when it perhaps began to be noticed by Arian logicians."[54] Once again, it was the non-trinitarian theologians that tended to be heavily influenced by ancient philosophy and the non-trinitarian theologians were eventually rejected by the church.

Now we can conclude the complicated theological controversies of the fourth century and the Arian contribution. Christopher Stead elaborated that the Arians were in the philosophical tradition of Platonism while the major Nicaean theologians were continuing to develop the biblical tradition. Stead explained Arian thought: "Arius appears to have taken the same view as Eusebius; he argued that the Logos himself experienced emotions of dismay and terror at the time of the Passion, and therefore fell short of the serene impassibility of the Father."[55] Christopher Stead then stated that this led Arius to believe "that the Logos was in some sense a creature, though unique in status and the foremost among God's works." In a similar manner Richard Bauckham concluded, "In the context of the Arian controversies, Nicene theology was essentially an attempt to resist

---

51. Stead, *Philosophy in Christian Antiquity*, 155.
52. Stead, *Philosophy in Christian Antiquity*, 157.
53. Stead, *Philosophy in Christian Antiquity*, 158.
54. Stead, *Philosophy in Christian Antiquity*, 159.
55. Stead, *Philosophy in Christian Antiquity*, 191.

the implications of Greek philosophical understandings of divinity and re-appropriate in a new conceptual context the New Testament's inclusion of Jesus in the unique divine identity."[56]

Cyril of Alexandria and Nestorius of Constantinople

The final move in this chapter will take us into the first half of the 5th century. The crucial debate was between Cyril, Archbishop of Alexandria (ca. 376–444), and Nestorius, Archbishop of Constantinople (ca. 386–450). Perhaps there is an important statement in the phrase regarding Cyril of Alexandria: "Cyril did not use technical terms. He taught, correctly that our Lord's humanity was real, and that it existed only in the Logos incarnate."[57] Here Cyril meant not simply the reality of the humanness of Christ but that it was a distinctly authentic humanity in Christ. It should be noted that Stead makes no comment on Platonic ontology at Chalcedon. Instead the Church was debating theological structure contained in the Church tradition.

One of the important doctrines in the debate between Cyril and Nestorius was how to use the concept of suffering in the definition of God. The Greek word was *pathos*, and in the Greek philosophical tradition it was often connected to change such as an emotion of anger or fear. It could also refer to less than admirable lust or vice. It may be conceived as not being part of one's rational choice but rather events or feelings that come upon a person. Alternatively, impassibility in Christian thought referred to the sovereignty of God that he cannot be overpowered by an outside force. Still, Christopher Stead recognized the word, impassible, ran the risk of making God to be insensitive approaching apathy towards creation.[58]

Nestorius asserted divine impassibility based on philosophical concerns. Paul Gavrilyuk asserted,

> The conclusion is reached that Nestorius asserted unqualified divine impassibility. Cyril, in contrast, held a qualified view of divine impassibility and maintained that neither divinity suffered alone, apart from humanity (in which case the assumption of humanity would be superfluous), nor humanity suffered alone, apart from and in sharp contrast to the impassable divinity (in which case the reality of divine involvement in the incarnation would be put at risk).[59]

---

56. Bauckham, *God Crucified*, 78.
57. Stead, *Philosophy in Christian Antiquity*, 214.
58. Stead, *Philosophy in Christian Antiquity*, 129–30.
59. Gavrilyuk, "Nestorius' Main Charge," 190.

Important to this is Cyril's controversial letter to Nestorius. In Cyril's letter which contained the twelve anathemas, the twelfth stated very clearly, "If any one does not confess that the Word of God suffered in the flesh and was crucified in the flesh . . . let him be anathema."[60] The Nestorian supporters consistently maintained that divine impassibility was crucial that divinity could not participate in human experience.[61] For Cyril qualifications on impassibility and passibility were necessary to understand the conditions within the Incarnation. For Nestorius to separate impassibility and passibility guaranteed the affirmation that divinity could not be influenced by any human conditions.[62]

The concept of impassibility was a philosophical one and, at times, Cyril insisted on impassibility as did the Nestorians, but Cyril corrected a rigid philosophical version through Christology. Nestorius accused Cyril of inconsistency and confusion on this matter since Nestorius insisted on the rigid philosophical version. Paul Gavrilyuk presented the case against Cyril from the point of view of Nestorius: "On this reading, Nestorius was a thoroughgoing philosophical impassibilist, whereas Cyril was an inconsistent and hesitating theopaschite. Were it not for his inadequate philosophical framework, Cyril would have seen the light and joined the circles of those who advocate unrestricted divine suffering today."[63] It was Philippians 2:6–11 that allowed Cyril to make his point on a readjusted impassibility.[64]

Gavrilyuk finally made his point: "Cyril's defence of the paradigm of the incarnation was not philosophically driven, but was motivated by the desire to articulate a distinctly Christian account of the divine involvement."[65] Then Gavrilyuk insisted, "We should also note Cyril's conscious reliance upon the NT in affirming both qualified impassibility and qualified passibility."[66] At the ecumenical Council of Ephesus in 431 CE the church sided with Cyril of Alexandria and this was reaffirmed at the following ecumenical Council of Chalcedon (451 CE). Platonic ontology was put to rest in favor of the biblical paradox of the Word made flesh.

---

60. Bettenson and Maunder, *Documents of the Christian Church*, 51.
61. Gavrilyuk, "Nestorius' Main Charge," 194.
62. Gavrilyuk, "Nestorius' Main Charge," 196.
63. Gavrilyuk, "Nestorius' Main Charge," 203.
64. Gavrilyuk, "Nestorius' Main Charge," 203.
65. Gavrilyuk, "Nestorius' Main Charge," 204.
66. Gavrilyuk, "Nestorius' Main Charge," 205.

Conclusion

The purpose of this chapter has been reached. The church dealt with three distinct approaches to the culture of Platonic philosophy. Firstly, there were those who accepted Platonic categories and used these categories to develop Christian theology. Secondly, there were those who employed Platonic language but changed the meaning of words to develop Christian theology. Thirdly, was a group of theologians who avoided philosophical categories completely and developed a more biblically oriented Christian theology. It appears from this analysis that the church recognized the legitimacy of the second and third methodologies to develop the authentic gospel.

Bibliography

Athanasius. *Letters to Serapion: Concerning the Holy Spirit*. Translated by C. R. B. Shapland. London: Epworth, 1951.

Bauckham, Richard. *God Crucified: Monotheism and Christology in the New Testament*. Carlisle: Paternoster, 1998.

Bettenson, Henry, and Chris Maunder, eds. *Documents of the Christian Church*. 3rd ed. Oxford: Oxford University Press, 1999.

Boersma, Hans. *Embodiment and Virtue in Gregory of Nyssa: An Anagogical Approach*. Oxford: Oxford University Press, 2013.

Evans, G. R., et al. *The Science of Theology*. Vol. 1. Basingstoke: Marshall, Morgan & Scott, 1986.

Gavrilyuk, Paul. "Nestorius' Main Charge Against Cyril of Alexandria." *Scottish Journal of Theology* 56.2 (2003) 190–207.

Greer, Rowan. "Introduction." In *Origen: An Exhortation to Martyrdom, Prayer, First Principle (Book IV), Prologue to the Commentary on Song of Songs, Homily XXVII on Numbers*, 1–40. Mahweh: Paulist, 1979.

Gregory of Nyssa. *On the Soul and the Resurrection*. Translated by Catherine Roth. Crestwood: St. Vladimir's Seminary Press, 1993.

Gunton, Colin. *Father, Son & Holy Spirit: Toward a Fully Trinitarian Theology*. London: T. & T. Clark, 2003.

———. *Yesterday and Today*. 2nd ed. London: SPCK, 1997.

Ludlow, Morwenna. "The Cappadocians." In *The First Christian Theologians: An Introduction to Theology in the Early Church*, edited by G. R. Evans, 168–85. Oxford: Blackwell, 2004.

Rainey, David. *The Argument for the Deity of the Holy Spirit According to St. Basil the Great, Bishop of Caesarea*. MTh thesis, Vancouver School of Theology, 1991.

Rist, John. "Christian Theology and Secular Philosophy." In *The First Christian Theologians: An Introduction to Theology in the Early Church*, edited by G. R. Evans, 105–14. Oxford: Blackwell, 2004.

Singer, Peter. *Practical Ethics*. 2nd ed. Cambridge: Cambridge University Press, 1993.

Stead, Christopher. *Philosophy in Christian Antiquity*. Cambridge: Cambridge University Press, 1994.

Unger, Dominic J., trans. *St. Irenaeus of Lyons: Against the Heresies*. Vol. I, Book I. Ancient Christian Writers 55. New York: Newman, 1992.
Ward, Keith. *A Vision to Pursue: Beyond the Crisis in Christianity*. London: SCM, 1991.
Williams, Rowan. *Arius: Heretic and Tradition*. Rev. ed. Cambridge: Eerdmans, 2001.

9

The Ideal of Faithfulness in Western Culture

—Diane Speed

Faithfulness lies at the heart of the Christian story of salvation. It is a key attribute expected of the people of God across both Testaments of the Bible and in the ingoing life of the church. Yet faithfulness has also been recognized as a major virtue in secular traditions.

Through an exploration of influential secular writing at focal points in the history of Western civilization, this paper will illustrate the persistent attachment of the ideal of faithfulness to both Christian and non-Christian secular society, and suggest ways in which faithfulness is still a feature of public discourse in the West, acculturated to contemporary Western secular attitudes. That faithfulness appears often to have been a focus for contention or debate, I would suggest, reinforces the centrality of faithfulness as a dynamic topic in human lives and societies in any generation, as each tells its own stories about itself.

The fact that the title of this Festschrift is a deliberate play on the title of John Wesley's great treatise, *A Plain Account of Christian Perfection*, invites us to begin by observing the close relationship of "faithfulness" to "Christian perfection" as ways of identifying, respectively, the process and the goal of the Christian journey through this life and of using this perception as a lens through which to read certain secular texts.

Wesley's understanding that it is possible to attain Christian perfection in this life is explicitly attached to biblical teaching of God's faithfulness to his word as that which draws human beings into faithfulness to him: for example, 1 John 1:9[1] (*Plain Account* 12.2;[2] also *Plain Account* 4.15, 4.16).

---

1. Biblical references are to the NRSV. Wesley's own quotations are from the KJV as the common English version of the day.

2. While Wesley concentrates on how and when perfection may be attained in this

The spiritual process through which human faithfulness may grow towards and then into perfection, that is, the process of sanctification, involves being "renewed in the image of God, in righteousness and true holiness" (*Plain Account* 5.17). Perfection may, according to Wesley, be fully achieved at a greater or lesser time before death through an act of faith. The overall process is summed up in the last chapter of the *Plain Account* (13).

The faithfulness of the human person is identified as faithfulness to "the grace given" (*Plain Account* 6.19), that is, the promise of salvific mercy from a faithful God who keeps his word. Human progress in faithfulness may be understood as the human reflection in time of God's infinite and eternal faithfulness in his ongoing dealings with humanity.

The love of God for humanity is not addressed focally in the discourse of the *Plain Account* but is woven into the treatise as a whole, surfacing, for example, in passing references to God's "pardoning love" and "one who had received the love of God" and the quoting of Romans 8:38–39 (all in *Plain Account* 8.24), as well as the human need to "abide in the love of God" (*Plain Account* 9.25).

While God's love for the person is manifested in his faithfulness, human faithfulness is expressed in love of God and neighbor, which is, arguably, the main overall exhortation of the *Plain Account*. Wesley declares repeatedly that to be a "perfect Christian" necessarily means to obey utterly the great commandment to love God and neighbor, referenced interchangeably to Deuteronomy 6:5, Deuteronomy 30:6, and Matthew 22:37 (all, for example, in *Plain Account* 5.17). Faithfulness growing into perfected faith is the goal of earthly life, but perfected faith means reaching the ultimate goal of life that is love, which alone continues forever from this life to the next. For faith and faithfulness, like hope, there is a role while one is on the journey but, in the end, these are subsumed by love: 1 Corinthians 13 (*Plain Account* 10.A.33).

The secular writing explored below, it will be shown, illustrates a thematic concern with faithfulness that may arise in either Christian or non-Christian society, and either have or not have an explicitly Christian purpose. Every story, however, is concerned in some way with questions about how faithfulness works in this world. For all the main texts adduced there is a wealth of scholarship available, which to a greater or lesser extent

---

life, the *Plain Account* overall refers to biblical teaching and a derived theology of faithfulness that is broadly in keeping with understandings across an ecumenical range: a comparable understanding of the perfection of the church is argued, for example, by Harkianakis, *Infallibility of the Church*. Some traditions would doubt the attainability of perfection for individuals in this life.

includes some discussion of issues of faithfulness. The readings offered here are related to each other in a longer historical context.

The confluence of Classical and Christian tradition from the earliest days of Christianity is well recognized as the foundation of Western thought, evident especially in Latin patristic writers such as Augustine of Hippo, but arguably discernible even in Pauline biblical texts. The confluence of these two great traditions reaches a high point, arguably, in major creative texts of the medieval period, and one manifestation of this confluence is discernible in the discourse of faithfulness that plays a significant part in texts from both periods.

From the Classical tradition, Virgil's *Aeneid* is both the culmination of the ancient Mediterranean world's dominant stories about itself and the basis of one of the most widely disseminated stories the West proceeded to tell about itself thereafter. The epic is pivotal in terms of cultural history for its repeating and transforming of ancient Greek literary mythology to express the new literary mythology of the Roman Empire and thence to exert a far-reaching influence on the literary mythologies of several other places and regimes in the West.[3]

Composed in the ten years or so before the poet's death in 19 BC and widely known from the outset, the *Aeneid* is not far in time from the period of Jesus's ministry at the other end of the Mediterranean. It retells the ancient Greek story of the city of Troy (Greek *Ilion*, customarily traced to a site in western Turkey), its fall to the Greeks, and the further story of the Trojan prince Aeneas, his escape, and his settling in Italy, to become the ancestor of the Romans, so that the fall of Troy is recapitulated in the rise of Trojan Rome. The first six of the twelve books recount the travels of Aeneas as the leader of those Trojans who have escaped the Greeks after the destruction of Troy. The remaining six books recount his arrival in Latium in Italy, ruled by its old king Latinus, whose sole heir is his daughter Lavinia. After a series of encounters with the Latins, Aeneas defeats their champion Turnus, suitor of Lavinia, in single combat. The work was not quite finished when Virgil died, but its narrative direction is clear enough: Aeneas has already won Lavinia (12.937), and he will now take the land as his own, for himself and his descendants.

The far-reaching outcome is foreseen at various points during the narrative. Aeneas is the son of the goddess Venus (Aphrodite) and the Trojan

---

3. The edition cited is that of Gian Biagio Conte. There are numerous English translations, such as that of Ahl, but translations of lines quoted here are my own. The concept of literary mythologies was developed particularly by Roland Barthes to explain the normative ideologies articulated in a text's reflection of its contemporary cultural ethos and its own further construction of that ethos: Barthes, *Mythologies*.

prince Anchises. Early in Aeneas's travels, Venus secures Jupiter's promise that her son will survive his current trials to reach Italy and achieve his destiny, which will lead to the foundation of Rome by his descendant Romulus and the subsequent rise of a later glorious descendant, Augustus Caesar (the triumphant first Emperor of Rome 27 BC–14 AD, under whose aegis Virgil was writing his masterpiece; *Aeneid* 1.229–96). Aeneas's travels in the first half of the poem include a retelling of the siege and fall of Troy, his sojourn with Queen Dido of Carthage, which temporarily threatens the completion of his mission, and his journey to the underworld, where he hears prophecies of his destiny aligning with the earlier predictions of Jupiter from the shade of Anchises, who has died on the way in Sicily (6.756–853).

The story of Troy was set out in the Greek *Iliad* of Homer from around the early eighth century BC and numerous other records show that it was widely known in the ancient world. Homer's *Odyssey*, recounting the extended travels of the Greek hero Ulysses on his way home from the Trojan War, probably provided a model for the travel narrative of Virgil's hero.[4] The *Aeneid*, however, has quite distinct discursive concerns and associated narrative elements, most obviously in its primary focus on Aeneas and his most emphasized quality, *pietas*, "piety."

In his limited appearances in the *Iliad*, Aeneas emerges as a great warrior demonstrating prowess, especially in single combat with the greatest of the Greek champions, Achilles (recounted in Book 20). He is also presented as being prudent and generally virtuous, having the support of some of the gods, and being destined to be the future leader of the Trojans. In the *Aeneid*, however, although Aeneas is still a great warrior, he is also endowed particularly with the quality of *pietas*, meaning "dutifulness" and "loyalty" to the gods, one's parents, or country. This is established as his main characterizing quality at the beginning of the work, in the poet's initial invocation of his Muse, where he announces as the subject of his poem *"insignem pietate virum"* (1.10: "a man marked by dutifulness"). The related adjective *pius* is used of him many times, mostly in the formulaic expression *pius Aeneas*, which is used both by the character Aeneas of himself and by the narratorial voice that directs the reader's response, to the point that *pius* is almost a cognomen.[5]

Pietas is the equivalent of English "faithfulness." *Pietas* in the *Aeneid* is commonly regarded by scholars as referring to Aeneas's faithfulness in three areas, all associated with patriotism: (i) dutiful care of his old father

---

4. For recent translations of the *Iliad* and the *Odyssey* see, respectively, those of Alexander and Wilson.

5. Lewis and Short, *Latin Dictionary*, *pietas* and the related adjective *pius*.

Anchises, bearing him on his own back to the ship that will enable them to escape from Troy, (ii) piety in taking with him the household gods of Troy, the Lares and Penates, actually carried by his father, to set them up in their new home, and (iii) faithfulness to his divinely inspired mission to establish Troy in Italy as its successful, enduring recreation, with his descendants its future rulers. His faithfulness in the third area is tested along the way as he dallies with Dido but, reminded of his duty by Mercury, sent by Jupiter, he leaves her, to continue his journey (4.279–583). The disastrous consequences for Dido are spectacular and political rather than emotionally compelling and attention is focused on the great destiny of Aeneas. The quality of Aeneas's *pietas* is not seriously questioned until Book 12, when the presenting problem does not have closure within the narrative.

This problem is the conduct of Aeneas when Turnus is finally disabled by Aeneas's spear (12.930–52). It has become a particular scholarly concern in recent years, though opposing approaches have marked the history of Virgilian scholarship since very early days. The two men have been depicted as great warriors evenly matched, Turnus armed with his sword, Aeneas with his spear, both breathing hard, standing face to face (12.788–90), and shouting bold challenges to each other (12.889–95), but the gods have agreed that the victory will go to Aeneas in accordance with his destiny (12.791–886). When Aeneas's spear wounds Turnus, he submits and appeals to Aeneas, on the grounds that Aeneas will understand how a father would grieve the loss of a son, to have pity and restore him to his old father as he is, either wounded or dead, without striking a final blow (12.930–38). The evenness of their strength means that, when one is at a disadvantage, the other has an opportunity to show his nobility in a magnanimity of more substance than simple pity for an inferior. Aeneas begins to feel pity; but, when he notices on Turnus's shoulder the baldric of his fallen comrade Pallas, taken as spoil by Turnus when he killed him (10.453–89), he is incensed. Terrifying in his anger, he cries out that Pallas will have revenge and, burning with rage, deals Turnus a fatal blow with his sword (12.946–47).

The question is whether the *pietas* that drives Aeneas towards his destiny and the future glory of Rome and its emperors is present in the revenge he takes for his comrade or absent in his refusal to withhold the fatal blow against an already-defeated enemy, who has appealed to him on grounds related to the first area of his *pietas*. It is not insignificant that the shade of Anchises has previously urged Aeneas to spare the defeated and finish the proud (6.853). One's preferred reading of this episode in turn affects one's view of the *Aeneid* as a whole, celebrating the values on which Rome is supposedly founded or doubting them.[6]

Read through the lens of a Christian, and Wesleyan, point of view, Aeneas's vengeful action would not be endorsed, and his journey, even if generally informed by faithfulness, would not have reached the point of the act of faith, in alignment with perfection, which, in turn, would mean alignment with the divine will. The unfinished text does not suggest that any awareness of Aeneas's part that he might have chosen mercy without changing the course of Trojan history, or any questioning of his action on the part of his fellows, only by the narratorial voice. The issue is complicated by the fact that the human narrative is driven by a metanarrative of conflicting wills amongst the Classical Pantheon, within which the gods themselves have limited moral understanding, rather than an overarching Providence.

In an effort to move beyond over-simple views of whether Aeneas acts rightly or wrongly, Richard Tarrant has suggested that his moral dilemma represents an "unresolvable contradiction," that for the poet "such contradictions are not problems to be solved, but irreducible tensions to be recognized and accepted," and that the poet is proposing a "moral entropy" in which "a good man can be driven by his own good qualities to perform horrifying actions."[7] This proposal might suggest either that the poet sees no intelligent purpose behind apparent chaos or that the poet recognizes the potentially dangerous effects of human failure to discern and adhere to integrity.

Open-ended debate without closure seems to be a promising approach to a challenging question, though Tarrant makes no formal distinction between the historical person of the poet and the textually constructed narratorial persona. Perhaps the poet is posing a question on the basis of a universal morality (for Christians, as expressed in Rom 1:18–23; 2:1–16).

The short study of some medieval literary texts below will show that the subject of faithfulness almost inevitably opens itself to questions about how it should be pursued, about how true faithfulness might manifest in different contexts.

Although the Virgilian story of Troy was widely disseminated though succeeding centuries, versions questioning the *pietas* of Aeneas and the glory

---

6. Tarrant provides a careful analysis of Book 12 in "The Last Book of the *Aeneid*." Putnam finds Aeneas to be without real *pietas*: "Anger, Blindness, and Insight in Virgil's *Aeneid*." Based on a substantial study of representations of Aeneas in many forms, Galinsky notes his "rather contradictory" character but indicates that Virgil intends praise for his *pietas*: "Pius Aeneas." I would like to thank Anne Rogerson for drawing my attention to these three works. For a comprehensive treatment of the poem's endorsement or non-endorsement of Augustan establishment values see Perkell, "Editor's Introduction" to *Reading Vergil's "Aeneid."*

7. Tarrant, "Last Book of the *Aeneid*," 122–25.

of Troy for reasons other than his treatment of Turnus were also popular. Of the numerous representations of key episodes in the story in monuments, coins, and documents from before and after Virgil, only a minority clearly endorse the *pietas* of Aeneas, typically representations from imperial circle and the emperors' association with Aeneas himself.[8]

A non-Virgilian story about Aeneas widespread in both the ancient and the medieval worlds depicted Aeneas as betraying Troy to the Greeks. This was disseminated particularly through two early pseudo-histories of Troy, the *De excidio Troiae historia* of Dictys Cretensis (fourth century) and the *Ephemeridos belli Troiani libri* of Dares Phrygius (fifth century), which together formed the basis of the two major accounts circulating in the medieval West, both counter-Virgilian: Benoît de Sainte-Maure's verse *Le Roman de Troie* (ca. 1155–60) and Guido delle Colonne's prose *Historia destructionis Troiae* (1287), this last the best-known version in medieval England.[9]

Tensions around the legend of Troy appear in numerous medieval texts, including some discussed below. In addition, the Trojan legend was linked with the emerging Arthurian legend, and uncertainty about the glory or failure of the Arthurian world echoed the uncertainties of the Trojan legend. Retellings of either legend also provided opportunities for critiquing contemporary national regimes.

Stories of King Arthur arose in the Celtic world of ancient Britain and were further developed in medieval England and France and thence elsewhere, flourishing in both chivalric and popular circles. The kings of Celtic Britain were said to have been descended from an eponymous ancestor called Brutus, a descendant of Aeneas, whose own travels led him, in turn, to found yet another Troy as what became London. Rulers of contemporary England traced their origins to the British, other rulers also traced their origins to the Trojans, and the extended story of Troy became effectively the supposed secular history of the known world, parallel with the biblical story of salvation as the religious history of the world.

The link between the two legends is first known from the ninth-century *Historia Brittonum*, partly anonymous, partly by Nennius, but a longer version is found in the *Historia Regum Brittaniae* of Geoffrey of Monmouth, completed ca. 1138 and very widely disseminated and adapted. In England this occurred in various forms of what was known generically as the "Brut," in both Anglo-Norman and English texts. The English prose *Brut* that from

---

8. Galinsky, "*Pius Aeneas*," 10.

9. For editions of these four works see, respectively, those of Eisenhut, Stohlmann, Constans, and Griffin. For translations see those of Frazer (Dares and Dictys), Burgess and Kelly (Benoît), and Meek (Guido). For late-medieval knowledge of Guido see Simpson, "The Other Book of Troy."

the late fourteenth century was added to in the manner of an historical chronicle across the next century.[10]

The first of the medieval English texts to be discussed for its concern with faithfulness is a long Arthurian romance by one of the "Ricardian" poets recognized as giants of the English literary canon.

The term "Ricardian" was introduced in 1971 to refer to certain English writers from, approximately, the reign of Richard II (1372–99):[11] two based in London and associated with the royal court, Geoffrey Chaucer, a public servant, and his friend John Gower, a lawyer; two regional poets from the West Midlands, William Langland and the so-called *Gawain*-poet. The works of the first three survive in many manuscripts and have remained well-known since their original composition. In the case of the fourth, what are commonly believed to be four works by the one unidentified man survive only in a single manuscript, but the story of the longest of them, *Sir Gawain and the Green Knight*, was popular enough to have been retold a century later, in a shorter romance called "The Green Knight," and *Sir Gawain and the Green Knight* itself has been reworked in many modern art forms since it was first edited and published in print in 1839, enjoying an extraordinary popular reception across through the twentieth century.

The opening lines locate the background of the story in Troy, with specific reference to Aeneas and his ambiguous approach to faithfulness:

> *Siþen þe sege and þe assaut watz sesed at Troye,*
>
> *Þe borȝ brittened and brent to bronde and askes,*
>
> *Þe tulk þat þe trammes of tresoun þer wroȝt*
>
> *Watz tried for his tricherie, þe trewest on erthe.*
>
> *Hit watz Ennias þe athel, and his highe kynde,*
>
> *Þat siþen depreced prouinces, and patrounes bicome*
>
> *Welneȝe of al þe wele in þe west iles.* (1–7)[12]

(After the siege and the attack were over in Troy, the city destroyed and burnt to firebrands and ashes, the man who carried

---

10. For summary details of the tradition see, for example, Allen's "Introduction" to her translation of Lawman's *Brut*, xii–xxxvi; and Speed, "*King Lear* and the *Brut*," 61–62. For a substantial overview of the tradition centered on a study of Geoffrey of Monmouth see Tatlock, *Legendary History of Britain*. Geoffrey's *Historia* is edited by Wright and translated by Thorpe.

11. Burrow, *Ricardian Poetry*.

12. The edition cited is that of Tolkien and Gordon. One modernization is that of Tolkien, published posthumously in 1975, but modernizations of lines quoted here are my own.

out the treasonous actions was tried for his treachery, the truest in the world. This was the noble Aeneas, and his lofty kindred, who afterwards subjugated realms and became lords of almost all the wealth of the western isles.)

An obvious difficulty is the juxtaposed descriptions of Aeneas as treacherous and yet the truest man in the world. Attempts to resolve the problem have included interpreting "trewest" as meaning "surest," with reference to his *tricherie*, which refers here to his disloyalty to the Greeks after committing to them.[13] It is more likely, however, that these words mean what they immediately appear to mean, and that the juxtaposition expresses the narrator's amazement that a man so highly principled should have acted so contrary to expectations. *Trewe* ("true") means "faithful," equivalent to Latin *pius*. The noun *treuth* has meanings extending from those related to modern "troth" to those related to modern "truth," but its primary sense is given in the *Middle English Dictionary* as "fidelity to one's country, kin, friends, etc., loyalty; allegiance; also, genuine friendship; also, faithfulness."[14]

The main theme of *Sir Gawain and the Green Knight* is thus announced in dramatic fashion at the outset. The plot devolves on two interconnected situations in which Gawain's *treuth* is tested.

On New Year's Eve, King Arthur's court is visited by a huge Green Knight, who issues a challenge that one of the company should strike him with his own axe in exchange for accepting the same treatment from him a year later at the Green Chapel. Sir Gawain loyally intervenes to stop the king from endangering himself by accepting but, when he cuts off the Green Knight's head, the latter picks it up and rides off. On the following All Saints' Day, Gawain sets off to find the Green Chapel and on Christmas Day, after a difficult wilderness journey, comes across a castle, where he is welcomed by its lord and invited to stay until the day of his appointment at the Green Chapel, which is nearby. To pass the time his host proposes a game according to which he will go out hunting each day and give Gawain his winnings and Gawain will stay behind and give his host whatever he has won, and

---

13. Tolkien and Gordon argue for "surest" treachery: *Sir Gawain and the Green Knight*, 70n3–5. Aeneas's betrayal of Troy for personal advantage was repeated in his failure to keep the pledge of cooperation he made to the Greeks when he broke his word and concealed Polixena from them: for this he was judged by the Greeks to be exiled from Troy forever: Guido, *Historia*, 31 (1936 edition).

14. See "Treuth" and "Treu(e)" from the *Middle English Dictionary*. The headnote to *treuth* observes that "the concepts it expresses defy rigid categorization." The words *feithful, feithfulness(e*, and related forms, borrowings from the French, are recorded from the fourteenth century, but are not nearly as often used as *trewe, treuth,* and related forms, from Old English (with some influence from similar French words): see *feithful, feithfulness(e*, and related forms.

Gawain agrees to this. On the first two days, in exchange for meat from his host's kills, Gawain gives his host the kisses he has been obliged to accept from the lady of the castle. On the third day, however, she foists on him also a green girdle that will protect its wearer from death. In the evening Gawain duly passes on the kisses but keeps the girdle a secret. On New Year's Day he sets off to the Green Chapel, finds the Green Knight, and prepares to accept the beheading. The Green Knight, however, only nicks his neck, then reveals that he is Bertilak, Gawain's host. The whole beheading game has been devised by Arthur's half-sister, disguised as an old lady at Bertilak's court, to test the pride of Arthur's court. The nick has been Gawain's punishment for concealing the girdle, Bertilak allowing that Gawain did this only, as he thought, to preserve his life. Gawain rides off home wearing the girdle as a baldric, a reminder of his failure to keep his word:

> Þis is þe token of vntrawþe þat I am tan inne,
> And I mot nedez hit were wyle I may last. (2509–10)

(This is a token of the unfaithfulness in which I have been caught, and I must needs wear it as long as I live.)

Arthur and his court do not share Gawain's view of the seriousness of his failure and adopt the baldric as a reminder of the renown of the royal court (2518), the very matter questioned by the whole test.

Faithfulness to one's word lies at the heart of both the beheading game and the exchange of winnings. Gawain behaves with extraordinary integrity with respect to king and country, but he fails insofar as his last-minute fear of death leads him to conceal the girdle from his host. The lady has insisted that he "loyally conceal" it ("*lelly layne*," 1863) from her lord and he agrees, so that there is a conflict of loyalty for him between the husband and wife, which he might have avoided if he had truly entrusted his life to God and Mary (to whom he is particularly dedicated: 644–50, 738). Unlike Virgil's Aeneas, however, his subsequent remorse shows that he is patently pressing on with his journey of faithfulness.

Gawain's individual failure in integrity pales alongside the public failure of the king and the rest of his court to act like responsible leaders, and text holds no promise that they will reflect and reform. Arthur himself is "child-gered" ("childlike," 86), unable to sit still for long (87–88), prepared to engage with a challenge he could have rejected. The court as a whole is portrayed as youthful and carefree, content in the beginning to let their king accept the Green Knight's challenge when he might well have lost his life and imprudently left the country headless, and it is unchanged in the end by Gawain's experience, not appreciating his high-minded regard for faithfulness throughout, only grasping the superficial glamour of his adventure, which they appropriate for themselves in misrepresenting his baldric.

The juxtaposition of Gawain's seriousness and the levity of the king and his court evokes a response of discomfort and a suspicion that this ruling class is a moral failure. The implication is that Aeneas's failure in *pietas*, or *treuth*, has been reproduced in the failure of his royal descendant to fulfill his princely obligations to those entrusted to his care and thus his duty to the God he ostensibly honors. One function of the individual's journey of faith has been to draw attention to the implications for public faithfulness on the part of national leaders. Although Richard II came to the throne as a boy-king, his sense of responsibility came under question as his reign progressed. It may well be that the inadequacy of Arthur alludes to the impropriety of the actual king of the day

A more overt use of the story of Troy to represent the state of the nation in Richard's day appears in Gower's great English poem, *Confessio amantis* ("The Lover's Confession," a long collection of exemplary tales within a frame-story, the circumstances of its composition explicitly placed in the later years of Richard's reign.[15] The original prologue, composed by 1390, identifies London as the "*newe Troie*" ("new Troy," *37), where the poet purports to have met the king on the river and accepted his commission to produce a book about love. This episode and its mention of Troy disappear in the revised prologue from just a short time later, 1392–93, with a new dedication to Richard's opponent and, in 1399, deposer, Henry of Lancaster (83–87), but the long narrative following the prologue was little changed between versions, and Troy may be taken throughout as code for London.

The *Confessio* is cast as a complaint about current corruption in all three estates—rulers, church, and commons. Gower's overt political concern is particularly evident in the obtrusive seventh book. The Lover of the frame-story, named John Gower, makes his confession to the priest of Venus, who provides instruction on various points in the tales and connecting discourse. The first six books address the first six of the seven deadly sins. The natural expectation is for a seventh book addressing lechery, but, instead, the seventh book provides a mirror for princes. An eighth book then addresses lechery.

Although the ostensible overall theme is love, the political theme is ubiquitous, as foreseen in the prologue (66–70). A number of the tales recount episodes from the story of Troy and, taken together, set out virtually

---

15. The edition cited is that of Macaulay. A modernization is that of Tiller. A more detailed analysis of the *Confessio* and argument for the reading that follows here will be found in my chapter, Speed, "*Translatio imperii* and Gower's *Confessio amantis*." A major study of the historical background to Gower is Fisher, *John Gower*.

the whole legend, pointing to the deceit and betrayal, treachery and folly, that characterize both personal and public life amongst the Trojans. The tales are largely based on the counter-Virgilian Benoît and Guido, along with Ovid, Virgil's younger contemporary, whose critical view of the Roman establishment earned him life-exile from Rome.[16] With regard to Aeneas, for example, the Greeks' cunning ploy in the tale of the Trojan horse succeeds in destroying Troy only because of the internal treachery of Aeneas and Antenor (1.1097, 1127, and1186), exacerbated by the inadequacy of an imprudent king. In the tale of Aeneas and Dido (4.73–142), the focus is on Aeneas's betrayal of Dido, with no mention of his divine mission.

In short, the inference from the Trojan and other tales, as well as the frame-story and the prologue, is a warning against the dangers posed by unfaithfulness in both public and private life.

Chaucer, on the other hand, focuses on faithfulness in individual human relations. His main rendering of the story of Troy is his *Troilus and Criseyde*, recounting the affair between Troilus and Criseyde, and Criseyde's unfaithfulness. Troy also features in two of the nine tales within the *Legend of Good Women*, those of Dido, betrayed by Aeneas, and Hypsipyle and Medea, both in turn betrayed by Jason. His most extended exploration of faithfulness, however, is found in the *Franklin's Tale* within *The Canterbury Tales*, his unfinished collection of tales within a frame story.[17]

The Franklin's Tale sets out an intricate web of dilemmas for four individuals. A knight called Arveragus woos a lady called Dorigen, swearing never to exercise mastery over her, though for his reputation's sake it will appear in public that he does. She responds by giving her word ("*trouthe*," 9) to be his faithful wife. When he goes off to seek honor in combat, she fears he may be shipwrecked on the terrible rocks along the coast. While passing the time with friends, she is importuned by a squire called Aurelius, but declares that she will never be an unfaithful wife ("*untrewe wyf*," 984). He presses his suit so intensely, however, that finally, in play, she gives him her word ("*trouthe*," 998) to love him best of all if he will remove the rocks. He seeks out a scholar of natural magic to make it appear that the rocks have gone. In exchange for his promise ("*trouthe*," 1221) of a great sum of money, the scholar obliges, and Aurelius reminds Dorigen of her promise. She is dismayed and shares the situation with Arveragus, who has returned. His

---

16. A major study is Otis, *Ovid as an Epic Poet*.

17. All Chaucer texts are cited from *The Riverside Chaucer*. *Troilus and Criseyde* is modernized by Windeatt, *The Canterbury Tales* by Wright. A more detailed analysis of the *Franklin's Tale* and its exploration of *trouthe* may be found in my article: Speed, "Character and Circumstance in the *Franklin's Tale*."

determination is that, although no one else must know about it, she should keep her "*trouthe*" to Aurelius, since

> *Trouthe is the hyeste thing that man may kepe.* (1479)

(Faithfulness [to one's word] is the most important thing to observe.)

Aurelius, however, moved by the nobility of Arveragus, foregoes his prize and gives his word ("*trouthe*," 1537) to bother her no more. He himself owes a vast debt to the scholar and determines to keep his "*trouthe*" (1577) to pay him, but the scholar is moved by the nobility of both Arveragus and Aurelius and forgives the debt. That the tale has been an intellectual game is evident in the Franklin's teasing question in conclusion:

> *Which was the mooste fre, as thynketh yow?* (1622)

(Which was the most noble, in your opinion?)

The plot is at least equally concerned with the dilemmas posed by conflicting obligations, whose finally resolution is more or less resolved by the exercise of nobility. In brief, Arveragus's integrity is threatened when he opts to split his private from his public intentions. The mutual faithfulness promised in marriage is threatened by Arveragus's decision to prioritize his knightly calling over his marriage for a time (the right priority being a favorite point of debate in medieval literature). Dorigen's rash and unnecessary promise to Aurelius creates a dilemma for Arveragus and herself. Arveragus determines a course of action that runs contrary to their marriage vows and common sense. Aurelius faces having to sell up his heritage, thereby denying his rightful place in society (1562–66). The scholar has to decide whether or not to claim his rights from Aurelius or meet the challenge to behave as nobly as his social betters.

Despite the happy ending, the conscious decisions to enter into contrary commitments have made clear the potential for disaster for the three nobly born characters.

Langland's *Piers Plowman* is an allegory of the Christian life and complaint against the church, in which the narrator named Will, possibly to be understood as representing the human will, has a series of dreams that take him on a journey through life to find Truth (*Treuthe*) and Do-Well (*Dowel*: "good works"), as he observes the pride and worldliness of the church.[18] Although *treuthe* occasionally means "faithfulness", the allegorical figure *Trewthe* seems to represent God or an aspect of God (as in John 14:6).

---

18. The edition and the translation cited are that of Schmidt.

Amongst many allegorical figures he meets is Piers (Peter) Plowman, who shifts between doing the work of Christ and being Christ in the world, as the church should ideally do and be. He experiences visions of key biblical events, including the fall and the crucifixion, and figures from the history of salvation, including Abraham, signifying faith, and Moses, signifying hope, both also seeking Christ. Conscience seeks grace and Piers Plowman, as Will wakes up to the church as it is.

The individual Christian journey of faith is seen to be, variously, helped and hindered by the church of the day, which has yet to commit as a whole to making the same journey.

This necessarily very short consideration of faithfulness in the literary mythologies of the West has shown that, when John Wesley placed faithfulness at the center of his understanding of what God requires of us, he was speaking into a discourse as old as time—certainly as old as the first records of Judaeo-Christian tradition depicting the fall. What this study has suggested is that a recognition of the centrality of faithfulness to the functionality of human relationships and society at large is actually deep-seated in the West, whether consciously contextualized in the Christian story of salvation or not.

In a mere snapshot of approaches to faithfulness in our own day, we turn finally to key forums for the expression of people's everyday concerns: the popular media and social media.

In the postmodern era, also referred to by some as a "post-Christian" era, it is undeniable that many Westerners are moving away from traditional forms of Christian observance to more generally "spiritual" engagement, or none, while a new set of heroes and ideals is emerging, a new vision of faithfulness, facilitated by what modern technology has to offer. Fantasy has never been more popular in the arts, with larger-than-life, single-minded heroes saving the world from evil in situations strikingly removed from everyday reality—pure escapism, doomed not to achieve anything lasting for its adherents, unless, perhaps, read allegorically.

Associated with this phenomenon is today's "cult of celebrity," which elevates individuals, in a typically transitory way, to the status of gods.

In medieval Europe the phenomenon of courtly love found expression in the appropriation of the religious vocabulary of the church, expressing admiration of one's lady as religious worship.[19] Today, one very similar development has been the appropriation of the religious vocabulary and meaning of the church by other activities of a hobby kind, above

---

19. Although there is extensive scholarship on this subject and some disagreement about exactly what is meant by "courtly love," the seminal work remains Lewis's *Allegory of Love*, in which a "religion of love" is identified as one of the main recurrent features.

all, and especially in Australia, sport. Faithfulness for many means faithfulness to one's sporting team, an individual within it, or the sport itself.[20] More broadly, the vocabulary of "following," as on Facebook or Twitter, actually transposes the language of Christian discipleship to adoration of human figures who have become newsworthy for one reason or another. The term "fans," abbreviated from "fanatics," itself previously used mainly of "religious fanatics," features commonly in both sporting and general celebrity reports to mean "supporters."

Beyond this again, one might point to the readily-observable decline in lifelong commitment to one domestic partner or employer. Faithfulness in present-day secular culture often involves quick change for short-term gain rather than life-fulfillment, promised by a journey of faithfulness.

The church has always had to address the broader cultural issues of the day to find the most effective ways of presenting the Christian faith to its own people and the wider world. It may be that comparing current approaches to faithfulness with approaches in the past might provide a useful rhetoric for fruitful discussion between traditionalists and moderns.

Bibliography

Allen, Rosamund. "Introduction." In *Brut*, translated by Rosamund Allen, xiii–xxxvi. London: Dent, 1992.
Barthes, Roland. *Mythologies*. Translated by Annette Lavers. London: Vintage, 1972.
Benoît de Sainte-Maure. *Le Roman de Troie*. 6 vols. Société des anciens textes français. Edited by. L. Constans. Paris: Firmin Didot, 1904–12.
———. *The "Roman de Troie."* Translated by Glyn S. Burgess and Douglas Kelly. Woodbridge: Brewer, 2017.
Burrow, J. A. *Ricardian Poetry: Chaucer, Gower, Langland, and the "Gawain"-Poet*. London: Routledge and Paul, 1971.
Chaucer, Geoffrey. *The Canterbury Tales*. Oxford World's Classics. Oxford: Oxford University Press, 1985.
———. *The Riverside Chaucer*. Edited by Larry D. Benson. 3rd ed. Oxford: Oxford University Press, 1988.
———. *Troilus and Criseyde*. Translated by Barry Windeatt. Oxford World's Classics. Oxford: Oxford University Press, 1998.
Dares Phyrgius. *De excidio Troiae historia*. Edited by Jürgen Stohlmann. *Mittellateinisches Jahrbuch* 1. Ratingen: Henn, 1968.

---

20. The subject has been explored in several popular publications of Barry Spurr, including articles in the *Sydney Morning Herald*, *The Age*, *Sydney's Child*, *Melbourne's Child*, and *News Weekly*. I would like to thank him for providing a copy of his unpublished keynote address to the Association of Australasian University Colleges and Halls of Residence, "Challenging the Obsession," drawing attention to the seriousness of the implications for education and the social good.

Dictys Cretensis. *Ephemeridos belli Troiani libri*. Edited by Werner Eisenhut. 2nd ed. Leipzig: Teubner, 1973.

Dictys of Crete and Dares the Phrygian. *The Trojan War: The Chronicles of Dictys of Crete and Dares the Phrygian*. Translated by R. M. Frazer. Rev. ed. Bloomington: Indiana University Press, 2019.

Galinsky, G. Karl. "*Pius Aeneas*." In *Aeneas, Sicily, and Rome*, 3–62. Reprint, Princeton: Princeton Legacy Library, 2016.

Geoffrey of Monmouth. *The "Historia Regum Britannie" of Geoffrey of Monmouth*. Vol. 1, *Bern, Burgerbibliothek, MS 568*. Historia Regum Britannie of Geoffrey of Monmouth 1. Edited by Neil Wright. Cambridge: Brewer, 1985.

———. *History of the Kings of Britain*. Translated by Lewis Thorpe. Reprint, London: Folio Society, 1968.

Gower, John. *Confessio Amantis: The Lover's Shrift*. Translated by Terence Tiller. Penguin Classics. Harmondsworth: Penguin, 1963.

———. *The English Works*. Edited by G. C. Macaulay, 2 vols. Early English Text Society Extra Series 81–82. Reprint, London: Oxford University Press, 1957.

Guido delle Colonne. *Historia destructionis Troiae*. Edited by Nathaniel E. Griffin. Medieval Academy 26. Cambridge: Medieval Academy of America, 1936.

———. *Historia destructionis Troiae*. Translated by Mary Elizabeth Meek. Bloomington: Indiana University Press, 1974.

Harkianakis, Stylianos. *The Infallibility of the Church in Orthodox Theology*. Translated by Philip Kariatlis. Sydney: Australasian Theological Forum and St Andrew's Orthodox, 2008.

Homer. *The Iliad*. Translated by Caroline Alexander. New York: HarperCollins, 2015.

———. *The Odyssey*. Translated by Emily Wilson. New York: Norton, 2018.

Langland, William. *"Piers Plowman": A New Translation of the B-Text*. Translated by A. V. C. Schmidt. Oxford World Classics. Oxford: Oxford University Press, 2009.

———. *The Vision of Piers Plowman*. Edited by A. V. C. Schmidt. Rev. ed. London: Dent, 1995.

Lewis, Charlton T., and Charles Short. *A Latin Dictionary*. Reprint, Oxford: Clarendon, 1969.

Lewis, C. S. *The Allegory of Love: A Study in Medieval Tradition*. Canto Classics. Reprint, Cambridge: Cambridge University Press, 2013.

Mynors, R. A. B., ed. *P. Vergili Maronis Opera*. Oxford Classical Texts. Oxford: Clarendon, 1969.

Otis, Brooks. *Ovid as an Epic Poet*. Cambridge: Cambridge University Press, 1966.

Perkell, Christine. "Editor's Introduction." In *Reading Vergil's "Aeneid": An Interpretative Guide*, edited by Christine Perkell, 3–38. Oklahoma Series in Classical Culture 23. Norman: University of Oklahoma Press, 1999.

Putnam, Michael C. J. "Anger, Blindness, and Insight in Virgil's *Aeneid*." In *Virgil's "Aeneid": Interpretation and Influence*, 172–200. Chapel Hill: University of North Carolina Press, 1995.

Simpson, James. "The Other Book of Troy: Guido delle Colonne's *Historia destructionis Troiae* in Fourteenth- and Fifteenth-Century England." *Speculum* 73 (1998) 397–423.

Sir Gawain and the Green Knight. Edited by J. R. R. Tolkien and E. V. Gordon, revised by Norman Davis. Rev. ed. Oxford: Clarendon, 1967.

Sir Gawain and the Green Knight, Pearl, and Sir Orfeo. Translated by J. R. R. Tolkien. Edited by Christopher Tolkien. London: Allen & Unwin, 1975.

Speed, Diane. "Character and Circumstance in *The Franklin's Tale*." *Sydney Studies in English* 15 (1989) 3–30.

———. "*King Lear* and the *Brut*." In *Imperfect Apprehensions: Essays in English Literature in Honour of G. A. Wilkes*, edited by Geoffrey Little, 56–73. Sydney: Challis, 1996.

———. "*Translation imperii* and Gower's *Confessio amantis*." In *"Booldley bot meekly": Essays on the Theory and Practice of Translation in the Middle Ages in Honour of Roger Ellis*, edited by Catherine Batt and René Tixier, 379–93. Turnhout: Brepols, 2018.

Spurr, Barry. "Challenging the Obsession: Australians and Sport." Keynote address to the Association of Australasian University Colleges and Halls of Residence. St Andrew's College, University of Sydney. 28 September 2005. Unpublished.

———. "The High Price of Winning." *The Sydney Morning Herald*, August 7, 1997.

———. "Nightmare Sporting Parents." *Sydney's Child*, June 2001.

———. "Sport 1 The Arts 0." *Sydney's Child*, April 2000.

———. "Sports Mad." *The Sydney Morning Herald*, February 5, 2000.

———. "Sport's Stranglehold on Australian Culture." *News Weekly*, January 1997.

Tarrant, Richard. "The Last Book of the *Aeneid*." *Syllecta Classica* 15 (2004) 103–29.

Tatlock, J. S. P. *The Legendary History of Britain: Geoffrey of Monmouth's "Historia Regum Britanniae" and Its Early Vernacular Versions*. Reprint, Berkeley: University of California Press and Gordion, 1974.

Virgil. *Aeneis*. Bibliotheca scriptorum Graecorum et Romanorum Teubneriana. Edited by Gian Biagio Conte. 2nd ed. Berlin: De Gruyter, 2019.

———. *Aeneid*. Translated by Frederick Ahl. Edited by Elaine Fantham. Oxford World Classics. Oxford: Oxford University Press, 2008.

Wesley, John. *A Plain Account of Christian Perfection*. Edited by Randy L. Maddox and Paul W. Chilcote. Kansas City: Beacon Hill Press, 2015.

10

Holiness as Happiness
A Plain Account of Sanctification

—GLEN O'BRIEN

Introduction

John Wesley's 1777 collation of much of his earlier material on Christian perfection into the rather optimistically named *Plain Account*, established a long tradition of explanation of the Methodist approach to sanctification.[1] Classical Methodist theologians such as Richard Watson and W. B. Pope followed the basic contours of Wesley's argument while introducing certain emphases of their own.[2] American holiness writers often adopted a polemical mode in efforts to keep the doctrine alive among mid-nineteenth-century Methodists who had replaced a desire for mystical union with God through perfect love with more prosaic and practical concerns.[3] Twentieth- and twenty-first-century scholars such as Albert Outler, Thomas Oden, Randy Maddox, Kenneth Collins, and many others have produced sometimes magisterial works that have closely explored Wesley's theology, examining its every nook and cranny.[4] Some of this work has attempted systematic treatments of Wesley's theology as if it were a completely cohesive and comprehensive system of theology, requiring only the correct interpretive approach. My own view is that Wesley's theology was occasional

---

1. Wesley, "Plain Account of Christian Perfection," 132–91.

2. Watson, *Theological Institutes*; Pope, *Compendium of Christian Theology*.

3. A new scholarly history of the American Holiness Movement is long overdue. In the meantime, the best available monographs remain: Dieter, *Holiness Revival*; Peters, *Christian Perfection*; and Jones, *Perfectionist Persuasion*. See also Kostlevy, *Historical Dictionary*. A recent study that includes the holiness origins of Pentecostal churches in the Southern United States is Stephens, *Fire Spreads*.

4. Collins, *Theology of John Wesley*; Maddox, *Responsible Grace*; Oden, *John Wesley's Teachings*; Outler, *Evangelism and Theology*.

in nature, completed on the run, not always consistent, and sometimes contradictory. For all that, it is marvelous to read, deeply spiritual, intellectually satisfying, and worthy of serious consideration. William Abraham has called for the end of Wesleyan theology, arguing that we should stop speaking of Wesley as a systematic theologian altogether, while insisting that he should be seen instead an ascetic theologian and a saint.[5] While I can't follow his argument all the way, I do think his voice is a healthy reminder to Wesleyan theologians always to remain open to the possibility that some of Wesley's theological conclusions may have been wrong. I have always felt, for example, that the idea of "the destruction of inbred sin" was a wrong-headed aspect of Wesley's teaching on sanctification and in the end unnecessary, since the central values of his teaching may be retained without an appeal to a doctrine that sits on the edge of orthodox belief.

The older language of "entire sanctification" and "Christian perfection" speaks to fewer and fewer adherents in spite of remaining embedded in official doctrinal statements. Recent attempts to develop a "relational Holiness" approach drawing on "postmodern" categories (in part an attempt to salvage the doctrine of entire sanctification by finding a new language for it) have produced a few fresh ideas but no substantial constructive work has emerged along these lines. Most of this has been written at the more popular level and tends toward oversimplification.[6] Thomas Noble in *Holy Trinity Holy People* provides a solid Trinitarian theology of holiness, understood as a "communion of love,"[7] and David McEwan has given us impressive treatments of Wesley's theology of sanctification in two detailed examinations of Wesley's theology of holiness.[8] In this essay I wish to provide a brief overview of the shape of Wesley's teaching about sanctification, before building upon a major theme in David's second book, *The Life of God in the Soul* (namely, the theme of holiness as happiness) to argue that, while Wesley is not to be slavishly followed in all respects, his eudaimonian concept of holiness continues to provide a valuable model for inviting people into the fullness of sanctifying grace.

---

5. Abraham, "End of Wesleyan Theology."

6. Lodhal and Oord, *Relational Holiness*.

7. Noble, *Holy Trinity, Holy People*. For other Trinitarian approaches see McEwan, "Continual Enjoyment"; O'Brien, "Trinitarian Theology."

8. McEwan, *Wesley Pastoral Theologian*; McEwan, *Life of God in the Soul*.

John Wesley on Christian Perfection

For John Wesley, salvation always meant more than the mere forgiveness of sin.

> By salvation, I mean, not barely (according to the vulgar notion) deliverance from hell, or going to heaven, but a present deliverance from sin, a restoration of the soul to its primitive health, its original purity; a recovery of the divine nature; the renewal of our souls after the image of God in righteousness and true holiness, in justice, mercy, and truth.[9]

Wesley accepted the Protestant doctrine of imputed righteousness but only with the insistence that any imputed righteousness was at the same time imparted. It is true that the believer is accepted "through the merits of Christ the Son"[10] and yet this acceptance leads necessarily to sanctification as an experienced reality. Believers are not only counted as holy but actually become holy in union with Christ through the Spirit. Wesley did not have to go outside his own Anglican tradition to discover this emphasis, since the Edwardian homilies, used as a model of Anglican preaching since the sixteenth century, insisted that salvation brings with it a power over sin.[11] Salvation is more than God restoring to humanity, through Christ, what has been lost through Adam (though it includes that). Sanctifying grace does not only look back to the created order by restoring the soul to its "primitive health," it also propels the believer forward to the new creation, to an eschatological destiny in which human life is taken up into the divine life and, along with all creation, transformed. Because he was a Western Christian, a Protestant and an Anglican, he drew upon the Patristic writers through that particular lens, and his theology was consequently quite eclectic. If I could be forgiven such broad generalizations (and to borrow from Steve McCormick) in Wesley's understanding of salvation, the Christian is pardoned (the Western Latin concern), in order to participate (the Eastern Greek concern), with the result being a "faith filled with the energy of love" (the Wesleyan synthesis of the two concerns).[12] Such a synthesis echoes the Macarian Homilies and most of the writers of the *Philokalia*, including Saint Maximus the Confessor, Saint Symeon the New Theologian and Saint Gregory Palamas, lending weight to those who see Wesley as especially influenced by the Eastern Orthodox tradition. However, Wesley's Anglican context should not

---

9. Wesley, "Farther Appeal to Men of Reason and Religion," 106.
10. Wesley, "Sermon on the Trinity," 385.
11. A good example is Cranmer's 1547 homily, "Short Declaration."
12. McCormack, "Theosis in Chrysostom and Wesley," 38–103.

be overlooked in considering his sources, nor the Western "holy living tradition" that was so formative in his spirituality.[13]

Wesley sometimes used unguarded language in speaking of "perfection" in ways that could be easily misunderstood. In the sermon *Salvation by Faith* he insisted (drawing on the First Epistle of John) that the one who is born of God does not commit sin.[14] He later carefully qualified such views in sermons such as *On Sin in Believers* and *The Repentance of Believers* where he made it clear that sin remains in the hearts of those who are justified, though they are no longer ruled by sin.[15] In his doctrine of "entire sanctification" or "Christian perfection," Wesley held out the possibility of a second work of grace which would purify the heart from all sin, and fill it with perfect love for God and neighbor. Many Methodists of the eighteenth century testified that they had experienced this second work, though significantly Wesley himself did not. Though we would want to avoid the errors of "perfectionism" today, Wesley's ideal of "Christian (not sinless) perfection" is a valuable one because it refuses to place limits on the power of God to transform the human heart. It is a genuine optimism of grace. We can avoid going to extremes when we consider "perfection" a theological rather than a moral category.[16] After all there is nothing "imperfect" about what God has done in Jesus Christ, nothing "imperfect" about grace and nothing "imperfect" about the human *telos*.

The idea of sanctification is used in the New Testament in at least three senses—to refer to a new status as children of God,[17] to refer to the ongoing process of spiritual growth or maturation,[18] and to refer to the completion, perfection or culmination of a process.[19] All Christians would agree with these three senses but there is debate over the extent to which the third sense is possible in this life. While Wesley taught that entire sanctification, understood as deliverance from all inward and outward sin, was possible in this life, he conceded that most believers are not entirely sanctified in this life; however, some are and these usually experience it late in life or just

---

13. See the comprehensive selection of spiritual writings in Rowel et al., *Love's Redeeming Work*.

14. Wesley, "Salvation by Faith," 123–25.

15. Wesley, "On Sin in Believers," 317–34; Wesley, "Repentance of Believers," 335–52.

16. I am grateful to Dr. Bruce Barber for this helpful insight.

17. 1 Cor 1:2.

18. Heb 12:14; Eph 4:1.

19. 1 Thess 5:23. The texts in this and the previous two footnotes are not provided as proof texts but merely as representative of the kinds of texts that support the three overall uses of the term "sanctification" in the New Testament.

prior to death. Still, all may receive it in an act of faith, and if by faith then why not right now? Believers should, therefore, daily seek to be delivered from all sin and wait on God to complete the work.

> Look for it (sanctification) every day, every hour, every moment, why not this hour? this moment? Certainly you may look for it now, if you believe it is by faith. And by this token you may surely know whether you seek it by faith or by works: If by works, you want something to be done first, before you are sanctified. You think, I must be, or do, thus or thus. Then you are seeking it by works unto this day. If you seek it by faith, you may expect it as you are, and if as you are, then expect it now. It is of importance to observe that there is an inseparable connection between these three points. Expect it by faith, expect it as you are, and expect it now.[20]

The kind of "perfection" Wesley has in mind did not free the believer from the possibility of sinning or from the many mistakes and infirmities that accompany the human condition. Wesley's limited definition of sin as a "willful transgression of a known law" made freedom from sin more of a possibility than if sin were to be defined as any degree of falling short of God's absolute perfection. According to Wesley, sin "properly so called" was limited to voluntary transgressions of a known law. This excluded involuntary transgressions, and transgressions of laws unknown to the individual. This more limited view of sin as willful transgression does not overlook the fact that human imperfections are a falling short of divine perfection which is why even the most fully sanctified believer must still rely daily on the atoning work of Christ. Even the "entirely sanctified" ought to pray daily "forgive us our trespasses as we forgive those who trespass against us."

During the nineteenth century, consecration at the altar became the central "motif" of the Holiness movement. This theological focus was to find practical expression in the "altar call," whereby seekers were urged to approach the "mourner's bench" or the "mercy seat" in a public setting, to obtain the blessing of either the new birth or entire sanctification. It is significant to note that this method was never employed by John Wesley. For Wesley, sanctification was never simply a "trip to the altar." It was always an experience obtained within the context of a strenuous application of the classical Christian disciplines. Furthermore, this pursuit was to be carried out within the context of the class meeting, and was, therefore, a corporate, rather than an individualistic pursuit. The later tendency to individualism and even unhealthy self-introspection was guarded against by Wesley in the

---

20. Wesley, "Scripture Way of Salvation," 153–69.

checks and balances of mutually enriching small group communities. The Methodist preachers met in conference at London in 1759 and gave themselves, partly, to the task of theological reflection and pronouncement. The question was posed at that time:

> How are we to wait for this change [i.e. entire sanctification] ... in vigorous, universal obedience, in a zealous keeping of all the commandments, in watchfulness and painfulness, in denying ourselves and taking up our cross daily; as well as in earnest prayer and fasting and a close attendance on all the ordinances of God. And if any man [sic] dream of attaining it in any other way (yea, or of *keeping* it when it is attained ...) he deceiveth his own soul. 'Tis true, we receive it by simple faith. But God does not, will not, give that faith, unless we seek it with all diligence in the way which he hath ordained.[21]

This last sentence indicates that Wesley did not deny that sanctifying grace was to be received by faith. On the contrary, this discovery (that we are sanctified by faith, even as we are justified by faith) was at the heart of his distinctive blending of the Catholic quest for perfection and the evangelical doctrine of grace. But for Wesley, faith was always something active. It was not to be understood as spiritual indolence or an excuse to disregard God's moral law, but rather as a dynamic lived experience enabling loving obedience.

David McEwan on John Wesley

In *Wesley as a Pastoral Theologian: Theological Methodology in John Wesley's Doctrine of Christian Perfection*, David McEwan revisited the so-called Wesleyan Quadrilateral, an approach to theology that has met with considerable critique from Wesleyan theologians though it is frequently cited by non-specialists as one of the more significant contributions that Wesleyan thought makes to theology. He argued that debates over the ordering of the sources of Scripture, reason, tradition (David prefers "community ethos"), and experience have little value and that the missing element in such debates is the role of the Holy Spirit as the energizing power behind the four sources.[22] Within a community of love, the Spirit guides theological reflection in a "dynamic neural network" in which the four sources of the quadrilateral function as "interlinked critical nodes" in a relational system of enquiry.[23] The

---

21. Wesley, *Works*, 13:403; 10:287–88.
22. McEwan, *Wesley as a Pastoral Theologian*, 5–36.
23. McEwan, *Wesley as a Pastoral Theologian*, 219–20.

survey of Wesley's doctrine of Christian perfection in this work illustrated Wesley's pastoral method and provided us with a long-overdue full-length account of Wesley's doctrine of entire sanctification that is a worthy successor to earlier works such as William Sangster's *Path to Perfection* (1943), and Harald Lindstrom's *Wesley and Sanctification* (1946).[24]

The central concern of this first work was to demonstrate that:

> Wesley is best understood as a pastoral theologian, whose concern is with the spiritual formation of his people. His vision of the nature of God, human beings and their interrelationship is remarkably consistent over his whole ministry and is centred in love, trust and relationships, rather than the intellectual comprehension of propositional truths about God, humans and the processes of salvation.[25]

This claim is convincingly argued throughout the book, but especially in chapters 4 and 5, through an exploration of Wesley's leadership of the Methodist people and his role as a spiritual mentor and guide.

Four years later this work was followed up by *The Life of God in the Soul: The Integration of Love, Holiness and Happiness in the Thought of John Wesley* which continued the methodological discussion to explore the essentially eudaimonian elements of Wesley's moral philosophy. In this work, the relational elements of our status as created beings are highlighted, as well as the intertwining of love, holiness, and happiness seen (along with freedom) as constitutive of the *imago Dei*.[26] Chapter 3 discusses Wesley's reading of the Sermon on the Mount as the principle location for the theme of holiness as happiness, and Wesley's status as a spiritual director of the Methodists once again comes into focus in chapters 4 through 6, illustrated through his extensive correspondence. The book concludes by asserting that "the life of God in the soul is essentially pure love filling the heart, expelling all that is contrary to God's nature. This love is fully and freely returned in an ever-deepening fellowship that fully participates in the life of the Triune God [and] equally embraces and shares in the life of the neighbour as an essential companion on the journey," making us both holy and happy.[27]

---

24. Sangster, *Path to Perfection*; Lindstrom, *Wesley and Sanctification*.
25. McEwan, *Wesley as a Pastoral Theologian*, 4.
26. McEwan, *Life of God in the Soul*, 9–36.
27. McEwan, *Life of God in the Soul*, 162.

Holiness as Happiness

The idea that holiness and happiness are to be equated may seem strange to those whose concept of holiness is tinged with legalism or dour self-control. When I teach this aspect of Wesley's thought in classes, students tend to fear that I am suggesting some kind of "prosperity gospel" or superficial kind of therapeutic religion for the self-obsessed middle class. Wesley's approach was grounded of course, in classical thought, with its concerns to establish the foundations for living an objectively good life. The ancient philosophical schools were in universal agreement that *eudaimonia* (literally "having a good guardian spirit") defined as "the state of having an objectively desirable life," was the supreme human good.[28] It should be distinguished from the idea of "happiness" as a passing emotional state of lightness or pleasure; *eudaimonia* is the good life objectively considered; it is, in effect, human flourishing. For the ancients, happiness was the *telos* of human existence, desirable for its own sake. If existence is always a positive good then to exist most fully is self-evidently a good to be pursued.

As a student at Oxford, before he began to take religion quite so seriously, Wesley enjoyed life's simple pleasures and has even been described as Epicurean in such enjoyment.[29] During his time at college he played tennis, read the classics, as well as contemporary novels and plays, tried his hand at poetry and frequented the theatre. All of these give us a picture of a young man with an ability to appreciate the aesthetic (more than the ascetic) side of life, an active seeker of innocent pleasures. He certainly took exception to the world-denying asceticism in Thomas á Kempis's *Imitation of Christ*. In a letter to his mother in 1725, he declared that God could never have made the world without the design that it should be enjoyed by humanity.

> I can't think that when God sent us into the world he had irreversibly decreed that we should be perpetually miserable in it. If it be so, the very endeavour after happiness in this life is a sin, as it is acting in direct contradiction to the very design of our creation. What are become of all the innocent comforts and pleasures of life, if it is the intent of our creator that we should never taste them? If the taking up our cross implies the bidding adieu to all joy and satisfaction, how is it reconcilable with what Solomon so expressly affirms of religion that her ways are ways of pleasantness, and all her paths peace? A fair patrimony indeed which Adam left his sons, if they are destined to be continuously wretched! And though heaven is undoubtedly a

---

28. See "Eudaimonia" in Honderich, *Oxford Companion to Philosophy*, 252.
29. Hoffman, "Moral Philosophy of John Wesley," 125.

sufficient recompense for all the afflictions we may or can suffer here, yet I am afraid that argument would make few converts to Christianity, if the yoke were not easy, even in this life, and such a one as gives rest, at least as much as trouble.[30]

If Christianity were a "sour religion" with a morose and gloomy ethos, Wesley, by his own admission, could never have been a Christian.[31] Jeremy Taylor's more ascetic ideal, with its insistence that all spare time should be used in religion, began to exert a powerful influence on Wesley from about the year 1725 and this acted as something of a counter to his Epicurean traits. The study of the ascetic ideals of the primitive church also increased in him and his fellow Oxford Methodists a tendency to detachment from this world. The writings of Henry Scougal presented a spirituality to be pursued over against, rather than through, creation. William Law's mystical writings further contributed to an ascetic tendency in the young Wesley so that by the time he traveled to Georgia in 1735 he had adopted an almost inhuman regime of ascetic behavior. In fact going to Georgia might itself be seen as a way of ensuring the kind of hardship and deprivation of comforts that the idealistic young Wesley thought necessary in order to be weaned off the pleasures of this world.[32] His mysticism at this time was stoic in nature as he found himself desiring to be made of stone so that he might be truly dead to the world. By 1739 he was clear on the difference between the affective nature of the Christian religion and the stark apathy of the stoic ideal.

> But who are "the meek"? Not those who grieve at nothing, because they know nothing; who are not discomposed at the evils that occur, because they discern not evil from good. Not those who are sheltered from the shocks of life by a stupid insensibility; who have, either by nature or art, the virtue of stocks and stones, and resent nothing, because they feel nothing. Brute philosophers are wholly unconcerned in this matter. Apathy is as far from meekness as from humanity. So that one would not easily conceive how any Christians of the purer ages, especially any of the Fathers of the Church, could confound these, and mistake one of the foulest errors of Heathenism for a branch of true Christianity.[33]

30. Wesley, *Works*, 25:162–63.
31. Ward and Heitzenrater, *Works*, 19:175–76.
32. For an important revisionist account of Wesley's time in Georgia, see Hammond, *John Wesley in America*.
33. Wesley, "Upon Our Lord's Sermon on the Mount," 488–89.

After his much-celebrated experience of the assurance of his salvation on May 24, 1738, Wesley's ascetic tendencies remained, but there was now the added note of the joy that accompanies the knowledge of forgiveness. The "faith of a servant" was exchanged for the "faith of a son" and his attitude toward the world-denying asceticism of the mystical writers became increasingly negative.[34] The path of "the dark night of the soul," found in such writers as Madame Guyon and William Law, seemed to run contrary to the doctrine of the witness of the Spirit, with the accompanying assurance of adoption into the family of God. For Wesley, the need for a person to pass through a sense of God-forsakenness was rendered unnecessary by an ever-increasing sense of God's reassuring presence as the characteristic mark of filial devotion. Neither the apophatic "cloud of unknowing" nor the ancient philosopher's life of reason were the sources of human happiness for Wesley, but rather, seeking and finding God. Happiness is thus a byproduct of the grace-enabled life. An ascetic strain remained in Wesley throughout his life, not as a means to the end of finding acceptance with God so much as an expression of loving obedience—the heart returning to the God in childlike delight. The whole of life is to be oriented toward God, and God is to be loved supremely, but this no longer meant that other things were not also to be loved.

Wesley translated the *makarioi* of the Beatitudes not as "blessed," but as "happy" and described the Sermon on the Mount as "a sweet invitation to true holiness and happiness . . . a persuasion to impart it to others [and] a description of true Christian holiness."[35] His views on happiness were in keeping with certain features of eighteenth-century philosophy, especially that of John Locke, of which Wesley was particularly well appraised. Locke, and the Cambridge Platonists before him, had asserted that happiness was the result of following an innate law of human nature and Wesley seems to affirm this approach to some extent.

> To bless men; to make men happy was the great business for which our Lord came into the world. And accordingly here he pronounces eight blessings together . . . Knowing that happiness is our common aim, and that an innate instinct continually urges us to the pursuit of it, he in the kindest manner applies to that instinct, and directs it to its proper object. Though all men [*sic*] desire, yet few attain, happiness, because they seek it where it is not to be found. Our Lord then begins his Divine institution,

---

34. Wesley's "love/hate" relationship with the mystical writers is surveyed in Tuttle, *Mysticism in the Wesleyan Tradition*.

35. Wesley, *Explanatory Notes*, 19.

which is the complete art of happiness, by laying down before all that have ears to hear, the true and only method of acquiring it.[36]

Even during the particularly ascetic period of his Georgia experience, Wesley was able to pen the following letter to Mrs. Chapman.

> You seem to apprehend that I believe religion to be inconsistent with cheerfulness and with a sociable, friendly temper. So far from it, that I am convinced, as true religion or holiness cannot be without cheerfulness, so steady cheerfulness, on the other hand, cannot be without holiness or true religion. And I am equally convinced that true religion has nothing sour, austere, unsociable, unfriendly in it; but on the contrary, implies the most winning sweetness, the most amiable softness and gentleness. Are you for having as much cheerfulness as you can? So am I. Do you endeavour to keep alive your taste for all the truly innocent pleasures of life? So do I likewise.[37]

In Wesley's multi-volume *Christian Library,* designed to bring together the best spiritual and theological resources for the informal theological education of his preachers, several pieces dealt with the theme of happiness. Howe's *Thoughts upon Religious and Philosophical Subjects* asserted that purity of heart effects a disposition of cheerfulness in the believer.[38] Dr Lucas's *Inquiry after Happiness* maintains that happiness is the most universal motivating principle of human action. Not even the suffering of the cross precludes human happiness, for beyond death lies the hope of eternal life.[39]

In spite of the eudaimonian emphasis in Wesley's moral philosophy, Methodist and Holiness Christians sometimes managed to find a way to render holiness as a painful search for unbending perfection marked by seriousness and often characterized by an emphasis on legalistic rule keeping. It may partly be for this reason that the concept of holiness as happiness is sometimes met with curious looks and frowns. Wesley provided members of classes and bands with rules designed to regulate the lives of his converts and aid them in the pursuit of perfection. Several of these rules included the avoidance of frivolous diversions.[40] The churches that formed out of the nineteenth-century holiness movement all developed "membership commitments" which were the rough equivalent of such rules. Where Wesley was keen to avoid

---

36. Wesley, *Explanatory Notes,* 19.
37. Wesley, *Works,* 25:92.
38. Wesley, *Christian Library,* 2:26, 33–63.
39. Wesley, *Christian Library,* 2:25, 151–52.
40. Wesley, "Nature, Design, and General Rules of the United Societies," 67–76, and "Rules of the Band Societies," 77–79.

legalistic applications of rules by stressing the need of the Spirit's anointing, holiness churches were not always as sophisticated in their understanding.[41] Wesley saw rules as "prudential means" to the end of obtaining a "constant ruling habit of soul, a renewal of our minds in the image of God, a recovery of the divine likeness, a still increasing conformity of heart to the pattern of our most holy Redeemer."[42] Holiness churches, on the other hand, often approach the rules as if they were ends in themselves.

Wesley's ethics had a means-end structure that was teleological rather than deontological in nature, so that the adoption by holiness churches of external markers of sanctification was at odds with Wesley's approach.[43] Randy Maddox identified the same tendency in regard to Wesley's moral psychology.[44] The holiness churches, in adopting a rationalist and decisionist moral psychology, moved away from Wesley's affective moral psychology, and in so doing disconnected the means of grace from the end of sanctification. Wesley adopted the eighteenth-century British empiricist model of voluntarism, which, contrary to heavily rationalistic Kantian models, stressed the affections as the most powerful motivators of human action. According to this model, a person is enabled to love only when they have experienced love. Love cannot simply be chosen; it is the response of those who have received love. Since Wesley defined Christian perfection as "loving the Lord your God with all the heart, and the neighbour as oneself," he understood obedience as flowing not from the reason (Descartes), or the will (Kant), but from the affections (Locke). These affections are planted in the human heart as seeds, but their full flowering can only take place through the application of the Christian disciplines, hence the need for "rules." It is here that Wesley's position is close to the "habituated virtues" tradition of Aquinas. Through the practice of the means of grace a *habitus* of the soul develops, so that loving and obeying God's commandments becomes more and more "instinctive" to the believer.

Kenneth J. Collins also sees a teleological orientation in Wesleyan ethics.[45]

---

41. Cited in Dunning, "Ethics in a Wesleyan Context," 3. See also Dunning, *Reflecting the Divine Image*.

42. Wesley, cited in Dunning, "Ethics in a Wesleyan Context," 8.

43. Dunning, "Ethics in a Wesleyan Context," 8. For Wesley's views as teleological in nature see also Collins, *Faithful Witness*, 169–70, 177.

44. Maddox, "Reconnecting the Means." The following paragraph relies heavily on Maddox.

45. Collins, *Faithful Witness*, 177.

> Indeed, failure to recognize that . . . Wesley's personal ethics . . . entails a means/end structure constitutes perhaps the most common way of distorting Wesley's moral views. For example, viewed in isolation, Wesley's prescriptions concerning time, money, dress, tobacco, and the reading of plays all appear unduly harsh, and this harshness has surfaced on occasion within the holiness movement in American Methodism. However, if Wesley's moral counsel, especially in the area of personal ethics, is viewed not as an end in itself, but as an appropriate means to a much higher goal, then legalism in the form of rules for the sake of rules and the spiritual immaturity which results from this can be avoided.[46]

The higher goal of Wesley's rules was perfect love for God and neighbor which meant that the personal ethic laid down by Wesley for the members of the Methodist Societies was "not self-directed . . . but . . . other-directed. . . . Needless self-indulgence, therefore, like using tobacco, is rejected, the expense of fine dress is quietly put aside, money is saved, sleep is curbed, and all for the suitable end of the love of neighbour."[47] Wesley's vision of the "good life" was not a personal ethic alone, but reached out to secure "the good life" for others.

Conclusion

The word "holiness" has virtually no usage in the present culture of the west. Nor does it have any real equivalent or synonym. It is simply not in the semantic field of most people. Even church people rarely use it outside of those denominations that identify as "holiness" churches. As a member of the Salvation Army/Uniting Church dialogue which produced a report on *Holiness and Social Justice*, I discovered that even members of the dialogue team (from both churches) needed to overcome something of an aversion to a word that seemed vaguely old-fashioned and had the faint aroma of sawdust trail revivalism about it.[48] "Perfection" is an even more difficult word to use in polite company and "perfectionism" is considered a destructive personality trait to be avoided at all costs. While "sanctification" is a central New Testament doctrine it appears to be receiving relatively little

---

46. Collins, *Faithful Witness*, 177.
47. Hynson, *To Reform the Nation*, 102, cited in Collins, *Faithful Witness*, 177.
48. Salvation Army and the Uniting Church in Australia, *Holiness and Social Justice Dialogue Report*.

attention from either biblical scholars or systematic theologians.[49] Perhaps we need a "New Perspective on Holiness" that reconsiders the use of the concept in the New Testament in the broader context of its use within Second Temple Judaism and the Greco-Roman world.[50] Certainly using well-worn tropes and clichés from our more recent revivalist past will not open us up to new understanding.

While the word "happiness" finds more favor in a therapeutic culture obsessed by wellness, little of the classical search for the fullness of being remains in the word. For most people, "happiness" refers to a pleasant disposition that puts a smile on one's face or to a sense that, all things considered, life has been good and there's little to complain about. The idea that happiness is found only in God is an ancient philosophical claim that now sounds no more than a religious hard sell or an evangelistic tract. Given these semantic obstacles, selling the idea that holiness and happiness, when properly understood, are essentially the same thing is a challenging task. In the eudaimonian spirituality of John Wesley we have a resource for connecting human longing to divine grace. David McEwan stands among the foremost interpreters of this Wesleyan approach to addressing human desire. He has given us a "plain account" of the Wesleyan resources needed to construct a contemporary theology of Christian perfection, not as a mere recitation of the teaching of John Wesley, but as a long overdue work of constructive theology.

Bibliography

Abraham, William J. "The End of Wesleyan Theology." *Wesleyan Theological Journal* 40.1 (2005) 7–25.
Allen, Michael. *Sanctification*. New Studies in Dogmatics. Grand Rapids: Zondervan, 2017.
Barton, Stephen C. *Holiness Past and Present*. London: T. & T. Clark, 2003.
Brower, Kent. *Holiness in the Gospels*. Kansas City: Beacon Hill, 2005.
———. *Living as God's Holy People: Holiness and Community in Paul*. London: Paternoster, 2010.

---

49. Some recent work in the Reformed tradition that appears an exception to this generalization include Allen, *Sanctification* and Kapic, *Sanctification*. John Webster's outstanding essays in *Holiness*, include a remarkable essay on the holiness of theology itself. Among Wesleyans, Kent Brower has published two helpful volumes on holiness in the New Testament, *Holiness in the Gospels* and *Living as God's Holy People*. Brower and Johnson, *Holiness and Ecclesiology*, brings together a number of quality essays on its twin themes.

50 My colleague Arseny Ermakov has called for just such a "New Perspective." The otherwise good collection of essays in Barton, *Holiness Past and Present* includes no discussion of holiness in the Jewish or Greco-Roman worlds of the first century.

Brower, Kent, and Andy Johnson, eds. *Holiness and Ecclesiology in the New Testament.* Grand Rapids: Eerdmans, 2007.
Collins, Kenneth J. *A Faithful Witness: John Wesley's Homiletical Theology.* Wilmore, KY: Wesley Heritage, 1993.
———. *The Theology of John Wesley: Holy Love and the Shape of Grace.* Nashville: Abingdon, 2007.
Cranmer, Thomas. "A Short Declaration of the True, Lively and Christian Faith." In *The Two Books of Homilies Appointed to be Read in Churches*, 36–47. Oxford: Clarendon, 1855.
Dieter, Melvin E. *The Holiness Revival of the Nineteenth Century.* Metuchen, London: Scarecrow, 1980.
Dunning, H. Ray. "Ethics in a Wesleyan Context." *Wesleyan Theological Journal* 5.1 (1970) 3–10.
———. *Reflecting the Divine Image: Christian Ethics in Wesleyan Perspective.* Downers Grove: IVP, 1998.
Hammond, Geordan. *John Wesley in America: Restoring Primitive Christianity.* Oxford: Oxford University Press, 2014.
Hoffman, Thomas G. "The Moral Philosophy of John Wesley: The Development and Nature of His Moral Dynamic." PhD thesis, Temple University, 1968.
Honderich, Ted, ed. *The Oxford Companion to Philosophy.* Oxford: Oxford University Press, 1995.
Hynson, Leon. *To Reform the Nation: Theological Foundations of Wesley's Ethics.* Grand Rapids: Asbury, 1984.
Jones, C. E. *Perfectionist Persuasion: The Holiness Movement and American Methodism, 1876–1936.* London: Scarecrow, 1974.
Kapic, Kelly M., ed. *Sanctification: Explorations in Theology and Practice.* Downers Grove: IVP Academic, 2014.
Kostlevy, W. ed. *Historical Dictionary of the Holiness Movement.* Lanham: Scarecrow, 2009.
Lindstrom, Harald. *Wesley and Sanctification: A Study in the Doctrine of Salvation.* Grand Rapids: Asbury, 1988.
Lodhal, Michael, and Thomas J. Oord. *Relational Holiness: Responding to the Call of Love.* Kansas City: Beacon Hill, 2005.
Maddox, Randy L. "Reconnecting the Means to the End: A Wesleyan Prescription for the Holiness Movement." *Wesleyan Theological Journal* 33.2 (1998) 29–66.
———. *Responsible Grace: John Wesley's Practical Theology.* Nashville: Abingdon, 1994.
———. *Wesley as a Pastoral Theologian: Theological Methodology in John Wesley's Doctrine of Christian Perfection.* Milton Keynes: Paternoster, 2011.
McCormack, K. Steve. "Theosis in Chrysostom and Wesley: An Eastern Paradigm of Faith and Love." *Wesleyan Theological Journal* 26.1 (Spring 1991) 38–103.
McEwan, David. "'A Continual Enjoyment of the Three-One God': John Wesley and the Life of God in the Soul." *Phronema* 33.1 (2018) 49–72.
———. *The Life of God in the Soul: The Integration of Love, Holiness and Happiness in the Thought of John Wesley.* Milton Keynes: Paternoster, 2015.
Noble, Thomas. *Holy Trinity, Holy People: The Theology of Christian Perfecting.* Eugene: Cascade, 2013.
O'Brien, Glen. "A Trinitarian Theology of Sanctification for the Wesleyan Tradition," *Phronema* 33.2 (2018) 63–81.

Oden, Thomas C. *John Wesley's Teachings*. 4 vols. Grand Rapids: Zondervan, 2014.
Outler, Albert C. *Evangelism and Theology in the Wesleyan Spirit*. Nashville: Discipleship Resources, 2003.
Peters, John Leland. *Christian Perfection and American Methodism*. Nashville: Abingdon, 1956.
Pope, William Burt. *A Compendium of Christian Theology*. London: Pantianos Classics, 1875–76.
Rowel, Geoffrey, et al., eds. *Love's Redeeming Work: The Anglican Quest for Holiness*. Oxford: Oxford University Press, 2004.
The Salvation Army and the Uniting Church in Australia. *Holiness and Social Justice Dialogue Report*. Melbourne: Salvo, 2018.
Sangster, William. *The Path to Perfection: An Examination and Restatement of John Wesley's Doctrine of Christian Perfection*. London: Hodder & Stoughton, 1943.
Stephens, Randall J. *The Fire Spreads: Holiness and Pentecostalism in the American South*. Cambridge: Harvard University Press, 2010.
Tuttle, Robert G., Jr. *Mysticism in the Wesleyan Tradition*. Grand Rapids: Asbury, 1989.
Watson, Richard. *Theological Institutes: Or, a View of the Evidences, Doctrines, Morals, and Institutes of Christianity*. 3rd ed. London: Mason, 1823.
Webster, John. *Holiness*. Grand Rapids: Eerdmans, 2003.
Wesley, John. *Explanatory Notes upon the New Testament*. Salem: Schmul, 1975.
———. "A Farther Appeal to Men of Reason and Religion." In *The Works of John Wesley: The Appeals to Men of Reason and Religion and Certain Related Open Letters*, edited by Gerald R. Cragg, 11:95–326. Nashville: Abingdon, 1989.
———. "The Nature, Design, and General Rules of the United Societies." In *The Methodist Societies: History, Nature and Design*, edited by Rupert E. Davies, 9:67–76. The Bicentennial Edition of the Works of John Wesley. Nashville: Abingdon, 1989.
———. "On Sin in Believers." In *The Works of John Wesley: Sermons I (1–33)*, edited by Albert C. Outler, 1:317–34. Nashville: Abingdon, 1984.
———. "A Plain Account of Christian Perfection." In *The Works of John Wesley: Doctrinal and Controversial Treatises II*, edited by Paul Wesley Chilcote and Kenneth J. Collins, 13:132–91. The Bicentennial Edition of the Works of John Wesley. Nashville: Abingdon, 2013.
———. "The Repentance of Believers." In *The Works of John Wesley: Sermons I (1–33)*, edited by Albert C. Outler, 1:335–52. Nashville: Abingdon, 1984.
———. "Rules of Band Societies." In *The Methodist Societies: History, Nature and Design*, edited by Rupert E. Davies, 9:77–79. The Bicentennial Edition of the Works of John Wesley. Nashville: Abingdon, 1989.
———. "Salvation by Faith." In *The Works of John Wesley: Sermons I (1–33)*, edited by Albert C. Outler, 1:123–25. Nashville: Abingdon, 1984.
———. "The Scripture Way of Salvation." In *The Works of John Wesley: Sermons II (34–70)*, edited by Albert C. Outler, 2:153–69. Nashville: Abingdon, 1985.
———. "Sermon on the Trinity." In *The Works of John Wesley: Sermons II (34–70)*, edited by Albert C. Outler, 2:378–86. Nashville: Abingdon, 1985.
———. "Upon Our Lord's Sermon on the Mount: Discourse the Second." In *The Works of John Wesley: Sermons I (1–33)*, edited by Albert C. Outler, 1:499–509. Nashville: Abingdon, 1984.

———. *The Works of John Wesley*. Vol. 1, *Sermons I (1–33)*. Edited by Albert C. Outler. Nashville: Abingdon, 1984.

———. *The Works of John Wesley*. Vol. 2, *Sermons II (34–70)*. Edited by Albert C. Outler. Nashville: Abingdon, 1985.

———. *Works of John Wesley*. Vol. 9, *The Methodist Societies: History, Nature and Design*. Edited by Rupert E. Davies. The Bicentennial Edition of the Works of John Wesley. Nashville: Abingdon, 1989.

———. *The Works of John Wesley*. Vol. 10, *The Methodist Societies: The Minutes of Conferences*. Edited by Henry D. Rack. Nashville: Abingdon, 2011.

———. *The Works of John Wesley*. Vol. 11, *The Appeals to Men of Reason and Religion and Certain Related Open Letters*. Edited by Gerald R. Cragg. Nashville: Abingdon, 1989.

———. *The Works of John Wesley*. Vol. 13, *Doctrinal and Controversial Treatises II*. Edited by Paul Wesley Chilcote and Kenneth J. Collins. The Bicentennial Edition of the Works of John Wesley. Nashville: Abingdon, 2013.

———. *The Works of John Wesley*. Vol. 19, *Journal and Diaries II (1738–1743)*. Edited by W. Reginald Ward and Richard P. Heitzenrater. Nashville: Abingdon, 1990.

———. *Works of John Wesley*. Vol. 25, *Letters I (1721–1739)*. Edited by Frank Baker. The Oxford Edition of the Works of John Wesley. Nashville: Abingdon, 1980.

Wesley, John., ed. *The Christian Library: Extracts from and Abridgments of the Choicest Pieces of Practical Divinity which have been Published in the English Tongue*. 30 vols. London: Cordeux, 1821.

Section 3 ⎯⎯⎯⎯⎯⎯⎯⎯⎯⎯⎯⎯⎯⎯⎯⎯⎯⎯⎯⎯

Pastoral Perspectives on Christian Faithfulness

11

The Church and Urban Justice

A Faithful Wesleyan Perspective on Caring for People with Lived Experience of Poverty within Cities

—*Deirdre Brower Latz*

Practical theology, at its best, joins Scripture with sources found in the world around us, offering a mode of conversation between ideas, Scripture, and context/s that shapes the church and creates frameworks for embodied practice. As a discipline, its starting place is the lived experience of theologians who, in brushing shoulders with neighbors and friends, living in streets and communities, find their theological frameworks challenged and shaped.

So—when asked to write something that would honor David McEwan—my mind started with experience and went to daily walks when coteaching with him in Bangalore. David and I share an intergenerational passion for Wesleyan theology as *practical* and *pastoral* and this has always encouraged me. We are convinced there is a possibility of crafting a deep theology, fit for twenty-first-century life, rooted in our shared tradition as Wesleyan theologians. Because David and my meeting places have been (mostly) three cities—Brisbane, Bangalore, and Manchester, in the leafy places of compounds and the streets near poverty—I wanted to think more about a Wesleyan shape to urban theology—particularly as it engages with the underside of cities. The kind of theology we dreamt of would change cities, transform communities, touch lives, and deepen the faith of those who encounter it.

But what is the shape of this theology? In an urbanized world, discovering God within and God's view of the/your city is an urgent imperative. This chapter describes a practical/pastoral theological framework, derived from a Wesleyan perspective, focusing on urban theology for, with, amongst, and by marginalized people, especially those experiencing poverty.

Wesley, Poor People, and the City: Why Wesleyans have a Head Start

London. Bristol. Manchester. Bangalore. Brisbane.

Our biographies shape us, and Wesley was marked by cities he visited. You can read his journals as a log of the people encountered and sermons preached—it's fascinating. But his presence in these places indicated something he assumed to be true: Christians are to be where people are. Being with people in their ordinary worlds shaped Wesley's vision, preaching and practice. The compelling vision of being with and demonstrating in word and deed that God is for people is manifest in Wesley himself, and in those who follow his theological vision for the world.

In the twenty-first-century cities—Bangalore, Manchester, and Brisbane—there are commonalities. Teeming with people, each is creative, energetic, engaged, and richly diverse. Education, development, and IT are valued. Religion is contested. Each has an underside: nighttime economies, a mixture of poverty and wealth, crime and criminal enterprise, corruption and poverty. They have politics, civic society, street dwellers, and housedwellers. Cities are complex. What does a Wesleyan perspective bring to thinking about these cities as representative of the church in the city and the way we care for its marginalized people?

Thinking through Scriptural Eyes

There's tension in the Bible about cities. City equals bad or city equals good: Which is it? If we lean one way, we cite Babel, Babylon, Sodom, Gomorrah, Samaria, Rome, Athens, Corinth, and Jerusalem-who-killed-the-prophets. Places of sinful practice, questing after god-status, disdain for the one-true-God, inhospitality, slavery, idol worship, and philosophy that doesn't think its way to God. If we lean the other, the mythic city enters our vocabulary— the city of life, beloved by God, the New Jerusalem, the place and hope of the city-as-beloved, no longer a place of pain. It's God's seat, where God's throne is, where God will finally gather all in worship. It's a conurbation of all good things, wealth pouring in, health recovered, restoration ours.

So, which is it?

The middle way, common to Wesleyans, is helpful. The city in Scripture is an interwoven tapestry of light and dark, good and bad, sin and grace, love and questing for love, of hate and acting in hate. The relentlessly negative view of a city that sees it as only depraved, deprived, and despised is not one I recognize as Wesleyan. Instead, there is good news of an attentive God whose eye is on the city. This God who weeps over the city with pain and offers its people forgiveness. The city as a place where people who need God gather, make life, love, society, and reflect something of God to one another is a compelling scriptural vision. Of course, there is nothing passive about God's approach to the city. God's active love sends people. Nineveh is in God's eye. God's people, even in exile, seek the welfare of the city.

Considering cities as the focus of God's love is not enough, however. It calls for participation in the mission of God in the city. The call is to *know* the city in the same way a wife knows her husband. It is possible to live in a city and never know it. In all three cities of David's and my walks—Brisbane, Bangalore, Manchester—it is possible only ever to encounter the rich, see the beautiful, and find entertainment that makes life seem just fine. Entire infrastructures protect the wealthy from their poorest neighbors. Masking realities of social, economic, and employment exclusion is prevalent. Brisbane Riverwalk, the Northern Quarter, the Lalbagh Botanical Park—all places of delight. Within the cityscape of most modern cities there is the celebrated and regenerative ability of the city as a source of learning, health, community, design, relevance, and wealth. Then there's Inala, Ashton-Under-Lyne, and Rajendra Nagar Slum—the other side. Places of hidden urban workers who contribute to the machinery of the city without necessarily benefiting from it. And, further still, the marginalized, socially and economically, who form a new underclass, or "precariat," often invisible(d).

But even in places marked by poverty and despair, a God's-spy view sees love and life, hope and grace. The rhetoric that sees places of poverty as devoid of God and hope must be challenged. Jesus is present there. John Brooks articulates something I think Wesley would recognize—there are no God-forsaken places, just church-forsaken places.[1] The desire of God's heart to meet, restore, renew, transform, remind, and re-clothe is one of the markers of Scripture. Those who were not a people are now God's people. In those places where life is hard, God is present, by God's spirit, to nudge goodness, prompt generosity, deepen faithfulness.

This is no romantic utopia: problems of poverty remain—cycles of hunger, despair, pain, brokenness. The problems of wealth also remain—cycles of trust in self, misplaced worship, wealth created through exploitation. Scripture and the Wesleyan way drives people into *both* places for true

---

1. Brooks, *Church-Forsaken*.

encounter, but, I argue, particularly to places seemingly on the margins—not away from them.

What's a Christian to do? We learn to see people experiencing poverty. We discover that those least able, the excluded, marginalized, and despised places of our cities are places of God's loving presence. We do this from amongst, within, and give voice and place to believers who have never left places of poverty—because they are home and belong to them.

God's View of the City: Poverty

In Wesley's eighteenth century the hallmarks of poverty were perceived from the standpoint of those who were not poor. The verdict was that for some poverty was inevitable (the ill, the old, the young, the widowed) and for others it was decisional idleness.[2] Echoes of these understandings of poverty still exist. "The legacy of a distinction between the deserving poor and the undeserving poor remains a potent element of academic and political debate on poverty."[3]

Predictably, the very young, old, women, and immigrants suffer acutely.[4] Poverty seems contagious; entire neighborhoods become "poor" ends of town. Higher crime, drug use, and rates of depression alongside lower life expectancy and poorer health build up a picture that suggests poverty as a daily reality inclines (only) some towards criminal behavior.[5] Poverty taints people's lives and blights their children and children's children. It "always means malnutrition, inadequate protection against the vagaries of climate, and homelessness—all defined in relation to what a given society perceives to be the proper standards of nourishment, dress and accommodation."[6] Additionally, poor people may be "marginalized from effective participation in mainstream economic, social and political life and concentrated into 'settlements of the marginal, the socially problematic and welfare-dependent.'"[7] Aspirational poverty, hopelessness in Christian terms, becomes embedded. In fact, poverty itself acts as an agent

---

2. Alcock, *Understanding Poverty*, 9–46.

3. Alcock, *Understanding Poverty*, 3. In twenty-first-century Britain, Australia, and India "the working poor," people who, while holding jobs, experience poverty, still exists. This kind poverty effects life choices, community engagement, and health.

4. Cf. "Poverty in Australia."

5. Barry, *Why Social Justice Matters*, 178. The causal link between poverty and crime is debated. See Pantazis et al., *Poverty and Social Exclusion*, 249–84.

6. Bauman, *Work, Consumerism, and the New Poor*, 37.

7. Atherton, *Public Theology*, 44.

of exclusion and isolation.[8] Worklessness as a habit becomes embedded in communities and creates further mechanisms of despair.

Naturally, poverty cannot be separated from wider social realities: values, tradition, philosophical questioning, the role of authority, politics, and the shape of society and culture. As in the eighteenth century, questions of marginalization, morality and poverty, acquisition and duty, the wider considerations of what it means to be poor are significantly interconnected in the twenty-first century.[9]

Common responses to urban poverty follow particular paths—in general and in the church. Poverty is fled, avoided, categorized, criminalized, relativized, and hidden. Professionalized responses are offered: study it, and potentially dehumanize those people experiencing poverty's captivity. Ethnography or poverty studies are often done to and for people. Truly understanding poverty demands multidisciplinary engagement, including giving voice to those for whom poverty is a reality. Who speaks for the poor?[10]

If we are to avoid easy answers, we must acknowledge that poverty relates to exclusion from agency, voice, access, participation, engagement, connection, hope, and expectation. This is profoundly dehumanizing and isolating. Othering occurs—those who are poor people are the "widow, orphan, and alien," "the poor," from the Bible, easily forgotten by the rich or scapegoated.

But there is a reality that must never be ignored. Poverty is not homogeneous, nor is a single response possible.[11] It is "a common condition but not a shared identity or characteristics. People in poverty may thus constitute a serial collectivity, without necessarily having anything in common other than their poverty and societal reactions to it."[12] There is no one *type* of poor person. Many urban poor people live and work in and with dignity, grace, sustained perseverance, and with a longing to be more than they currently are. Many people with lived experience of poverty are more than able to speak for themselves and cocreate solutions given the

---

8. Seabrook, *No-nonsense Guide to World Poverty*.

9. There is a developing "global environmental apartheid" (Shiva, "World on the Edge," 112). See McIntosh, *Soil and Soul*; Gorringe, *Harvest*; Lynas, *High Tide*; Kennedy, *Crimes against Nature*; and Lovelock, *Revenge of Gaia*.

10. See Bonino, "Poor Will Always Be with You," 191.

11. Hutton and Giddens, *On the Edge*, 28. Lister, *Poverty*; Seabrook, *No-nonsense Guide to World Poverty*; and Alcock, *Understanding Poverty*, all support this.

12. Lister, *Poverty*, 152. Australian, Indian, and UK poor people face different realities. Globally the city is not the primary location of poverty. The focus on the urban poor is not to over-claim the city as the sole place of poverty. However, it is an arena where poverty becomes visible in a new way.

opportunity. Such a complex problem demands a breadth of response: in social policy, in the ways the non-poor respond to poverty, personally and socially, and in how the church engages with marginalized people, including hearing the voice of poor people.[13]

Reading the City

So, what is a Wesleyan theology for the church in the city: and for the poorest parts of the city? What are Wesleyan trajectories for creative responses? What of Wesley's theology do we need to reflect in our life and practice as Wesleyans serving the city?

From Ephesians to reflections on Matthew 25, and the powerful call in sermon 98, "On Visiting the Sick," Wesley serves as a master on engaging in mercy:[14]

> One great reason why the rich, in general, have so little sympathy for the poor, is, because they so seldom visit them. Hence it is, that, according to the common observation, one part of the world does not know what the other suffers. Many of them do not know, because they do not care to know: they keep out of the way of knowing it; and then plead their voluntary ignorances an excuse for their hardness of heart. 'Indeed, Sir,' said person of large substance, "I am a very compassionate man. But, to tell you the truth, I do not know anybody in the world that is in want." How did this come to pass? Why, he took good care to keep out of their way; and if he fell upon any of them unawares "he passed over on the other side."[15]

Embedded in Wesley's understanding was the idea that person-to-person connection was essential. The top-down approach of Wesley's day is evident: It is the wealthy, those with power, who must exert effort to see, connect, and "know." In the arguments that follow, I am suggesting a corporate response that stresses that people who experience poverty themselves and live in settings regarded as the poorer communities of cityscapes, must also be active participants in the church's response.

---

13. Age, racism, disability, and feminization are associated with aspects of poverty. See Lister, *Poverty*; Seabrook, *No-nonsense Guide to World Poverty*; and Alcock, *Understanding Poverty*.

14. Eph 2:10.

15. Wesley, "On Visiting the Sick," 387.

What Might a Church Faithful to Wesleyan Trajectories of Thought Do?

1. Learn to See Again

The church must see "the poor" as people: visible, named, known as beloved, and worthy. For Wesley keeping poor people out of sight is entirely possible—and an indictment. People experiencing poverty are pursued by God and are encouraged to see for themselves the beauty and oppression of the circumstances in which they find themselves. This "seeing" is scriptural because God sees all people as cherished.

2. Learn to Listen to Poverty's Story and Respond to Deep Needs

Stories of people experiencing poverty must be heard, and listening takes time, attentiveness, compassion, and is a pastoral and congregational responsibility. Many church structures mitigate against hearing the voices of the people. Quiet voices must be amplified. This offers agency, and the decision to invite representatives of poverty to the table.[16] Of course, questions remain: Who offers the invitation; who provides the vocabulary; and who decides who is poor? How is the role of asking itself given away? This is not easy.

3. Learn to Reflect on Poverty with Others

Sustained and disciplined theological reflection on poverty, narratives of oppression and freedom, power and liberation, is necessary.[17] Theological perspectives dealing with cultural issues and local community observation, renewed engagement with social sciences, and rereadings of Scripture can lead to persistent cultural critiques, and prophetic responses being developed. Matching theological reflection to an awareness of praxis is vital.[18] This must be amongst, alongside, and within poor and urban communities.[19]

---

16. See the Social Policy Research Unit based at the University of York (https://www.york.ac.uk/spru/), the Joseph Rowntree Foundation (http://www.jrf.org.uk/), the Townsend Centre for International Poverty Research based in the University of Bristol (https://www.bristol.ac.uk/poverty/), and the Chronic Poverty Research Centre (http://www.chronicpoverty.org/) amongst others.

17. For example, Dewi Hughes, Walter Wink, Walter Brueggemann, John Atherton, and Daniel Bell Jr. provide sustained reflection in this area alongside liberationists Gustavo Gutiérrez, Jon Sobrino, Theodore Jennings, etc.

18. See Gutiérrez, *Power of the Poor*, 15–17.

19. Graham et al., *Theology Reflection Methods*, 138–69.

Christians must renew their willingness to engage in the public sphere.[20] While this does not guarantee an emphasis upon poverty and its issues, enfolding poverty in discussions about church and city-life and can offer new directions for the church.

4. Engage in a Series of Rejections

Rejecting any assumptions in relation to poverty is important. Currently, those apart from the poor determine their value, and sit in judgement upon their circumstances. The narrated life is excluded from the decision-making process. Rejecting this approach demands recognizing the power of language and labels to create and form reality, and supposes an alternative approach is possible. Resisting seeing "the poor" as not us, not people, not named, and not known, who live elsewhere; resisting seeing them as statistical objects worthy of investigation is vital.[21] Since poverty is heterogeneous, with differing causes, responses and realities, realizing that poor people are each unique in their story and circumstance is imperative. In this rejection of difference, the church practices equalizing—all are welcome to speak, to be heard, to shape the future. No longer "Other"—now Us.

5. Return, Remain: Locate to the Margins

To truly see, and hear, one must be amongst and connected to people with lived experience of poverty. The church hears a friends' stories of poverty—not a stranger's story. The faces of poverty known and beloved. Challenge then comes to the church: to stay; to be alongside; to remain; to return. This resists a prosperity aspiration to move away from communities of poverty and holds to "prosperity" as God's hope for *each* community. That the church is *here*. The church is poor.

Thus, relocation from poverty to affluence, from city to suburb, from engaged-with community to drive-into community, is resisted. The church's faithful commitment to the city and its people, its presence in neighborhoods, its hope and corrective imagination is invaluable. The decision to remain embodied/embedded in cities is a theologically driven commitment made in full awareness of challenges this presents. The operant stance[22]

---

20. Lister, *Poverty*, 102.

21. This can be compared to Martin Buber's thinking relating to "I–It" contrasted with "I–Thou."

22. That is, the way a group enacts its practice.

of a group that stays may reflect their espoused theology of incarnation, embodied presence, sacrificial love, and commitment to the poorest, least, and lost. (Of course, it may be nothing of the kind, they stay because they're demotivated, or declining, waiting out death, or bounded for other reasons of convention or tradition.)

For congregations that "stay" the commitment they portray is powerful. Engaging its members locally, mutuality developed through shared acts of service, food-eaten and drinks shared, learning together to speak truth to power, practicing transformation through cross-cultural encounter (whether racial or fiscal, educational or caste-based), organizing together so that no one is hungry or naked or nameless or alone—all this is a vital witness to Christ. Clearly, this does not mean merely a *building* remains. Rather, the *congregation* commits to remaining. "Redemption and lift" for new converts is real: a shift in values often leads to greater education, opportunity, options, and wealth (both personally and corporately), which can make it challenging to stay. However, theologically, the transformation of the person, transforming a community demonstrates how yeasting works.

Reverse options, of deliberately relocating to the margins as an act of embodied mission, is significant too. Such relocation, however, can be read in multiple ways: from hope-filled and a gift, to taking away necessary housing and patronizing. Resistance may come from the receiving culture. Moving towards places of poverty is a personal decision which may be as significant as a congregation's commitment to rootedness or relocation.

A Wesleyan trajectory, then, is to stay, or be where the neediest are and creatively help connect God and God's beloved people and the communities in which they dwell.

6. Challenge Oppressive Practices

It is not enough to see, to listen, to reject othering, to remain amongst, or go to—we also need to identify oppression and reject it.

Many Christians are activists. Need compels us to respond by clothing, feeding, aiding, sheltering, physically supporting, and enhancing lives. However, a danger is collusion in acts of oppression by masking its harm, smoothing over rough places by our intervention and hiding from speaking truth to power. The church, therefore, must move from activism alone to naming and challenging structures and systemic evils that create and inhabit systems that captivate and destroy. Whether governmental or societal, culturally normative, or based on kinship structures, the role of the church is to have an ethic of incarnational presence and speaking truth to power. Jesus's words in Luke 4 symbolically enacted in the present.

Such challenge is difficult. Oppression wears guises and takes many forms, some seemingly legitimate ones.[23] But the church as a collective has the possibility of prayerfully and thoughtfully identifying places that silence and dehumanize people. The church has the capacity to name, know, and voice with others sins that crush and bring death through poverty.

However, such a response—vital though it is—risks making "the poor" into a cause. "The poor" are again Othered. Well-meaning attempts to speak on behalf of can disempower, discourage, speaking alongside or from within. Instead, poverty-ridden people must be equipped and empowered to serve the kingdom in their settings, dissatisfied with the poverty they experience and becoming part of redeeming and restoring the city-spaces they inhabit as God's work.

7. Encourage Personal Engagement: "A Plain Duty"

Congregations are made up of people. The professionalization of care risks transactional engagement which is detrimental to mutuality. Our care cannot be only on a caring-professional basis. The pastoral leader cannot be the sole visitor, contact, or advocate. The removal of "neighborly" care from within a congregation can shift the understanding of poverty towards abstraction. People need to engage with one another, enter each other's homes, converse as equals, and encounter one another's realities. Through personal empathetic experience the genuine circumstances that bring about poverty can be challenged, explored, and transformed. This is a hurdle: to engage with people experiencing urban poverty "they" must be encountered as people coequal in Christ. Of course, policy, social work, agencies of transformation are also part of the solution. However, the need for grassroots connectivity, for people to encounter one another as persons is also vital; without this, transformation that recognizes one another as agents and subjects is limited.

8. Develop Disciples Together

Small-group intimacy, where church is relational and interdependent, where high—and equal—expectations are placed on each person who

---

23. For example, market economies can influence and lead to poverty, but are embraced by many, including Christians, as the best form of life.

claims to belong to Christ, is vital. In settings of intimacy people are known, active participants, open to correction and correcting. The church as a place of profound discipleship exhorting each to become more than they are—transformed beings—is a powerful Wesleyan dynamic.

What Does this Mean for Our Trajectories?

As a biblically-shaped church, God's holy people, our mandate to be amongst people, advocating for the flourishing of the city, engaging in practices of justice and redemption is clear. *If* theologically Wesleyan, we believe good news is for all, all can be redeemed, sin can be vanquished, and assurance of salvation known. We believe the Holy Spirit can, and does, transform people; they can become more than their circumstances proscribe. We believe lifestyles that reflect Christlikeness, corporately and personally, bear witness to Christ's Lordship and authority over all elements of our lives. As organizations that celebrate the priesthood of all believers, believe in lay ministry, and encourage congregations to equip and enable, we believe anyone may be called to lead, speak, and minister. Therefore:

1. Power

We must be genuinely empowering. This may begin through advocacy and shaping spaces that give away power, but it must lead to people speaking on their own behalf, so the voice of those typically voiceless may be heard. The church, in hearing, responds with acts that develop dignity and liberation from oppression. Since marginalization creates powerlessness, which "circumscribe what people in poverty are able to do in all the dimensions [of life] . . . It can also affect what they think and feel so as to cramp their worldview and stunt their aspirations for something better, individually, and collectively,"[24] it is imperative to empower. Of course, this is thorny: what empowerment is, who offers it, how it is experienced, and to what degree it actually enables or offers actual power is contested.[25] However, the church

---

24. Lister, *Poverty*, 173.

25. Empowerment can be a "chameleon 'feel-good' term that means different things to different people in different contexts, reflecting in part, which meaning(s) of power inflect its articulation" (Lister, *Poverty*, 173). Nevertheless, the currency of empowerment is the language of social policy and welfare, at times thinly disguising punitive cessation of support, leaving families bereft and at other times serving to enhance the development of lifestyles away from poverty.

must recognize people experiencing poverty embody values, insights, and qualities that need to be heard and need to lead us.[26]

This leads to an awareness of the power of language. Words and labels used to show whom we believe to be our neighbor, our community, with claims on us. Poor people are people like us, our neighbors; we share with them a nature and a destiny; we are bound together in community.[27] The language the church uses must reflect the humanity of each person. Recategorization is significant; we are no longer those who Other and categorize into "the poor," or the "adjective here" (deserving, lazy, violent, etc.) poor. Instead, in the church each person is equally identified as truly human, rehumanized by participation in Christ and Christ-in-them.

Supporting leadership development for those from least privileged homes, and creative tent-making leadership in churches that otherwise could not have pastoral leadership, may be small ways of working to this end. The wealth/power of the church must be employed in consistently working for the sake of the poorest, creatively enabling money and power to serve rather than be served.

2. Solidarity and Advocacy

The recognition of communal solidarity and corporate responsibility[28] emerge as important. Christians rediscovering "who is my neighbor?"[29] recapture a sense of care, redefining holiness in the direction of compassion. This realigns poverty as an issue in which we are complicit and to which we contribute, and ensures we take responsibility for breaching codes of caring for the oppressed proscribed by God. Relative wealth is recognized as being at the expense of others.

Within this Wesleyan response, the church engages in advocacy for economic justice alongside increasing sustainability matters.[30] The complexity of economic justice means the church should be wary of simplistic answers. Still, suggestions of redistribution alongside adequate welfare support, linked to better opportunities, better pay, more legislated forms of long-term loans, and so on, are aspects of economic justice to be considered.[31]

---

26. Forrester, *Christian Justice*, 91.
27. Forrester, *Christian Justice*, 87.
28. Corporate social responsibility is meant theologically as a "body of Christ" term.
29. Luke 10:29.
30. Bosch, *Transforming Mission*; and Myers, *Walking with the Poor*.
31. See for example: Barry, *Why Social Justice Matters*; and Gorringe, *Harvest*.

Economic justice and reform is essential if the issues facing the poorest can be redressed alongside spiritual transformation.

We must therefore practice resistance to elements that construct cyclic realities of poverty for those least able to break free without intervention. At points, compassion-welfare[32] has proven detrimental. Ironically, it is often "hard for people to move out of poverty without losing resources in the process."[33] Advocacy in this sense considers justice issues such as regulating debt and supporting changing circumstances so that people can spiral up as well as down. Intervention—when practiced—is time limited and evolves so as to reject collusion in the problems we are mitigating against—even by the church. Advocacy helps name, as congregations, what the systemic reality is. Sin infects even our best solutions, so we never "get it fixed." Congregations need to understand the ethos of social action and recognize aspects of oppression in which we collude. We must practice resistance to elements that construct cyclic realities of poverty for those least able to break free from it without intervention.

3. Embodiment and Identity

We resist relocation to places of wealth, which means we must reflect our locale. The Wesleyan expectation that God is at work in places before we attend them, that God is ceaselessly for people, means we must seek ways of demonstrating that. Challenging the ways churches structure themselves (including in literacy, leadership, music styles, etc.) to be compatible with the real culture of its community is important. Meeting the culture with grace is a Christian call (see Acts 17).

We must consider again our corporate identity—we are children of God. Our primary Christian identity, rooted in community, is a fictive family, shaped by those amongst us who are poor, as well as those who are rich. How do we ensure the gospel's non-preferential treatment of the rich is encoded and enshrined within the communities we serve? How do we teach and equip the congregation so that those with the most power are able to self-empty and serve? How can we ensure we enact the radical egalitarian DNA of participation in Christ (Gal 3:28) and Wesley, who emphasized preaching to the poor people of the day and enabled them to be equal in Christ? Empowering people to take leadership roles; engage in responsibility for one another; ensuring public worship draws on those

---

32. This can be toxic unless read as Jeremiah 29 intends, not a program of government (though government may live out Jeremiah 29).

33. Forrester, *Christian Justice*, 102; Putnam, *Bowling Alone*.

from a range of backgrounds to serve; creating spaces for stories to be told; mutuality in prayer or side-by-side service; all foster an identity of shared practices that reflect Christ's body.

4. Imagination and Symbolic Action

We must stretch our imagination(s). Can we weave a hope-filled perspective into our preaching, teaching, and practices? Can we align ourselves with God's vision of the city as a place of peace, home, haven, and worship? What would enable an enacted holy vision so that the city becomes a place of regenerative hope where those within it (poor or rich) restore wholeness to broken and fragmented places? The church identifying co-laborers in hope within systems that seek to restore cities, and practices of community that enable restoration to spread as an alternate contagion of holiness, are all part of the imaginative and prophetic practices we can engage in.

We must reflect corporately on our symbolic action and ethics and ceaselessly speak truth. The role of the church necessarily involves bearing an ethic, holding the world accountable, being a plumb line for justice. The tensions that challenge us in our desire to help poor people and simultaneously participate in systems that may continue cycles of poverty must be addressed. Truth-telling and repentance will be part of our story.

5. Co-laboring

We must support Christian professionals, holding them accountable to be mindful of poor people and conscious that they are to serve Christ and the least. We must take seriously the global issues of environmental poverty, food poverty, the implications for our own lifestyles, and encourage those who take positions of power to reflect on the plight of poor people—wherever they are found. We must concern ourselves with the ethics of consumption, renewal of place, and environmental concerns. Accepting that poverty is different in Brisbane, Bangalore, and Manchester, the church must support those working for the sake of poor people. Wesley had a predilection for equating the good news with the restoration of the whole world. Although the issues facing his world were vastly different, Wesley (who could not have imagined a world like ours) was always committed to the eschatological vision of ultimate restoration.[34]

---

34. Oden, *John Wesley's Scriptural Christianity*, 128–31.

The Pastoral Implications

The pastoral implications for all of this are profound. In the complexities of congregational life, we need to practice discipleship beyond a worship service and into a daily sojourning alongside those often viewed as the Other. The Church must draw together disparate people—the rich and the poor—into one congregation where mutual regard and a vision for unity is upheld. We must foster a kenotic space of co-equals, identifying injustice and challenging it, reshaped into a community that reflects the Holy Spirit's transformation of the lives of people, who through encountering Christ become reshaped into an identity based on faith, not socio-economic strata. For Wesley, unless the Christian was engaged with poor people (which he acknowledged was discomforting and less and less likely as his people were lifted from poverty themselves), they were not properly Christians. One of the deepest theological challenges that he gives is that ministry amongst the poor is a means of grace, *not* to the poor only, but to those Christians engaged with them. It mutually enables one another to reflect more of the life of God than would otherwise be possible.

The truth of the city and its poorest people, when taken from a Wesleyan framework, necessitates a reconsideration of the relationship of Christianity to every aspect of urban poverty and its attendant issues. Doing so reframes this relationship in the light of both new and ancient truths. This draws on historical features of Christianity suggesting that the poor are blessed[35] (Luke 7) and that Jesus came to proclaim good news for the poor (Luke 4), and it affirms this as a central reality of Christian practices. This includes ways of seeing and attending to the city around us. It also includes the Christian virtues, disciplines, and practices: hospitality, voluntary poverty, tithes and alms, cross-boundary relationships, pastoral care, morality, personal and public engagement, redistribution of wealth, redefinitions of neighbor, and issues of personhood, humanity, and community. Indeed, a new recognition on the part of Christians that the poor are people, loved by

---

35. "Pre-modern Europe came closer than its modern successor to finding an important function for its poor. The poor like everybody else and everything else in pre-modern Christian Europe, were Children of God—an indispensable link in the 'divine chain of beings'; a part of God's creation and, like the rest of the world before its modern desacralization or 'disenchantment', saturated with meaning and purpose. The poor suffered, and their suffering was the repentance for original sin and a warrant of redemption. It was, though, up to the more fortunate to bring succour and relief to the sufferers and so to practise charity and gain in the process their own share of salvation. The presence of the poor was therefore God's gift to everybody else: an occasion to practice self-sacrifice, to live a virtuous life, to repent sins and to earn heavenly bliss." Bauman, *Work, Consumerism, and the New Poor*, 87.

God, created in God's image, and with high standing in God's eyes[36] enable those Christians willing to engage with poverty to do so in the certainty that they are realigning themselves with our deeply rooted faith. It draws on Scripture and tradition, supported by compassionate reason and (re-) affirmed as an integral part of the experience of Christianity, and seeks not just the welfare of the one but the many, and the "least." The kind of responses to such acute and growing needs will ultimately recognize that Christians must "be at the service of all people, especially the poor."[37] This is, I am contending, faithfully Wesleyan and entirely Christlike.

Bibliography

Alcock, Pete. *Understanding Poverty*. Basingstoke: Palgrave Macmillan, 2006.
Atherton, John. *Public Theology for Changing Times*. London: SPCK, 2000.
Barry, Brian. *Why Social Justice Matters*. Cambridge: Polity, 2005.
Bauman, Zygmunt. *Work, Consumerism and the New Poor*. Buckingham: Open University Press, 1998.
Bonino, José Míguez. "'The Poor Will Always Be with You': Can Wesley Help Us Discover How Best to Serve 'Our Poor' Today?" In *The Poor and the People called Methodists*, by Richard P. Heitzenrater, 181–94. Nashville: Kingswood, 2002.
Bosch, David. *Transforming Mission: Paradigm Shifts in Theology of Mission*. Maryknoll: Orbis, 1992.
Brooks, Jonathan. *Church-Forsaken: Practicing Presence in Neglected Neighborhoods*. Downers Grove: InterVarsity, 2018.
Forrester, Duncan B. *Christian Justice and Public Policy*. Cambridge: Cambridge University Press, 1997.
Gorringe, Timothy. *Harvest: Food, Farming and the Churches*. London: SPCK, 2006.
Graham, Elaine, et al. *Theological Reflection: Methods*. London: SCM, 2005.
Gutiérrez, Gustavo. *The Power of the Poor in History*. Translated by Rober R. Barr. London: SCM, 1983.
Heitzenrater, Richard P. *The Poor and the People called Methodists*. Nashville: Kingswood, 2002.
Hutton, Will, and Anthony Giddens, eds. *On the Edge: Living with Global Capitalism*. London: Vintage Digital, 2012.
Kennedy, Robert F., Jr. *Crimes against Nature: How George W. Bush & His Corporate Pals are Plundering the Country & Hijacking Our Democracy*. London: Penguin, 2004.
Lister, Ruth. *Poverty*. Cambridge: Polity, 2004.
Lovelock, James. *The Revenge of Gaia: Earth's Climate Crisis & the Fate of Humanity*. London: Allen Lane, 2006.
Lynas, Mark. *High Tide: News from a Warming World*. London: Harper Perennial, 2004.
McIntosh, Alistair. *Soil and Soul: People versus Corporate Power*. London: Aurum, 2001.

---

36. Forrester, *Christian Justice*, 105.
37. US Catholic Bishops, "Pastoral Letter."

Myers, Bryant L. *Walking with the Poor: Principles and Practices of Transformational Development*. Maryknoll: Orbis, 2005.
Oden, Thomas. *John Wesley's Scriptural Christianity: A Plain Exposition of His Teaching on Christian Doctrine*. Grand Rapids: Zondervan, 1994.
Pantazis, Christina, et al. *Poverty and Social Exclusion in Britain: The Millennium Survey*. Bristol: Policy, 2006.
"Pastoral Letter on Catholic Social Teaching and the US Economy." http://www.osjspm.org/economic_justice_for_all.aspx.
"Poverty in Australia." http://povertyandinequality.acoss.org.au/poverty/.
Putnam, Robert D. *Bowling Alone: The Collapse and Revival of American Community*. London: Simon & Schuster, 2000.
Seabrook, Jeremy. *The No-nonsense Guide to World Poverty*. Oxford: New Internationalist, 2003.
Shiva, Vandana. "The World on the Edge." In *On the Edge: Living with Global Capitalism*, edited by Will Hutton and Anthony Giddens, 112–29. London: Vintage Digital, 2012.
Wesley, John. "On Visiting the Sick." In *The Works of John Wesley: Sermons III (71–114)*, edited by Albert C. Outler, 3:384–98. Nashville: Abingdon, 1986.
———. *The Works of John Wesley*. Vol. 3, *Sermons III (71–114)*. Edited by Albert C. Outler. Nashville: Abingdon, 1986.

12

Faithful Preparation for Ministry
Exploring a Synthesis of Educational Models

—Bruce G. Allder

Introduction

Theological education is at the heart of the discipleship process.¹ The Great Commission (Matt 28:19–20) is directed to Christ's disciples. The task then for all who would claim to be followers of Jesus is to be a disciple maker. While Christ has promised to build the church, we are specifically called to make disciples. A faithful Christian is a faithful disciple-maker, and a faithful theological educator is one who prepares others to be disciple-makers. It is my assumption that discipleship is a deeply contextual engagement, and so to make this task manageable, I identify the context in which the following reflections are made. Firstly, my "tribe" is the Church of the Nazarene with its Wesleyan-Arminian theological emphasis. Secondly, I live and work mainly within the Asia-Pacific region with all its cultural diversity and challenges.

The Asia-Pacific Region Church of the Nazarene has as one of its strategic priorities "cohesive education ministerial preparation." The full document related to this strategic priority sets the parameters for further thought. Critical phrases include the following: "begins with discipleship in the local church . . . accessible, applicable, affordable and approved . . . strategies of outcomes based educational delivery within the context of new communities of learning . . . help overcome the obstacles of bi-vocationalism, language, distance and culture . . . a sustainable educational system that addresses an organic approach to evangelism . . . constantly updated."²

---

1. Theological education here is to be understood in its broadest sense. This includes formal and informal approaches.
2. Louw, "Regional Priorities."

The coherency addressed here includes both a concern for the theological coherence of content as well as coherence in educational process. The complexity of this issue is exacerbated by the multicultural context in which this conversation is taking place within the Asia-Pacific. For example, the term "accessible" includes not just the opportunity to gain entry to the education system used, but also that the pedagogy, financial requirements, and the educational processes be appropriate for the student in their context. This accessibility includes involvement in an accredited program that is recognized beyond the student's own setting. If the educational process is to fully empower the student to take on leadership and become a theological thinker in their own context and beyond, this is essential. Otherwise we unwittingly create a dependent graduate who can simply operate within their own context and within the parameters set by the educational process or system.[3] The word "approved" also fits with this idea and implies a Nazarene orthodoxy acceptable to the entire regional and global church. This wider purview prevents a purely parochial theological stance that may lead away from mainline theological tenets. The word "applicable" is loaded with educational outcomes and pedagogical implications. The outcome of contextual relevancy and an experience-based, on-the-job pedagogy is a way of giving substance to this.

The regional strategic priority also implies changes in the environment in which ministry is conducted. Such challenges as bivocational ministry, the need to address distance, culture, and language, and the requirement that graduates be able to work and think through rapidly changing contexts demand a robust educational process. Simply using a basic skills or competencies approach to theological education will be insufficient education for this kind of context. To be truly empowering, the educational system needs to be sustainable. In our changing world, with competing priorities, and changing economic structures, this may well be the ultimate test of whether an educational system is effective. Propping up these enterprises with resources from afar may limit the ability to respond contextually as needed.

Given the many issues ripe for investigation, this paper is focused on two broad themes: Firstly, the intentional, coherent theological education process that begins at the local congregational level and extends through to and includes formal theological studies; secondly, the contextuality of such a system that responds to both the accessibility and the formational elements required to be organic.

3. If the goal is to equip a genuinely indigenous education and leadership, the ability to speak into the educational system and our theology as an equal is essential. Otherwise a colonial mentality keeps the educational system teacher-centric (and, dare I say, current church leadership centric).

Theological Educational Models

While these issues may appear to be unique to our context, generations before have had similar conversations, and responded in a variety of ways. Based upon the work of Robert Banks, Brian Edgar, Darren Cronshaw, and others, Rupen Das has summarized various approaches (which he calls models) of theological education that have been developed over the years.[4] Several groups within the evangelical theological tradition have tended to adopt Bank's missional model ("Jerusalem") so that ministry preparation finds its coherence around mission and the *missio Dei*.

The "Athens" model, which Banks prefers to call "Classical,"[5] is assumed to have its genesis in the early Christian centuries. Citing Chrysostom, Ambrose, and Gregory the Great, Andrew Bain says the overriding concern in this period for ministry preparation was personal character and godliness.[6] The Scriptures were understood to be central to the process of formation in ministry preparation. Bain contends that there was a focus on relating Scripture to one's own life and to the lives of others which was positive and engaging.[7] At face value the "Athens" model appears to hold all that is necessary for a sustainable ministry preparation process. However, Banks (along with Farley[8]) argues that a fragmentation of theological education occurred in "the separation of the disciplines that accompanied the emergence of the universities in the twelfth century."[9] This created a dichotomy between theory and practice and an education which has become dominated by academic norms and values, clarity over charity, and a relegation of moral formation to simply one of several foci to be addressed.

Other models have been developed in response to these perceived limitations and changing contexts which Das refers to as the "Berlin" and "Geneva" models.[10] However, a review of these responses is beyond the scope of the current essay. What is of more interest here is Banks's "Jerusalem" model, which has been embraced, either wittingly or unwittingly, by several evangelical groups. The emphasis on mission alongside its penchant for an inclusivity that takes seriously the doctrine of the priesthood of all believers, is inherently attractive to the mind of the Evangelical. Banks bases

---

4. Banks, *Reenvisioning Theological Education*; Edgar, "Theology of Theological Education," 208–17; Das, "Connecting Curriculum with Context."
5. Banks, *Reenvisioning Theological Education*, 19.
6. Bain, "Theological Education," 50.
7. Bain, "Theological Education," 58.
8. Farley, *Theologia*.
9. Banks, *Reenvisioning Theological Education*, 25.
10. Das, *Connecting Curriculum with Context*, 17.

his model on two important elements. Firstly, learning is based on active involvement in ministry so that reflective practice is an essential pedagogical component. Secondly, theological education is not understood as a higher stage of Christian education, but as a part of everyone's Christian education. The rate determining step in the substance of the education is the student's stage in life and calling.[11]

At its best it appears that the "Jerusalem" model brings together the best of the "Athens" model while ensuring educational practice is informed by the mission of the church. So why look to another model? What is it that has promoted yet another rethinking of theological education in the evangelical context? Denise Austin and David Perry articulate the educational journey of the Australian Pentecostals through their emphasis on mission which, in their view, has been based on a practical pragmatism and even an inherent anti-intellectualism.[12] I suspect that the experience of the Pentecostals is a similar one for several of the evangelical movements within Australia.[13] In my own tradition, an inherent pragmatism that is resource driven, an impatience with the perceived slowness of ministry preparation, and a desire to be inclusive, have driven us to a distortion of Banks's model. The result has been a competency-based educational process that has left behind character formation. While this has been unintentional, there is a groundswell for change.

Austin and Perry make an appeal for the Pentecostal movement to adopt the "Athens" model. "One of the characteristics of the 'Athens' model is that the goal of pedagogy is not simply the acquisition of knowledge, but rather the application and appropriation of knowledge and experience for the purpose of personal transformation. This model of pedagogy fits well within a Pentecost world view."[14] However, a more effective response to this pragmatic missional approach can be found in a synthesis of models, rather than a return to a preexisting model that was developed in a different context for a different time. As such this proposed model is nothing new, but rather a bringing together of desirable aspects of two models in a fresh articulation that responds to our current context.

In response to the desire for change, such a synthesis needs to include:

1. character formation at the core of the educational process

---

11. Banks, *Reenvisioning Theological Education*, 157.

12. Austin and Perry, "From Jerusalem to Athens," 46.

13. Ball, *Transforming Theology*, gives a snapshot of theological education in Australia as institutions have wrestled with providing genuinely transformative education. See also Ball and Harrison, *Learning and Teaching Theology*.

14. Austin and Perry, "From Jerusalem to Athens," 49.

2. a missional perspective which embraces the passion (heart) and skills (head) throughout

3. inclusion of lay and clergy

4. a spiritual dynamic that is empowered by God's Spirit and has a strong experiential orientation

5. sustainability that is in terms of reproducibility

The Basis for the Proposed Emmaus Model

The name for this proposed model comes from the New Testament narrative (Luke 24:13–35) of two early Christian disciples walking home to the village of Emmaus after the tumultuous events of the first Easter morning. There are at least six features in this narrative that reflect a synthesis of educational models for ministry preparation. Firstly, Jesus came alongside the disciples as they discussed the events (Luke 24:14–15). While confused, they attempted to make sense of all that had just happened. It was a current event in which they had more questions than answers. Jesus coming alongside is an important pedagogical statement. Banks's key shift to a missional center in theological education places discipleship and discipling as the pedagogical centerpiece.

> This would require us to focus less on how to integrate spiritual formation into theological education, and more on theological education—at both the initial and more developed level—[to] illuminate and facilitate a contemporary form of discipleship. Rather than concentrating on the inner life of the believer, this orients it to, and contextualizes it in, the here and now of daily life in the service of the kingdom.[15]

Such coming alongside to help process the events in their lives is the platform for education that Paul Whetham and Dean Eaton[16] use in their approach to discipling in a post-Christian world. Terms such as coaching, respect for each other's context, and genuine dialogue move us away from technique and a simple transmission of content, to meaning making.[17] "This is . . . co-learning which aims at discovery of the grace of God together

---

15. Banks, *Reenvisioning Theological Education*, 162.
16. Whetham and Eaton, *Lighthouses*.
17. Smith, "Moving from Instruction to Inquiry," shows the various types of knowledge encountered in the world and how the processes toward meaning-making vary according to the context and types of knowledge encountered.

with people, not mere proclamation to them, as if we ourselves do not 'sit under' the Word we preach."[18]

While not all contexts are post-Christian, the student-centered approach that finds the curriculum within their context, shifts the focus from the teacher and a content driven-ness. This fits well with a desire to shape character and personal development within the formal educational process. This process allows for variation from a predetermined mold.

Secondly, there is the centrality of the Scriptures; Jesus explained the events in the light of the Scriptures (Luke 24:25–27). The scaffolding for meaning making is found within the Scriptures. This prevents the coming alongside being simply a subjective exchange of untested opinions. Klaus Issler says that the formative engagement with Scripture occurs as we approach the task with both head (analytical) and heart (meditative).[19] This allows for what ultimately becomes reflective practice as key questions are asked in the experience and meaning-making takes place with the assistance of the scaffolding of Scripture. A word of warning, though, to the exclusive application of Scripture in the process of meaning-making. A rigid or closed hermeneutic of Scripture is arguably inadequate to the full engagement within the educational process.[20]

Thirdly, as the disciples shared a meal with their guest the opportunity for further recognition and engagement at a genuine community level was possible (Luke 24:29–31). Hospitality and grace become an important element to this educational engagement indicating a holistic approach. Pedagogically, the teacher is on a similar journey as the students and learning happens while participating in the everyday occurrence. In modeling grace and hospitality, people (students) are the focus and teacher and student learn together. The development of learning communities appears essential to effective personal and community transformation. Traditionally the classroom has been the place of developing learning communities. However, with the intervention of technology, the means of delivering the content of a class no longer requires personal contact. The possibilities of developing community in online settings is a focus of many studies but it is not my intention to debate this issue here. The point is that a community is needed for effective reflective practice to occur.[21] In our individualized

18. Whetham and Eaton, *Lighthouses*, 9.

19. Issler, "Approaching Formative Scripture," 117–34.

20. The Church of the Nazarene, in article 4 of its constitution, reveals a high view of Scripture while maintaining a humility and openness in its interpretation (Blevins et al., *Manual*, 27). See also King et al., "Report of the Study Committee."

21. There are passionate presentations on both side of the argument about whether genuine community can be established without personal, direct contact. See Spencer,

Western educational endeavors, reconnecting with fellow-learners may well be a very Christian thing to do. Modeling a lifestyle and embodying truths taught become an important means of teaching. In the words of the apostle Paul: "You yourselves are our letter, written on our hearts, to be known and read by all; and you show that you are a letter of Christ, prepared by us, written not with ink but with the Spirit of the living God, not on tablets of stone but on tablets of human hearts" (2 Cor 3:2–3).

Fourthly, the lessons learned were more than a cognitive insight that was interesting to catch. The disciples' response at having made sense of their confusing experience on that first Easter morn was to testify to the "burning of their hearts within" (Luke 24:32). There is a passionate engagement with the truths encountered in the person of Jesus Christ. Transformative theological education will ignite fires in the hearts of students that will ultimately transform learning communities and in turn transform wider communities and even cultures. The engagement of the whole person is such that a sterile engagement with content will no longer be an option. Rather than have people encounter material in a way that has them losing faith in Christ and his work, the student is energized and transformed by such an encounter. It is all in the context of faith seeking understanding, rather than understanding seeking faith. As the teacher walks through the journey of confusion and doubt with a student, there is a new encounter with the Truth in the person of Jesus Christ.

Fifthly, so impacted were the disciples, that despite the potential danger of traveling back to Jerusalem that same evening, they hurried back to share what they had learned (Luke 24:33–35). The joy of discovery and the deepening relationship that they discovered in Jesus was impetus enough to spur them on. Their message was simple: "Yes, Jesus is alive, and the reports of his resurrection must be true as a result!" In educational terms, their learning changed their worldview, their behavior, and their mission. The change from confusion to assurance and uncertainty to confidence was remarkable. Oh, that our teaching will have similar outcomes!

Sixthly, once the lessons were learned, Jesus disappeared from their sight (Luke 24:31). Theologically we know that Jesus ultimately sent his Holy Spirit to come alongside the disciples (John 16:12), but there is a sense here that the students (disciples) are no longer dependent on the teacher (Jesus). They get to think for themselves and reason through new events based upon the lessons learned from Jesus. Empowering students to "step up" as witnesses to the reality of Christ and beginning to make sense of their

---

"Time Is Up," 105–13, for an appeal to maintain the physical contact; while Denoyelles et al., "Strategies for Creating," claim that with intentional, appropriate strategies such community is possible. These are just two of many such conversations.

own confusing circumstances ensures that they are ready to step into this amazing journey called ministry.

Features of the Emmaus Model Compared

Perhaps the best way to describe the Emmaus model is in terms of comparison with the Athens and Jerusalem models. Using Das's comparative table of theological models[22] the same major categories are used to describe the features of the proposed Emmaus model.

Table 1: Comparison of Models

Symbol	Athens	Jerusalem	Emmaus
Model	Classical	Missional	Journey in the company of others
Context	Academy	Community	Community of faith living in the wider diverse world
Goal/ Purpose	Transforming the individual	Converting the world	Discipled "disciple-multiplier" as a lifelong learner
Emphasis	Personal formation: knowing who . . .	Mission, partnership: knowing for . . .	Personal and group formation toward Christlikeness in the *missio Dei*
Formation	Individualized and focused on inner personal, moral, and religious transformation	Learning has to have reference to all dimensions of life, family, friendships, work, and neighborhood	Shaped by encounter with Christ and his community
Theology	Theology is the knowledge of God, not about God	Missiology is the mother of theology. It involves action—mission.	A theology of embodiment of the gospel, i.e., incarnation of kingdom-of-God principles and servanthood

---

22. Das, *Connecting Curriculum with Context*, 17. Under the symbol of "Teacher" for the Emmaus model, see Banks, *Reenvisioning Theological Education*, 171.

Symbol	Athens	Jerusalem	Emmaus
Teacher	Provider: of indirect assistance through intellectual and moral disciplines to help students undergo formation	Practitioner/missionary: the teacher is not removed from practice; teaching involves sharing lives as well as truth	Discipler/Mentor/Coach/fellow-learner—sharing life as well as knowledge
Student	Cultivates the mind, character, and spirit	Discipled to become a disciple-maker	Discipled to be a disciple-maker and shaper of culture

The Emmaus Model also needs to be read in conjunction with the following grid adapted from Das's work[23] outlining the target audience of such education. One of the key priorities for the Asia-Pacific Church of the Nazarene is a coherent educational program that reaches from the local church at lay level right through to the high-level academic whether it be lay or clergy. This comprehensive vision for discipleship seeks a curriculum that can embrace all levels of student and the diverse vocations of students. While the scaffolding to aid learning may become more sophisticated as the student progresses academically, coherence would require no substantial shift in emphasis from intentional transformation of the person and community while expressing that transformation missionally. Notice that a separate category of the Christian training for the marketplace is in place to emphasize a non-clergy track that intentionally seeks transformation of society through the traditionally considered non-religious vocations. This broadens the focus of theological education and addresses one of the new realities of mission—a sense of bi-vocationalism that may or may not lead to a clerical status within the Christian church.

---

23. Das, *Connecting Curriculum with Context*, 21.

Table 2: The Target and Implications of the Emmaus Model

	Key Questions	Theology Training for Laity	Theology Training for Christians in the Marketplace, Professions, etc.	Training for Ministerial Theology	Training for Professional Theology	Training for Academic Theology
Target / Focus	Who is the target?	Local faith community; new Christians	Professionals who sense a call to be in the workplace as their ministry	Lay Leadership in local faith communities	Clergy/ Leadership	Teachers of clergy and researchers
Distinctive Content	What is the content of the training?	Spiritual and character formation. Understanding the faith community and its place within the wider community	Understanding the faith community and its place in the community; the nature of being a culture-maker and culture-shaper	Christian leadership, hermeneutics and understanding the faith community and its place within the wider community	Biblical studies; theology; theological reflection; critical thinking;	Research skills; theological reflection; discernment; critical thinking
Purpose	Why is this training being done?	To disciple and be a disciple-maker / multiplier	To be a disciple-maker / multiplier and reflective practitioner	Equip for service as a disciple-multiplier and equip others as reflective practitioner	Equipping others for ministry as disciple-multipliers; specialist ministry and study	Equipping others as disciple-multipliers; specialist studies
Method	How is this training to be done?	Small groups at congregational level; learning by doing in mission; short term classes	Small groups (formal cohorts); seminars; workshops	Small groups (formal cohorts); seminars; workshops	Learning cohorts in ministry contexts	Academy

	Key Questions	Theology Training for Laity	Theology Training for Christians in the Marketplace, Professions, etc.	Training for Ministerial Theology	Training for Professional Theology	Training for Academic Theology
Distinctive Ethos	What *values* and *spirituality* permeate the training?	Growing together toward Christlikeness in mission	Growing together toward Christlikeness; spiritual discernment	Growing together toward Christlikeness; spiritual discernment	Growing together toward Christlikeness, discovery; spiritual discernment; community of faith formation	Growing together toward Christlikeness; critical thinking and inquiry
Context	Where is the training conducted?	Homes and local faith communities	Homes, local churches, workplace	Local faith communities; academy; faith community networks	Local faith communities; academy; faith communities; networks	Local faith communities; academy
People	Who. How does the faith of those involved define the education?	Members of the community of faith	Members of the community of faith involved in the marketplace; pastors; leaders	Some members of the community of faith; leaders	Pastors and leaders / mentors	Pastors and leaders / mentors

The Difference between the "Jerusalem" and "Emmaus" Models

It may perhaps be argued that the "Emmaus" model is really a rebadged "Jerusalem" model for there are key elements that appear the same. There is no doubt that we owe Banks an enormous debt in the conversation on theological education as he has brought mission into the conversation of ministry preparation. However, in a way to focus on the difference between the two models, I use a description of theological education developed by Robert

Woodruff (see Figure 1).[24] The key component in this description is the lens through which the content, context, competency, and character elements are filtered. Woodruff understands the lens to be the curriculum. In the case of Banks's "Jerusalem" model, the lens or the unifying element for the curriculum could be considered as "mission." In the case of the Emmaus model the lens is "Christlikeness for mission" (character formation with a specific focus), and, arguably, has a more overt character formation element.

Figure 1: Focus in Education[25]

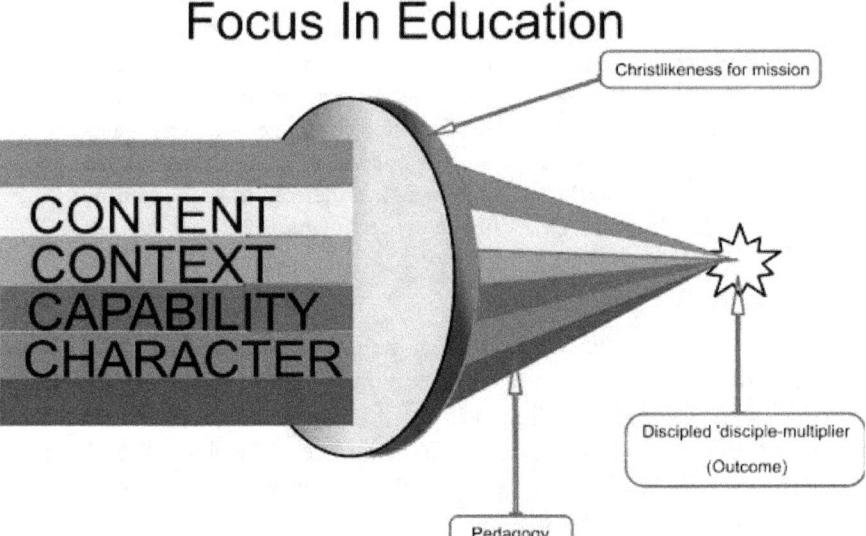

The specific outcome that is sought in the Emmaus model is a disciple multiplier who is on a lifelong journey of transformation within Christian community. Perhaps the "disciple multiplier" is code for "mission." If the entire curriculum is shaped by the lens of Christlikeness, then discipleship is at the core of the educational process rather than subsidiary to it. An identity in Christ develops a deeper appreciation for the reality of being part of a "kingdom of priests" (Exod 19:5–6; 1 Pet 2:9) and this is inherently missional. The lens becomes the unifying focus of the education process regardless of where the student is on that journey because the lens stays the same through the

24. Woodruff, *Education on Purpose*.
25 Adapted from Woodruff, *Education on Purpose*, 8.

entire journey.[26] Since this is to be lived reality, and not just an abstraction, integration of learning and action become the hallmarks of transformation. Each of the units taken in a formal program have elements of the focus, so that it is not simply a "add-on," which can lead to superficiality. It is the emphasis on the lived reality in community that avoids sidelining the missional aspects in the educational process.[27]

Defining Christlikeness more closely, and from the beginning, is needed to give substance to the curriculum: for example, questions like, what does it mean to be Christlike as an individual, as a community, and as an institution? Perhaps more telling is the way in which this development as an individual, community, and institution takes place.

> Christians start with certain "givens" and scriptural principles that form the basis of their belief system. We then encounter a whole range of experiences that often challenge these beliefs and force us to reinterpret Scripture or look at it in new ways. . . . We take action on the basis of our new understanding . . . and this is the elaborating part of the process of meaning-making. . . . It is through this testing out or action phase that we are able to tighten our meanings.[28]

The aspect of Banks's model that the Emmaus model embraces wholeheartedly is that education takes place along the way. "Rather than concentrating on the inner life of the believer, this orients it to, and contextualizes it in, the here and now of daily life in the service of the kingdom."[29] In other words, the student's context is both the place in which the learning takes place as well as the source of much of the material for reflection. This latter element is a significant challenge for curriculum design.

Implications to consider

Firstly, relationships in a learning community are a key feature in the context of this model. While content for learning may be delivered in a variety

---

26. This particular focus for theological education is one of several that have been proposed for theological education. A more recent articulation of a different lens to missional Christlikeness is found in Benson's "God's Curriculum." His theological orientation is evangelical and has similar goals.

27. The *Australian Journal of Mission Studies*, June 2018 edition, devotes most of the articles to theological education and mission, specifically focused on the New Zealand experience of the Presbyterian church.

28. Whetham and Eaton, *Lighthouses*, 20.

29. Banks, *Reenvisioning Theological Education*, 162.

of ways that do not necessarily involve relationships in community, the processing of the material most definitely does. Wilhoit describes experiential learning in community in four major dimensions.[30] He speaks of the cultivating of a spiritual openness that is cultivated in corporate worship, prayer, and participation in the sacraments; teaching that leads to a profound awareness of being part of God's community through preaching, meditation, and small groups; formation through acts of service that develops discernment and relational commitments that change attitudes and worldviews; and finally a transforming that takes place through hospitality, handling conflict well, and living authentically. None of this can be done effectively without the cultivation of relationships in Christian community. These dimensions are the purview of the local faith fellowship. Here the local community of faith is the locale of experiential learning. An educational structure that potentially enfolds this is a "cohort of students" approach where the supportive environment comes not only from the relationships with teacher and assistants, but also from fellow students.

In Fowler's developmental view of faith formation, there are key moments of confusion and dissonance.[31] It can be argued that this dissonance is a necessary precursor for genuine transformation. Keeping such experiences and education in the crucible of relationships helps prevent the loss of faith that can so often accompany such dissonance. Such tension is understood as an inevitable part of this journey.

> Now such a development would require a very different type of approach to education and personal formation to that generally imagined and practiced in many settings today. This approach would be much less along the lines of paternalistic oversight, with teachers and leaders dispensing confidently predetermined formulas of faith and patterns of personal formation, and more along the lines of a mentor's, or facilitator's, oversight. Educators, as fellow travellers, need to trust that people transitioning beyond stage 3 faith will find their way within a caring and supportive environment.[32]

These safe places to test new perspectives and to try and make sense of disorienting experiences in ministry are central to this process of education.

Secondly, the experiential learning that takes place does so within the context of active ministry. Rather than have the student withdraw from service in a local faith community, the student remains actively involved

30. Wilhoit, *Spiritual Formation*.
31. Fowler, *Faith Development*, 68.
32. Smith, "Growing Pains," 10.

and learns on the job. Learning the art of theological reflection and cultivating its mature application becomes a pillar of this process as this brings the scaffolding of content and concepts alongside the experiences. Educators sometimes refer to this assisted learning as a zone of proximal development. Knowledge beyond the reach of a student learning alone becomes accessible with the assistance of a more knowledgeable other. Such a conception fits the coaching and mentoring model of teaching that is implied in the Emmaus Model.

Experiential learning with all its pedagogical theory and implications has developed from Kolb's and others' work, on the experiential learning cycle.[33] As this is embraced an instruction-action-reflection model becomes possible. As such, cultivating the experiential learning within the community of faith as spiritual formation can also create possibilities for learning within the context of serving (ministry). This way the activity of ministry becomes a significant source of the curriculum.

Thirdly, the scaffolding needs to be grounded in Scripture if Christlikeness is to be the educational lens. Douglas John Hall, reflecting on the Canadian experience, says,

> theological education in Canada, in my view, often evinces a loss of confidence in scripture, central doctrinal loci and historic Christian practices as these could nourish the formation of thoughtful, engaged and generous leaders in the church at this time. Too often liberal (mainline) Protestantism in the Canadian context attaches itself to a series of causes and issues, all of them laudable, and "strong theory" from departments of critical and cultural studies instead of first becoming "more knowledgeable about the scriptures and traditions," in order to support spiritual formation for the life of Christ's church and for the sake of the world.[34]

There is a need to ensure a robust and wise hermeneutic of Scripture for an adequate Christian conceptual scaffold.[35] Times of community engagement with God's Word is needed. Banks speaks of reframing the curriculum toward a missional approach by placing the "Bible in the center . . . and then encircle it with history and tradition, . . . church and mission, . . .

---

33. Kolb, *Experiential Learning*.

34. Topping, "Troubling Context," 40.

35. In my own Nazarene tradition, a high view of Scripture is embraced with a careful hermeneutic that stays thoroughly Wesleyan and avoids the narrowness of a fundamentalism that can often be associated with a high view of Scripture. See King et al., "Report of the Study Committee."

experience and culture."[36] The purpose is to prevent the fragmentation of the educational experience into seemingly small unrelatable parts. If we are serious about a fully integrated approach from local church onward, then the local church itself will need to bring the effective use of Scriptures back into the life of the congregation. Teaching congregants how to engage with the Scripture in meaningful and formational ways is a precursor for the centrality of Scripture in the educational (discipleship) process.

> The common assumption is that the role of the Christian canon may be defined as epistemic in nature, so that one may assess the validity of Christian doctrine by what the Bible states. . . . However, the canonical process itself suggests the incorporation of the biblical texts into the Christian canon had more to do with their formative rather than their epistemic role.[37]

This has profound implications for pedagogy. Mark Maddix suggests, firstly, the interpretative process of Scripture involves more than the historical meaning contained in the text. There must be a convergence between text and reader that brings life beyond mere information—there is the engagement with the Spirit. Secondly, the Scriptures function authoritatively within the church community and the confessional context within which the reading and interpretation takes place. Thirdly, there is the necessity to live out of the church's engagement with the Scripture. There is a focus upon and a response to the text in Christian community.[38]

Fourthly, the role of the teacher is more the mentor and coach in a dialogic pedagogy. In the age of the flipped classroom, this is becoming increasingly familiar territory, although an ethos change in theological schools may still be needed for this to be effectively grasped. Clarifying the roles for teachers and staff in this new reality is essential for teachers to be adequately resourced. Jennifer Roberts identified a ranking of importance of current roles and of future roles in in a study of distance education teachers. While "knowledge expert" and "student support" rank first and second in both current and future roles, the roles of "technology expert" and "instructional design" jumped significantly in importance for future roles.[39] Class sizes need to be appropriate to work with the relational aspects of this style of learning. Teaching assistants, facilitators, and teachers journey with students through the processing of material and the

---

36. Banks, *Reenvisioning Theological Education*, 235.
37. Maddix and Thompson, "Scripture as Formation," 81.
38. Maddix and Thompson, "Scripture as Formation," 81–83.
39. Roberts, "Future and Changing Roles," 44–45.

dissonance that is often created through experiences within the student's world of ministry. Managing the content becomes secondary to processing content in a way that allows preconceived ideas to be challenged, worldviews examined, and critical thinking emerge from the experience. Rather than take a "know all, tell all" approach, the teacher becomes the asker of questions and provider of learning scaffolding at appropriate times through the ministry and educational journey.[40]

Fifthly, assessments in the educational program can be shaped for application in the student's context as they work in their own setting. The emphasis is on the livability, applicability, and effectiveness of the insights for ministry. While this is nothing new, the emphasis is in line with Banks's reconceiving teaching as a missional practice.[41] As curriculum is developed around student-related concerns, teaching is done in the context of the teacher and student, and reflection-in-action models.[42] Another aspect of assessment that will need further exploration is that of group assessments. In a highly individualized ethos that tends to come with Western higher education, work needs to be done on how to effectively formatively and summatively assess students' progress. This becomes an issue as a consequence of doing education in the context of the student—presumably in the life of a faith community. As cohorts of student work within their contexts, group projects and collaborative learning experiences raise possibilities of group assessments.

As relational learning becomes a focus, then a shift to formative assessment will be needed and perhaps a rethinking of method and timing of summative assessment. Perhaps leaving the summative assessment of a student until the end of a major section of the educational program may allow more room for formative assessments through the bulk of the educational journey. This may help limit the siloing educational content as more than one academic discipline is summatively assessed at the same time.

Sixthly, an educational system needs to be intentionally provided that will enhance this relational approach in theological education. Avoiding a depersonalized institution, working holistically with the student in their context, and ensuring an organic process will require a change of ethos.

> [T]he rising costs of providing traditional campus-based programmes, coupled with increasing doubts about the extent to which graduates are suitably prepared for dynamic

---

40. See Taylor and Dewerse, "Curiosity and Doubt," for a number of practical examples and experiments in innovative teaching practice.
41. Banks, *Reenvisioning Theological Education*, 169–86.
42. Kreminski and Frost. "Theological Education," 184.

technology-ubiquitous twenty-first century contexts, has triggered greater interest in more open, flexible, technology-mediated and cost-effective ways to address the demand. . . .

We believe there is a real danger that in the process of convergence of modes of provision the unique quality concerns of distance provision, regarding, for example, the issues of access, success and cost, and the implications for how people learn and work, may be lost.[43]

The important role of the congregation and the local church in this coherent approach to theological education requires rethinking how it is structured.[44] What has been traditionally thought of as field work needs to be related more closely to the educational enterprise. The field work itself and assignment of students could reorganize around cohorts for group theological reflection and action-reflection. The physical meeting places could be in local congregations, decentralizing the educational facilities. At this point some could be tempted to think that the place of an educational institution is no longer required. While some have toyed with this idea, there are key quality concerns that require investment of time and resources that an institution with an appropriate vision is best placed to address. Mays suggests the following are key concerns:

- recognition of the need for investment in the interplay between quality learning resources, decentralized student support and decentralized assessment;
- institutional adjustments in terms of policies, systems, procedures, and service-level agreements related to curriculum and materials development and renewal, support for both students and staff, robust systems making appropriate use of appropriate technology, cross-border provision, and different financial models;
- and centrally robust systems for program design, evaluation, and renewal.[45]

Concluding Remarks

Theological education is an area that is deeply embedded in context. This is one of the reasons that it continues to be subject to the stresses and strains of

---

43. Mays et al., "Deconstructing Dual-Mode," 136.
44. Banks, *Reenvisioning Theological Education*, 229–30.
45. Mays et al., "Deconstructing Dual-Mode," 137.

various educational forces—both traditional and contemporary. The challenge is to be faithful in the task of theological education and not simply move into whimsical popularist perspectives or stay entrenched in perspectives of the past that have outlived their service.

In this chapter I have attempted to give attention to two themes relevant to ministry preparation arising out of the Church of the Nazarene's strategic priorities, by synthesizing the Athens (classical) and Jerusalem (missional) models of theological education. The synthesis has taken the focus on character and spiritual formation of the Athens model along with the missional impetus of the Jerusalem model and placed the emphasis on Christlikeness in mission. This model has tried to be true to both emphases as a result. Using Woodruff's model of a lens to focus theological education, the unifying theme in the proposed Emmaus model is Christlikeness in mission. The implications of this refocus are profound and require further development. Pedagogy, institutional ethos and policies, the qualities of the teachers, and the context of the learning all require an intentional rethinking of the process. Rather than have distance education and digital approaches in education be driven by an operational pragmatism, it is hoped that this discussion can spark further conversation in what appears to be an inevitable trend in theological education.

A robust, informed process in ministry preparation demands our best thinking in these areas, especially as we seek to be faithful in our preparation and development of people for intentional ministry. Faithfully keeping missional Christlikeness the focus of all preparation will ultimately lead to a reevaluating of the processes used. Let's also be faithful to the context in which we find ourselves.

Bibliography

Ackerman, David. "The Journey Model of Theological Education." Unpublished, 2017.
Austin, Denise, and David Perry. "From Jerusalem to Athens: A Journey of Pentecostal Pedagogy in Australia." *Journal of Adult Theological Education* 12.1 (2015) 43–55.
Bain, Andrew M. "Theological Education in Early Christianity: The Contribution of Late Antiquity." In *Theological Education: Foundations, Practices, and Future Directions*, edited by Andrew M. Bain and Ian Hussey, 47–59. Eugene: Wipf & Stock, 2018.
Ball, Les. *Transforming Theology: Student Experience and Transformative Learning in Undergraduate Theological Education*. Australia: Mosaic, 2012.
Ball, Les, and James R. Harrison, eds. *Learning and Teaching Theology: Some Ways Ahead*. Australia: Morning Star, 2014.
Banks, Robert. *Reenvisioning Theological Education: Exploring a Missional Alternative to Current Models*. Grand Rapids: Eerdmans, 1999.

Benson, David M. "God's Curriculum: Reimagining Education as a Journey towards Shalom." In *Reimagining Christian Education: Cultivating Transformative Approaches*, edited by Johannes M. Luetz et al., 17–38. Singapore: Springer, 2018.

Blevins, Dean G., et al., eds. *Manual 2017-2021: Church of the Nazarene*. Kansas City: Nazarene Publishing House, 2017.

Das, Rupen. *Connecting Curriculum with Context: A Handbook for Context Relevant Curriculum Development in Theological Education*. Carlisle: Langham Global Library, 2015.

Denoyelles, Aimee, et al. "Strategies for Creating a Community of Inquiry through Online Asynchronous Discussions." *MERLOT Journal of Online Learning and Teaching* 10.1 (2014) 153–65.

Edgar, Brian. "The Theology of Theological Education." *Evangelical Review of Theology* 29.3 (2005) 208–17.

Farley, Edward. *Theologia: The Fragmentation and Unity of Theological Education*. Philadelphia: Fortress, 1983.

Fowler, James. *Faith Development and Pastoral Care*. Edited by Don S. Browning. Philadelphia: Fortress, 1986.

Issler, Klaus. "Approaching Formative Scripture Reading with Both Head and Heart." *Journal of Spiritual Formation & Soul Care* 5.1 (2012) 117–34.

King, Thomas, et al. "Report of the Scripture Study Committee to the Twenty-Eighth General Assembly, Church of the Nazarene." *Didache* 13.1 (2014) 1–13. http://didache.nazarene.org/index.php/volume-13-1/892-didache-v13n1-01-scripturestudycommitteereport-king1/file.

Kolb, David. *Experiential Learning: Experience as the Source of Learning and Development*. Englewood Cliffs: Prentice-Hall, 1984.

Kreminski, Karina, and Michael Frost. "Theological Education for Missional Leadership." In *Theological Education: Foundations, Practices, and Future Directions*, edited by Andrew M. Bain and Ian Hussey, 175–86. Eugene: Wipf & Stock, 2018.

Louw, Mark. "Church of the Nazarene Asia-Pacific Regional Priorities." https://asiapacificnazarene.org/regional-priorities/.

Maddix, Mark, and Richard Thompson. "Scripture as Formation: The Role of Scripture in Christian Formation." *Christian Education Journal* 3.9 (2012) 79–93.

Mays, Tony John, et al. "Deconstructing Dual-Mode Provision in a Digital Era." *Distance Education* 39.2 (2018) 135–39.

Roberts, Jennifer. "Future and Changing Roles of Staff in Distance Education: A Study to Identify Training and Professional Development Needs." *Distance Education* 39.1 (2018) 37–53.

Smith, Dean. "Growing Pains: A Reflection on the Experience of Suffering an Epistemological Crisis." *Crucible* 7.2 (2016) 1–11.

Smith, Stephen. "Moving from Instruction to Inquiry: How Complexity Theory Informs Work-Integrated Learning." In *Wondering About God Together*, edited by Les Ball and Peter G. Bolt, 35–51. Australia: SCD, 2018.

Spencer, Gregory. "Time Is Up and Space Is Down." *Journal of Spiritual Formation & Soul Care* 10.1 (2017) 105–13.

Taylor, Steve, and Rosemary Dewerse. "Curiosity and Doubt in Researching the Future: The Contribution of Flipped Learning to Sociality in Theological Innovation." In *Wondering About God Together*, edited by Les Ball and Peter G. Bolt, 426–52. Australia: SCD, 2018.

Topping, Richard. "Troubling Context: Theological Education and Formation in Canada." *Encounter* 76.3 (2016) 39–57.

Whetham, Paul, and Dean Eaton. *Lighthouses: Christian Coaching in a Post-Christian World*. Adelaide: Lutheran Church of Australia, 2018.

Wilhoit, James. *Spiritual Formation as if the Church Mattered: Growing in Christ through Community*. Grand Rapids: Baker Academic, 2008.

Woodruff, Robert. *Education on Purpose: Models for Education in World Areas*. Brisbane: QUT, 2001.

13

Faithfulness in the Face of Differences

John Wesley's Catholic Spirit and One-Heartedness

—RICHARD GIESKEN AND ERIK GROENEVELD

Introduction

This essay will focus on Wesley's well-known sermon "Catholic Spirit,"[1] which opens and closes with an emphasis on love—first for one another and then even for enemies and strangers. Wesley admitted that such a love was easily expressed but wondered how it was to be practiced. We will, therefore, explore the implications of such a love for church life, both within and beyond the church circle. Wesley's sermon has been used to advocate theological tolerance and even misunderstood to blur theological distinctiveness. In keeping with Wesley, we do not seek to stir up heated zealous debates but wish to explore how the spiritual condition of the heart provides a crucial starting point for unity that does not demand uniformity in all things doctrinal. If your heart is with our hearts, read on.

What Is the "Catholic Spirit" All About?

Although John Wesley's sermon on the "Catholic Spirit" is famous, the biblical story on which he based it is not as well known. Wesley taught (and continues to teach) us a spiritual lesson on being one in the kingdom of God, based on a strange encounter found in 2 Kings 10. The encounter is between King Jehu and Jehonadab, the son of Rechab, and takes place in a setting full of violence and murder. In chapter 9, on behalf of the prophet Elisha, Jehu is anointed king over the Northern Kingdom of Israel. The task Jehu receives from the Lord is as follows:

1. Wesley, "Catholic Spirit."

> ⁷ You shall strike down the house of your master Ahab, so that I may avenge on Jezebel the blood of my servants the prophets, and the blood of all the servants of the Lord. ⁸ For the whole house of Ahab shall perish; I will cut off from Ahab every male, bond or free, in Israel. ⁹ I will make the house of Ahab like the house of Jeroboam son of Nebat, and like the house of Baasha son of Ahijah. ¹⁰ The dogs shall eat Jezebel in the territory of Jezreel, and no one shall bury her." Then he opened the door and fled. (2 Kgs 9:7–10)

In the verses following, and in the next chapter, it becomes clear how Jehu accomplishes his task with zeal; he slaughters all who remained of the house of Ahab in Jezreel. Amidst the blood, limbs, skulls, arrows, and swords, Jehonadab appears. Jehu asks him this seemingly ironical question: "Is your heart right, as my heart is toward your heart? . . . If it is, give me your hand" (2 Kgs 10:15, NKJV[2]). Now consider for a moment what your answer would be; someone, having been busy with killing one after the other, comes up to you and stretches his bloody hand towards you and asks you to shake it. What would you do? It is likely that not only your hand would be shaking, but your whole body would be trembling in fear! Jehonadab, however, confirms his heart is right with Jehu and the one-heartedness is sealed with a firm handshake. For John Wesley, this handshake and oneness of heart symbolized the true catholic spirit.

We will now consider what this story and Wesley's application of it might mean for the twenty-first century church?

The Context of the "Catholic Spirit"

Wesley began his sermon with a reminder of Jesus's words from Matthew 5:44—"But I say to you, love your enemies, bless those who curse you, do good to those who hate you, and pray for those who spitefully use you and persecute you" (NKJV). How ironic to address your audience with these words after having read the bloody narrative of Jehu and the house of Ahab.

Fortunately, within the audience of today's local churches there is seldom the literal shedding of blood. But that doesn't mean there are no verbal fights in the congregation! Fights, sometimes out of egoism, selfishness, and stubbornness, but often as a result of the passion and zeal we have for the Lord. When others have a different way of thinking, or a different approach for expressing their zeal, a huge conflict can be the result. In French such a

---

2. We have chosen to use the NKJV here as it matches the language of "heart right" used by Wesley in this sermon, while having modernized language.

conflict is poetically phrased "*incompatibilité d'humeur*," a euphemism for clashing characters.

It is interesting to notice how Jehu and Jehonadab, despite their oneness of heart, have opposite characters. Jehu's character has already been seen, and is confirmed in 2 Kings 9:20 where his chariot driving is characterized as "maniac." For Jehonadab's character, we turn to Jeremiah 35:5–10. There we see how Jehonadab commanded his children not to drink wine, not to build houses, not to sow seed, not to plant a vineyard. Rather, his children should dwell in tents all of their lives. When we compare the lives of Jehu and Jehonadab, we see two very different people: the extroverted, maniac Jehu on the one hand, and the introverted, minimalistic, self-controlled Jehonadab on the other. Yet, these two opposite characters are shaking hands to confirm their oneness of heart. Apparently, the key in this story is the spiritual condition of the heart.

John Wesley and Holiness Theology: A "Heart Religion"

It can be argued that the distinctiveness of Wesleyan theology is that the starting point is not a specific doctrine or method, but rather a disposition and way of being. In other words, the disposition is about the spiritual condition of the heart. Nathan Crawford states that, "This disposition is one of love, both love of God and love of neighbor. . . . [It is] a hermeneutic of love that begins from the place of both loving and being loved; this becomes the beginning point of any theology that marks itself as Wesleyan."[3] In a similar way, Wesleyan scholar Kenneth Collins states:

> Faith, then, as great as it is, is not seated on the throne, and in one sense it will pass away in the world to come. But love, the greatest mark of the new birth, so celebrated in Wesley's practical theology, will never and can never pass away. The relation between faith and love is essentially instrumental, the one ever points to the other. That is, faith is in order to love. It is the servant of love. Consequently, the holy love of God so richly displayed in Jesus Christ is not only the point of it all, the nature of true religion, but also the very substance of the Christian faith.[4]

Where Crawford and Collins focus on love as the core of Wesleyan theology, others focus on the dwelling place of love, which is the heart. David McEwan points out that it is possible to intellectually comprehend the nature of love in terms of description and application, but this is a poor substitute

---

3. Crawford, "Sketching a Fundamental," 111.

4. Collins, *Theology of John Wesley*, 228. See also Clapper, *As If the Heart Mattered*, 62.

for an actual personal experience. Wesley, therefore, was convinced that Christianity was more about the heart than the head, about a lived relationship than an intellectual comprehension.[5] And from that perspective, it is surprising how Wesley explained and explored this heart religion from the story of Jehu and Jehonadab. Apparently, opposing characters can have the same spiritual condition of the heart; opposing characters can comply with God's calling in Leviticus 19:2—"*be holy, for I the Lord your God am holy.*" In this commandment God uses the verb "to be" rather than the verb "to do." He is not commanding us "to *do* holy, for I the Lord your God *do* holy." Although we have stated elsewhere how holiness can be conceived as three-dimensional ("being," "doing," and "thinking"), the focus here is first of all on our being, our spiritual condition of the heart and secondly about our actions.[6] This focus on "being" becomes clear in an encounter between Moses and God in Exodus 33–34. Moses asks God "show me your glory!" Given God's response, Moses could also have asked "show me who you are," since God's response does not consist of a long list of God's holy deeds like the plagues in Egypt or dividing the waters of the Red Sea. Rather than referring to his powerful and mighty actions or doings, God shows his being to Moses. This should not surprise us, however, since God's name is derived from the verb "to be" (Exod 3:14). In Exodus 34, God reveals his being; God reveals his heart to Moses:

> The LORD passed before him, and proclaimed, "The LORD, the LORD, a God merciful and gracious, slow to anger, and abounding in steadfast love and faithfulness, keeping steadfast love for the thousandth generation, forgiving iniquity and transgression and sin, yet by no means clearing the guilty." (Exod 34:6–7a)

The heart of God, his glory, his holiness, is full of love, patience, forgiveness, and justice. That heart is revealed in his son Jesus Christ, who is the image of God (Col 1:15). Could it be that our creation in the likeness of God (Gen 1:26) should also be defined in terms of God's heart condition? To answer this question, we need to return to Genesis 1. This first chapter of the Bible suggests that our creation in the image of God can be defined in what we do; we have the God-given power to create and to rule. But it also suggests that our reflection of God can be found in who we are. Genesis limits our being to our gender: we are male or female. But Paul, in Galatians 5, elaborates on our being by stating who we can be in the power of the Spirit. A life that shows the fruit of the Spirit is a life of love, patience, peace, goodness, and faithfulness. And although the Bible is not a book on mathematics,

---

5. McEwan, *Wesley as Pastoral Theologian*, 88.
6. Giesken, "Holiness in Community," 399.

the similarity between God's heart condition according to Exodus 34 and our heart condition, living a Spirit-filled life, according to Galatians 5, is remarkable. As God's children, created in his image, we are called to reflect who God is. Therefore, the authors of this article argue that Wesley's catholic spirit and Paul's Spirit-filled life refer to the same spiritual condition of the heart. In the following paragraphs, we will elaborate on the practical consequences of such a heart condition in the life of the congregation. It should have a positive impact on those inside and those outside the congregation. In both groups we will find friends, enemies, and strangers.

Application of the Catholic Spirit within the Congregation

Society and social life consist of groups. There are groups we feel comfortable in, like a group of friends, and, hopefully, the family. We can pick friends ourselves. But most of the time, we cannot select the members of a group, like work and church. More often than not, these groups consist of diverse characters like Jehu and Jehonadab. Such a context of diversity can lend itself to disagreements where specific and significant issues are at stake. The following table makes clear why people within organizations ("actors") have different interests, objectives, and opinions. Some of them are not participating in conflicting issues, the sleeping and stray dogs, but others will react like biting and barking dogs.[7]

Table 1: Overview of Different Types of Actors

	Dedicated actors		Non-dedicated actors	
	Critical actors	Non-critical actors	Critical actors	Non-critical actors
Similar/ supportive interests and objectives	Actors that will probably participate and are potentially strong allies	Actors that will probably participate and are potentially weak allies	Indispensable potential allies that are hard to activate	Actors that do not have to be involved initially
Conflicting interests and objectives	Potential blockers of certain changes (biting dogs)	Potential critics of certain changes (barking dogs)	Potential blockers that will not act immediately (sleeping dogs)	Actors that need little attention initially (stray dogs)

7. Table derived from Enserink et al., *Policy Analysis*, 96–99.

Often, people with similar opinions or interests will form alliances. Paul Sabatier refers to these alliances as "advocacy coalitions," which he defines as "a composition of people . . . who share a set of normative and causal beliefs and who often act in concert."[8] When we apply the table and the insights of Sabatier to the local congregation and to Wesley's sermon, it should be the church's focus to keep the hearts of the Jehus and Jehonadabs right![9] This will imply the pruning of egos and personality styles, since it is not easy to work alongside others.[10]

Along these same lines Edward Collins Vacek elaborates on group dynamics. Vacek states that it is possible to not only love individuals, but also to love a community of persons.[11] Vacek labels the groups we love as "personal groups" or "corporate persons." They have "an identity over and beyond that of the individual members, even though they are embodied in those members and could not be without them. . . . In a corporate person, the normative pattern is one of mutual dependence of individual and group."[12] Vacek argues that the church is such a group for Christians. He considers the church to be a corporate person with Christ as its head in which church members participate, even when these church members have diverging characters:

> [T]he Church not only necessarily must include great diversity within itself, it will also foster that diversity (1 Cor 12:12–31). Since individual Christians are members of the Church, they will of course accept the received identity of the Church (1 Jn 1:3). Since they are not the Church itself, they cannot make the Church whatever they want it to be. But since they participate in the Church, they must take responsibility for the ongoing formation of the Church's ever-developing identity. Both conformism and schism are failures of love. If genuine participation is present, there will be unity in difference between Christ and his Church and between the Church and its members. If genuine participation is not present, fanaticism, self-denigration, or totalitarianism results. . . . Thus, on the one hand, the Church

---

8. Sabatier, "Advocacy Coalition Framework," 129–68

9. An application for other (nonprofit) organizations than the church can be found in an article by Groeneveld and van Den Dool, "Let Love Rule," 23–57.

10. Groeneveld, "Renovating Holiness Includes," 280.

11. Vacek, *Love, Human and Divine*, 60.

12. Vacek, *Love, Human and Divine*, 82–83. Vacek explains: "We can love corporate persons. This love is not the same as love for each of the individuals who are members of the group. Indeed, we often love the group without loving all the individuals of the group. We also can love individual persons because of their membership in a group."

should love its members. That is, it should unite its destiny with theirs and aim at their enhancement. Communities rightly have a special love for "their own." On the other hand, members should unite their destiny with the Church and direct themselves to its enhancement.... Individuals rightly give and receive in different ways, but "even those members of the body which seem less important are in fact indispensable" (1 Cor 12:22).[13]

Vacek sees genuine participation as the key to establishing unity in diversity. Like Jehu and Jehonadab join together in their zeal for the Lord, so should the members of the local church. In addition to this, Vacek makes clear that in a congregation we should not only listen to biting and barking dogs, but also to stray and sleeping dogs. We should consult all fellow members "not just because they may have better insights, but also because we want *their* views to influence and form our own."[14] Sharing together is an expression of (*philia-*) love and it is a concern when people are unable or unwilling to receive the self-disclosure of people they should care about. Applied to the church, Vacek comments: "A church ... that will not permit its members to speak is not a philia-based group. A God who will not listen cannot be a 'friend.' Philia requires all members, to the degree they are able, to try to disclose themselves to the others and to receive the others' self-disclosure."[15]

Like Vacek, Dan Boone comments on how to deal with opposing views in his book *A Charitable Discourse*. He draws a picture of how discussions on a variety of issues can split the church in two. Boone presents a long list of topics that potentially can cause a schism in the congregation. In the end, however, he concludes:

> I think these are important issues. But none of them call for de-Christianizing someone. None of them need to separate brothers and sisters in Christ. I like to think of the day when God, in Christ, makes all things new.... On that day, the ... debate will end. My guess is that we will all be utterly amazed, and our opinions will melt into worship of the Creator.... I think those among us who dug in their heels over nonessential issues will finally be able to lay down the burden of needing to be right and will be able to embrace those they fought unnecessarily. So why not now? Can we love enough to trust? Within the boundaries

---

13. Vacek, *Love, Human and Divine*, 85–86.
14. Vacek, *Love, Human and Divine*, 288, emphasis his.
15. Vacek, *Love, Human and Divine*, 290–91.

of unity in essentials, can we find grace and charity in the nonessentials? Can the kingdom begin to break today?[16]

Boone pleads for the breaking of God's kingdom by accepting each other's differences and still being one of heart. It is interesting to note that a similar call to unite the "kingdom," is done by an American organization called *Better Angels*. This national citizens' movement is concerned with how the "kingdom" of the United States of America is torn in two, caused by the sharp division between the Republican and Democratic Party. The goal of *Better Angels* is "to reduce political polarization in the United States by bringing liberals and conservatives together to understand each other beyond stereotypes, forming red/blue community alliances, teaching practical skills for communicating across political differences, and making a strong public argument for depolarization."[17]

Where the *Better Angels* indirectly draw on love as the key to unity, Vacek and Boone directly go back to love as the key to unity. In fact, both authors go back to the being of God, whose heart is full of love expressed in patience, forgiveness, and grace. And, as we have seen, Paul shows us how we reflect this heart of God by obeying the Spirit who dwells in us. It is a matter of the heart, as Wesley rightfully states in quoting Jehu's question to Jehonadab: "Is your heart right, as my heart is toward your heart?" In the end, of course, our heart needs to be right with God. That is the surprising but at the same time tragic development in the story of Jehu. In 2 Kings 10:30 the Lord compliments Jehu, saying, "you have done well in doing what is right in My sight, and have done to the house of Ahab all that was in My *heart*"[18] (NKJV). The following verse, however, describes the divided heart of Jehu, where it says: "But Jehu took no heed to walk in the law of the LORD God of Israel with all his *heart*; for he did not depart from the sins of Jeroboam, who had made Israel sin"[19] (2 Kgs 10:31, NKJV).

The story of Jehu and Jehonadab shows that the heart should be right in a triple way: with God, with your brother and sister, and also within yourself. This condition of the heart is also the core of the Great Commandment as found in Matthew 22:37–39. In these words of Jesus, love

---

16. Boone, *Charitable Discourse*, 160–61.

17. See the website of Better Angels: https://www.better-angels.org/our-story/#our-approach. Elsewhere on the site it reads: "We unite red and blue Americans in a working alliance to *Depolarize America*. Instead of asking people to change their minds about key issues, we give all Americans a chance to better understand each other, to absorb the values and experiences that inform our political philosophies, and to ultimately recognize our common humanity."

18. Emphasis by the authors.

19. Emphasis by the authors.

should also be extended to the neighbor. But the next logical question then is, given the context of twenty-first-century multiculturalism and mass-migrations of people in an increasingly pluralistic world, can this "one-heart" principle be extended beyond the church and practiced towards strangers and even enemies?

Pushing the Boundaries

Thus far, we have argued that people tend to draw circles of comfort around themselves, defining those who are "us" and who are "them." This inner/outer language orientates our dealings with those who are "other" so that it is not simply how we speak about others but also the way we treat others. In the context of John Wesley's "Catholic Spirit" sermon our discussion has focused primarily on relationship with those within our own congregational or faith circle. It is easy to see the one-heart principle at work when dealing with other Christians. Even though we may not agree on all points of doctrine, there is a perceptible essential in our faith that binds us together. Whether predestinarian or a believer in free will/grace, there is enough space to extend the hand of fellowship and cooperation.

Wesley's principle of the catholic spirit can be extended beyond his initial application and become the framework for interactions with people who intentionally stand outside our own defined theological frameworks. In fact, Wesley opened his sermon on the catholic spirit by referencing Jesus's call to "love your enemies." Clearly this call drives us towards a reconciliatory relationship with even the most antagonistic of people.

Wesley also addressed love for enemies in Sermon 23, which is on the Sermon on the Mount. There he interpreted love as "tender good-will" towards those who were opposed to us and encouraged interaction with them in a way that would reveal to them a better way. We are even instructed to "say all the good [we] can, without violating the rules of truth and justice."[20] This demeanor towards an "enemy" should not simply be a performance or a pretense. Wesley admonished his listeners to be "as real in love as they (our enemy) in hatred." His strongest exhortation with regards to loving our enemy was to pray for them, even if they were repeat offenders and had no repentance in their hearts. This approach indicates Wesley's intense earnest toward people who disagree with us at the most fundamental level possible.

While Wesley's context was less pluralistic than those generally encountered today, it was not without significant insider/outsider distinctions. Methodists often faced derision and ridicule, which even turned physical

20. Wesley, "Upon Our Lord's Sermon on the Mount."

at times.[21] Yet, Wesley's perspective on love was not simply goodwill and affection, but concrete action. It was no less so regarding love for enemy. Love for one's enemy in his teaching was not simply theoretical, he expected it to result in positive behaviors toward those who opposed and could be deemed enemy or stranger. No action was no love.

The one-heart principle is founded upon the notion of an active love for all people—neighbor, stranger, friend, or enemy. It is such love in desire and action that Wesley used as a paradigm for one-heart fellowship. It is a unity of purpose that will not allow the nonessentials to disrupt. He raised the question, "Though we cannot think alike, may we not love alike? May we not be of one heart, though we are not of one opinion?" His answer is a very emphatic, "Without all doubt, we may."[22]

Enemies and Strangers

Wesley's theology of love is not restricted to the confines of the church. How are we to love our enemy if not by engaging in life together? Today's world has brought enemies into close proximity in many urban neighborhoods. Sometimes they are literal enemies, but in many cases, they are simply strangers in our midst—people with good hearts, despite their differences in religion, culture, or any other external delineator. There are many good people among those who are labeled by a different religion than our own. For many there is a reverence for the creator, which could be recognized as love. There is a humane treatment of others that could be taken as love of neighbor. In short, there is in these strangers a heart which could be described as "with mine."

In the encounter between Jehu and Jehonadab there was an initial ignorance, at least on the part of Jehu, of the deeper heart orientation of the other. Many social encounters today take place in such ignorance. People function at a level of necessary interaction but often fail to understand the person with who they are transacting. Much of modern living does not call for deep heart-to-heart exchanges for the social or economic transaction to occur smoothly. Thus, people live at arm's length from each other while living shoulder to shoulder.

As people begin to discover that the stranger is not so strange, friendships develop as they realize "the other" is surprisingly similar to themselves. Common desires, common fears, common frustrations are revealed

21. Goodwin, *Vile or Reviled*.
22. Wesley, "Catholic Spirit."

as conversation deepens beyond the perfunctorily. These areas of commonality provide the substance for one-heart cooperation.

One Heart not One Mind

Wesley recognized the limitations of human knowledge and experience. He addressed this in the sermon—that to be human was to be confined to certain ignorance.

Randy Maddox claims that for Wesley, "opinions" indicated an "*individual's personal* understanding, appropriation, or rejection of authoritative Christian teachings."[23] He argues that Wesley's understanding rests on the Enlightenment notion of the "disjunction between human ideas and their objects."[24] As has previously been shown, Wesley emphasized the "religion of the heart" rather than the certainty of human reason. This is not to say that human reason was not significant in Wesley's theological framework; he only recognized it was fallible. He recognized that this could lead to fractious relationships between people, and therefore cautioned against excessive zeal. These divisions are for Wesley of greater concern than holding wrong opinions,[25] perhaps because, while in relationship, wrong opinions can be corrected or at least exposed, but the divisions that occur through "uncharitable" schisms extinguish such potential.

Doctrine and theology appear to be harnessed for pastoral concern of the human person rather than a theoretical understanding of God. This does not mean that Wesley was unconcerned for good theology—quite the opposite. Reading any of Wesley's works leaves one in no doubt that he was certain of the positions he held. That can clearly be seen in the "Catholic Spirit" as his insistence that such a spirit is not indifferent to theological positions giving rise to "*speculative* latitudinarianism." This relativism was even harshly labeled "the spawn of hell." To counter any such lack of solid theological foundation, Wesley implored his listener to "Go, first, and learn the first elements of the gospel of Christ, and then shall you learn to be of a truly catholic spirit."[26]

Certainly the basics provide the structural framework for one-heart fellowship—unity does not always need uniformity. Though Jehu was a man of war and violence and still followed in the way of Jeraboam, Jehonadab was able to ascend into the chariot of Jehu and apparently offer

23. Maddox, "Opinion, Religion," 65.
24. Maddox, "Opinion, Religion," 69.
25. Wesley, *Explanatory Notes*, 107–8, based on 1 Corinthians 11:18.
26. Wesley, "Catholic Spirit."

him godly counsel. This illustration contains interpretive trajectories that may offer pathways toward joint initiatives of justice with agencies and individuals who are not of the same mind theologically but who seek to bring hope and healing to a range of situations such as social injustice, environmental concerns, mental health care, and interfaith peace initiatives—despite the fact that in the original text one-heart results in the annihilation of Ahab's family and supporters.

Give Me a Hand

It is becoming increasingly important for the church to be able to interact with people of different faiths, as well as those with no faith, in a way that is both respectful and uncompromising. While this seems to be contradictory to the mission of the church, Wesley makes the point that where there is a deep mutual respect, even though people have fundamentally different religious views, space for grace and cooperation is created. The zeal of Jehu was tempered by the righteousness of Jehonadab, and while Jehu was not fully "converted" he found blessing from God.

Wesley reveals his perspective on people of other religions in his sermon "On Faith." He writes: "But with Heathens, Mahometans, and Jews we have *at present* nothing to do; only we may wish that their lives did not shame many of us that are called Christians."[27] Here we recognize that there was little interaction between Wesley and those of the other faith-groups he mentioned. However, it is significant that he acknowledged that at times their lives were lived better than Christians. In this recognition there is fertile soil for the seeds of the one-heart principle, for if there is a life lived well, surely there is a heart that desires good.

A generous reading of Wesley provides a starting point to explore how to extend the hand of cooperation to those whose hearts demonstrate the universal language of love. Perhaps the optimism that springs from the doctrine of prevenient grace affords Wesleyans a unique way forward in this venture. If indeed we value and affirm this doctrine, it should be normal for us to look for its actuality in the lives of others. While Wesley was primarily focused on nurturing a greater sense of unity among all churches, our context today requires an extension of that hand of fellowship beyond our own circle of faith and toward fostering righteousness among people who may not know what the word means, but still have a deep desire to see its reality in the world.

27. Wesley, "On Faith."

In Wesley's context there were far fewer agencies and much less public funding for social services and social justice than is available in many countries today. Much of the work done by the early Methodist pioneered protocols for addressing poverty, lack of education, and social inequity. Reforms in government have since increased public spending in these areas, often taking over the work that was done by churches in the past. There is often more funding available from government and business sectors than can be raised by churches for investing in social capital. Therefore, partnership with non-church agencies has become a necessity to deliver services that will have significant impact on social needs.

Cooperation with agencies of justice seems to reflect the spirit of cooperation underlying the passage from 2 Kings. It is possible to partner with non-Christians and secular agencies in a way that does not compromise theological integrity. There are some suggestions that the opposite is true. By clarifying defining doctrines, common values become clearer, and if that common value is love for God and neighbor, then let cooperation be vigorous. Thomas Oden points out, however, that this is not simply an "emotive matter that can brush aside scriptural doctrine, but requires pressing these questions with inward intensity and honesty."[28] This was exactly Wesley's point: he clearly rejected diluting or compromising one's own theological position, and yet used a text that demonstrated how two unlikely characters could forge exactly such a pluralist partnership without either compromising their own integrity.

Mission Split and Shift

Catholic spirit is catholic love. The goal of the mission of God is to "make all things new." Too often Evangelical Christianity sees the mission of God as convincing people that Jesus is God. While this has significant theological and practical implications, it is not the purpose of the mission. Jesus is the means by which God is bringing to fulfillment the work of God's creation and thus the mission of the church is to cooperate with the Spirit of God in doing such.

That is not to say that worship and the gathering of the church is secondary to the work of social justice. But Wesley kept it balanced by insisting that a person motivated by the catholic spirit would "assist them to the uttermost of his power in all things, spiritual and temporal. He is ready 'to spend and be spent for them;' yea, to lay down his life for their sake." The human being is not divided between spiritual and physical—neither

---

28. Oden, *John Wesley's Scriptural Christianity*, 94.

should the mission of the church. By presenting a wholistic, cooperative model of religion, the church can offer a valuable witness to the activity of God in this world.

Some church-based development agencies are exploring more effective models of Christian witness that seek to build cooperation with non-Christians. Lindy Backues, associate professor of economic development at Eastern University, describes such a model, which has yielded some success. Backeus's model calls together people who have a commitment to see "betterment of the poor populations irrespective of the religious vision or grand world view" of both the worker and the target audience.[29] The model demonstrates the possibility that people of different religious backgrounds can participate in what Wesley called the catholic spirit. It focuses on community empowerment, recruiting diverse local workers who demonstrate particular defining characteristics and shared values—one crucial value being a commitment to regarding work as worship. By focusing on the marginalized and neglected and encouraging mutual respect and open discussions on matters of faith, people are able to cooperate without feeling that their theological integrity is being compromised. Backues concludes that the effectiveness of this development model comes from a "confluence of message and task,"[30] which reflects the incarnational model of Jesus.

God is not the God of the Christians only but cares for all humanity. The incarnation of Jesus broke the religious stereotypes of his day, as did John Wesley some seventeen centuries later. Today we do not seek to simply copy Wesley but to appropriate his insights for a new context. Taking seriously the notion that the "world is our parish," we should not be content to sit in the comfort of the fellowship of the saints. We must extend the circle to include all—showing perfect love for God through perfectly loving his creation and cooperating with God's prevenient grace at work in ordinary and extraordinary places in this world.

Conclusion

Wesley's bookending of his sermon on the "Catholic Spirit" with a call to love, first for neighbor but also for our enemies, has set the parameters for our exploration of the implications of Wesley's catholic spirit for the contemporary Church. While it is clear that one-heart fellowship is demanded within the family of faith, while maintaining doctrinal integrity, the question of how far cooperation with those outside the church may be pursued is more

---

29. Backues, "Interfaith Development Efforts," 74.
30. Backues, "Interfaith Development Efforts," 78.

contentious. However, there is sufficient fuel within the illustration of the one-heartedness of Jehu and Jehonadab to encourage an extension of such practical love towards non-Christians who might answer in the affirmative to the question, "Is your heart right, as my heart is toward your heart?"

Bibliography

Backues, Lindy. "Interfaith Development Efforts as Means to Peace and Witness." *Sustainability* 26.2 (2009) 67–81.
Boone, Dan. *A Charitable Discourse: Talking about the Things that Divide Us*. Kansas City: Beacon Hill, 2010.
Clapper, Gregory S. *As If the Heart Mattered: A Wesleyan Spirituality*. Nashville: Upper Room, 1997.
Collins, Kenneth J. *The Theology of John Wesley: Holy Love and the Shape of Grace*. Nashville: Abingdon, 2007.
Crawford, Nathan. "Sketching a Fundamental Wesleyan Theology: Pursuing a Hermeneutic of Love with Augustine's De Doctrina Christiana." In *The Continuing Relevance of Wesleyan Theology: Essays in Honor of Laurence W. Wood*, edited by Nathan Crawford, 111–22. Eugene: Pickwick, 2011.
Enserink, Bert, et al. *Policy Analysis of Multi-Actor Systems*. The Hague: LEMMA, 2010.
Giesken, Richard. "Holiness in Community." In *Renovating Holiness*, edited by Josh Broward and Thomas Jay Oord, 397–400. Nampa: SacraSage, 2015.
Goodwin, Charles H. "Vile or Reviled? The Causes of the Anti-Methodist Riots at Wednesbury between May 1743 and April 1744 in the Light of New England Revivalism." *Methodist History* 35.1 (1996) 14–28.
Groeneveld, Erik. "Renovating Holiness Includes Renovation of Leadership." In *Renovating Holiness*, edited by Josh Broward and Thomas Jay Oord, 278–80. Nampa: SacraSage, 2015.
Groeneveld, Erik, and Leon van Den Dool. "Let Love Rule: Opportunities and Impediments for Cooperation in Network Organizations." In *The Contribution of Love, and Hate, to Organizational Ethics*, edited by Michael Schwartz et al., 23–57. Bingley: Emerald, 2016.
Maddox, Randy. "Opinion, Religion, and 'Catholic Spirit': John Wesley on Theological Integrity." *Asbury Theological Journal* 47.1 (1992) 63–87.
McEwan, David. *Wesley as a Pastoral Theologian: Theological Methodology in John Wesley's Doctrine of Christian Perfection*. Milton Keynes: Paternoster, 2011.
Oden, Thomas C. *John Wesley's Scriptural Christianity: A Plain Exposition of His Teaching on Christian Doctrine*. Grand Rapids: Zondervan, 1994.
Sabatier, Paul A. "An Advocacy Coalition Framework of Policy Change and the Role of Policy-Oriented Learning Therein." *Policy Sciences* 21 (1988) 129–68.
Vacek, Edward Collins. *Love, Human and Divine: The Heart of Christian Ethics*. Washington, DC: Georgetown University Press, 1994.
Wesley, John. "Catholic Spirit." http://wesley.nnu.edu/john-wesley/the-sermons-of-john-wesley-1872-edition/sermon-39-catholic-spirit.
———. *Explanatory Notes upon the New Testament*. Vol. 2. 11th ed. London: Mason, 1831.

———. "On Faith." http://wesley.nnu.edu/john-wesley/the-sermons-of-john-wesley-1872-edition/sermon-122-on-faith.

———. "Upon Our Lord's Sermon on the Mount: Discourse Three." http://wesley.nnu.edu/john-wesley/the-sermons-of-john-wesley-1872-edition/sermon-23-upon-our-lords-sermon-on-the-mount-discourse-three.

14

A Faithful Father's Acceptant Love and Healing of Shame-Proneness
The Prodigal Son and John Wesley

—Neil Pembroke

It is a very great pleasure and honor to provide an essay in this fine collection celebrating David's highly significant contribution to theological scholarship. I have chosen to focus my reflections on the word of God and on Wesley's life because these constitute two of David's great passions; research grounded in the gospel and in the life and thought of Wesley has strongly animated and deeply fulfilled him for very many years.

The prodigal son and John Wesley, to be sure, are strange bedfellows. The younger son in the parable displays a flippant, irresponsible, devil-may-care approach to life. John Wesley was an earnest, extremely conscientious, and serious-minded man. The parable tells a story of a young man marked by most unholy ways. For most of his life Wesley fully committed his body, mind and soul to the pursuit of holiness. These are indeed two very different characters. But there is a golden thread that ties them together. In the course of this study it will become evident that they both suffered from shame. Moreover, we will observe that each man, in his own particular way, experienced the healing power of acceptant love.

The choice of shame as the main theme of the study stems from a major research interest of mine. For a pastoral theologian, it holds a great deal of significance. It is widely acknowledged by psychologists, therapists, and pastoral theologians alike that pervasive feelings of unworthiness, inferiority, and defectiveness are widespread today and constitute a major source of mental and emotional dis-ease.

I have set two major goals for the essay. First, I aim to identify moral shame in the prodigal son's experience and the origins and manifestations of a propensity for shame and doubt in John Wesley. Second, I attempt to show that the Lucan parable and certain pivotal personal experiences of Wesley join forces to point up in a most compelling and inspirational way the healing and transforming power in divine love expressed in grace-as-acceptance.

Attention is given in the first place to the parable of the prodigal son. Though most naturally enough approach it through the frame of sin-guilt-repentance-forgiveness, I suggest that there are good reasons to engage it from the perspective of shame and acceptance. Certain key events in the life of John Wesley are treated using this same general frame. I argue that his Aldersgate experience, coupled with the very positive reception of his field preaching at Bristol, contributed significantly to the healing of the shame-proneness that had dogged him in his early years.

A Prodigal Son and a Father's Acceptant Love

What follows is a psycho-theological reflection on the parable; I am not qualified to provide a technical exegesis. As a starting point, let me acknowledge that the parable *is* about sin, guilt, and forgiveness. My argument, however, is that there is also a shame-acceptance dynamic operating that is rarely acknowledged. In order to prepare the ground for this alternative take on the parable, it is necessary to become acquainted with the various types of shame. Over the past twenty years, there has been significant research conducted by pastoral theologians on shame and its healing.[1] In any discussion of shame, it is necessary to acknowledge that we are dealing not with a unitary concept but rather with a case of family resemblance. That is, there is significant variation in the way people experience shame. There are at least five members in the shame family—namely, situational shame, aesthetic shame, inherited identity shame, inferiority shame, and moral shame.[2] It is only the last two that we will concern ourselves with here. Inferiority shame is the type that is given the most attention in the psychotherapeutic literature. In broad terms, a sense of inferiority may be related either

---

1. See, for example, Capps, *Depleted Self*; Fowler, *Faithful Change*; Pembroke, *Art of Listening*; Pattison, *Shame*; Goodliff, *Unveiled Face*.

2. Two leading shame researchers who have developed typologies are Robert Karen and James Fowler. The former suggests four categories, namely *existential shame* (the individual suddenly becomes aware of his failings), *class shame* (related to my category of *inherited identity shame*), *narcissistic shame* (one's personal identity is shame-based), and *situational shame* (a category I also use). See Karen, "Shame," 58. Moving from "normal" shame to increasingly pathological variations, James Fowler describes five types and degrees. These are: *healthy shame, perfectionist shame, shame due to enforced minority shame* (cf. my *inherited identity shame*), *toxic shame* (cf. Karen's *narcissistic shame*), and *shamelessness*. See Fowler, *Faithful Change*, 113–31.

to talents and abilities or to personal qualities. A person may feel shame because she judges herself to be incompetent. That is, she is unhappy about the level of skill she has in certain key areas of her life. An individual may also feel shame because she considers that she is boring, timid, socially inept, lacks a sense of humor, to list just a few of the possibilities. Or she may feel ashamed on both counts.

With reference to moral shame, we note that moral failure represents a transgression against the personal and social orders. Awareness of the harm that is done to these orders makes us ashamed. There is a strong argument that shame rather than guilt is the truly moral feeling. As Gary Thrane puts it, "Those who merely dread the punishing voice of conscience (guilt) are not moral. Only those who love their virtue and dread its loss (shame) are moral."[3]

My argument is that it is moral shame rather than the inferiority type so commonly addressed in psychotherapeutic literature that is clearly evident in the case of the prodigal. As far as we can tell from the evidence provided, the shame that the wayward son experienced is related neither to his personal incompetence nor to dissatisfaction with his personality. His emotional distress is not caused by perceived incompetence in certain key activities. Nor do we have any evidence that he is disgruntled with his personal makeup. His major problem is not that he thinks he is dull and uninteresting, for example. The primary source of his shame is his moral failure and the dishonoring of self and family that goes with it. He fails in several ways. He treats his father as if he is already dead. In squandering his property, he fails to make provision for the future care of his father. And he makes himself unclean by working with swine.

In the experience of moral shame, guilt also features. This contrasts with inferiority shame. There is no guilt associated with cooking awful lasagna or with being clumsy in social situations!

It is important for our analysis to distinguish between shame and guilt. Shame researchers consistently use the global aspect of the shame experience to differentiate it from its cousin in the affect family. A person feels guilty over actions (or omissions) which have caused harm to others. Guilt can be localized in a certain aspect of the self—namely, that which is associated with a moral transgression. A person who gambles excessively on occasion may say, "I like the person that I am. I just get carried away sometimes when I go down to the track." Shame, though, cannot be tied to a discrete act that can be separated off from the self. The difference may be expressed this way: "I am guilty of this bad act; but I *am* my shame."

---

3. Thrane, "Shame," 154.

As Leon Wurmser observes, shame has a global quality because it is evoked by a discrepancy between a tested self and an ideal image.[4] This image is not simply constructed out of a delimited reality such as actions, but out of all the components which define a self. It is through shameful events that the self is revealed. Personal identity is shaped in this way. The shame events throw up the contours of a person's selfhood and of the world of reality she inhabits. Guilt may be assuaged by confession or restitution, but the experience of shame may be transcended only by a re-shaping of identity.

With all this in mind, I offer the suggestion that the father offers both forgiveness and acceptance to his lost son. Acceptance is affirmation and approval of a person and of his or her basic identity. The father knows this son well. He knows all about his serious personal flaws and deficiencies. And yet he is prepared to run out and embrace him and then to throw a party for him. Through these actions, he welcomes back this deeply flawed son into the family and into the community. This is what a person experiencing deep shame desires most. He or she wants to be accepted in his or her weakness and deficiency. It is possible to reform wayward tendencies; it is not possible to transform oneself into a completely new identity. The only hope for healing for a person plagued by shame is acceptance.

I am aware that some might object that in turning to contemporary pastoral psychological and psychotherapeutic literature to interpret the shame experience of the prodigal, I miss the fact that he lived in an honor-shame culture. I hope to show that in fact both losing face and moral conscience featured in the prodigal's experience (as it does in modern industrialized societies). Honor is a claim to worth made by an individual that is recognized by the social group. It can either be acquired passively (by birth or inheritance) or actively (through excellence in fulfilling one's kinship and communal obligations and in meeting challenges from others). Dishonor, or shame, is the result of a loss of precedence or face. Since the time of Margaret Mead, there has been a tendency amongst anthropologists to contrast shame and guilt cultures. Shame is associated with small communities featuring face-to-face relations in which the disapproval of others is feared. Guilt is linked to Western, diversified, and industrialized societies and is said to result from an internal sanction related to a moral transgression. This neat distinction disregards, on the one hand, the fact that shame features in modern developed, socially differentiated, and anonymous societies (e.g., in the dock of a criminal court, in the tabloid press, and in public "naming and shaming" campaigns prosecuted by community leaders and

---

4. See Wurmser, "Shame," 86.

lawmakers); and, on the other, that internalized sanctions against morally wrong actions feature in ancient cultures.[5]

In a culture in which honor is the primary value and shame is the major source of distress, individuals are not bereft of a moral conscience. They feel the weight of internal sanctions when they fall into moral transgression. I contend that both the shame of losing face and the guilt associated with transgression of divine law featured in the life of Israel and of the earliest Christian community. Both these dynamics can be clearly seen in the parable. The prodigal confesses to his father, "I have sinned against heaven and before you" (Luke 15:18). He is guilty of sin. It is clear that guilt and shame are tied up together in the wayward son's experience. It is also the case, further, that the sins of the prodigal represent a breach of the honor code. Through treating his father and the Jewish community so disrespectfully, he dishonors both himself and his family. The father wishes to spare him the shaming stares of the villagers, so he runs to the outskirts to greet him. The fact that the old man runs constitutes a loss of face. The robe, the shoes, and the ring, finally, have to do with conferring honor and status.

There was also an honor-shame system operating in eighteenth-century English society, albeit of a quite different kind to the Ancient Near Eastern one. Our second featured character, John Wesley, took duty and maintaining honor most seriously. However, it is again the modern psychological understanding of shame that will feature in my interpretation of some of the most significant events in Wesley's life and ministry. Erik Erikson's understanding of shame and doubt will be employed in the analysis.

Wesley's Journey from Shame-Proneness to Assurance

In reading the early life of John Wesley, what stands out is his tendency to denigrate himself in terms of his discipleship. He often seemed to long for assurance that he was a true Christian. This aspect comes through particularly strongly in his published journals. However, we need to approach this with some caution; Wesley had a tendency to devalue his pre-conversion discipleship in order to accent his newly acquired sense of assurance. Nevertheless, more reliable sources, such as his letters and descriptions written by contemporaries, confirm this general perspective. This tendency to shame, doubt, and despair is identified by leading Wesley scholars. Henry Rack comments that Wesley's early life was "marked

---

5. See Cairns, "Representations of Remorse"; Siebert, *Construction of Shame*, 15–16; and Peristiany and Pitt-Rivers, "Introduction," 8.

by agonizing self-reproach for his lack of Christianity."[6] In reviewing the whole of Wesley's life, Richard Heitzenrater makes this observation: "In his own spiritual pilgrimage, Wesley's attempt to 'press on to perfection' seems to be marked by a continuing desire for a sense of assurance. The first experience of assurance in 1738 seems not to have had an abiding satisfaction for his heart. . . . The periods of despair and *angst* became less frequent but apparently no less intense as time went on."[7]

In what follows, an attempt is made to draw a connecting line between this dimension of Wesley's spiritual life—the need for assurance—and his psychosocial experience. I argue that the psychological roots of Wesley's tendency to shame and self-doubt can be found in his mother's method of conquering the will of her children. In this approach to parenting, Mrs. Wesley shows the influence of the prevailing social milieu. Her "conquer the will" method was in fact a strict version of the "bend the will" approach that was popular in the day.

Significant for my interpretation of Wesley's childhood experience is Erik Erikson's theory that parental over-control leads to a propensity for shame and doubt. This is precisely the tendency that we see in the young John Wesley. He would set up a strict regime of piety, but then doubts over the authenticity of his discipleship would come, so he would get tougher with himself. He could never convince himself that he was a true Christian.

The second proposition to be argued is that Wesley came to a point of significant, though certainly not complete, transcendence of his battle with shame feelings through the assurance he received from two key events: the Aldersgate experience and the success of his field preaching at Bristol. While the attacks of shame and doubt would continue throughout his life, they would be much less frequent and intense.

Since we are working with Erikson's developmental psychology here, it is necessary to provide a brief sketch of it. Erikson produced a highly influential eight-stage model of human development.[8] It is the second stage that is relevant for our investigation. The "autonomy vs shame and doubt" crisis takes place in the second and third years of life. Decisive in this stage is "Who decides?" The child approaches her experience of the world in terms of "I" and "you," "mine" and "yours." It is a decisive stage in terms of the ratio between working-with and struggling-against, and between expressing freely and restraining self-expression.

6. Rack, *Reasonable Enthusiast*, xii.

7. Heitzenrater, *Elusive Mr. Wesley*, 198.

8. See Erikson, *Childhood*, 222–47; Erikson, *Insight*, 111–33; Erikson, *Identity*, 91–139.

While the child needs to learn to accept the control of others, the parents need to give her some breathing room as she attempts to stand on her own two feet. Parental over-control—the "Always me, never you" approach—has the potential to produce a lasting propensity for shame and doubt. Shame for Erikson is largely a feeling of self-consciousness; it is associated with dreams in which one finds oneself in a state of undress in a public setting. There is a vague sense that something has been left undone; "a vague diffuse sense of falling short of some ideal."[9] Doubt is closely related to shame in Erikson's thinking. It has to do with the consciousness of having a front and a back, and especially of having a "behind."

The virtue of will emerges during the autonomy crisis.[10] Will is the capacity to decide, to make free choices, while also exercising self-restraint. The fact that it was the *will* of her children that Susanna aimed to conquer is therefore most significant.

With this brief overview of Erikson's theory of autonomy versus shame and doubt in hand, we progress to a psychological interpretation of some vitally important experiences and events in Wesley's life. The starting point is his childhood. Here we will attend particularly to the parenting style of Mrs. Wesley.

The Conquered Son: Epworth

Samuel Wesley was a somewhat rigid and dictatorial Anglican priest. It seems that he and his wife, Susanna, had strong and opposing political views. Mrs. Wesley, having as she did Jacobite sympathies, refused to say "Amen" when her husband prayed for William III. Samuel promptly exclaimed: "[Y]ou and I must part: for if we have *two* kings, we must have *two beds*."[11] He left Epworth for London on church business and stayed there a year. When the Stuart queen, Anne, took the throne he decided to return. It was in this period of reconciliation that John was born, on June 17, 1703.

Susanna Wesley was a harsh disciplinarian. Her guiding principle was "conquer the will":

> In order to form the minds of children, the first thing to be done is to conquer their will, and bring them to an obedient temper. . . . Whenever a child is corrected, it must be conquered; and this will be no hard matter to do if it be not grown headstrong

---

9. Lowe, *Growth of Personality*, 62.
10. See Erikson, *Insight*, 119.
11. Clarke, *Memoirs*; cited in Crutcher, *John Wesley*, 28.

by too much indulgence. And when the will of a child is totally subdued, and it is brought to revere and stand in awe of the parents, then a great many childish follies and inadequacies may be passed by.[12]

Susanna Wesley's parenting style was by no means a unique one in her day. On the contrary, she was influenced by the socio-religious milieu of the time. This approach of getting on top of the will was common among serious-minded Christians living in eighteenth-century England and Europe. In studying a situation not too far removed from the world of Mrs. Wesley, John Demos records these words of John Robinson, a Puritan living in Plymouth Colony: "For the beating, and keeping down of this stubbornness parents must provide carefully . . . that the children's wills and wilfulness be restrained and repressed, and that, in time, lest sooner than they imagine, the tender sprigs grow to that stiffness that will rather break than bow."[13] However, Susanna's method does seem to represent a particularly strict version of this dominating style of parenting. After having acknowledged the influence of John Locke's bestseller, *Some Thoughts on Education*, with its recommendation that the will of a child needs bending, Tomkins makes this comment: "[T]his by no means indicates that most parents followed the principle with such rigour and Susanna was harsher than Locke in a number of ways."[14] Heitzenrater concurs: "[A]lthough John Locke does assume 'correction by the rod' as an acceptable method of punishment, he seems to have more moderate views than Susanna on the propriety and frequency of corporal punishment."[15]

I contend that Susanna's vigorous effort to "conquer the will" is of the utmost significance in relation to the autonomy crisis. The crucial question here, as we have seen, is "Who decides?" Parental over-control—"the always me, never you" approach—is very likely to result in a propensity for shame and doubt. Others have made this link between the repressive parenting style common in seventeenth- and eighteenth-century Western societies and the autonomy crisis.[16]

Erikson avers that shame "supposes that one is completely exposed and conscious of being looked at: in one word, self-conscious."[17] Gordon Lowe sums up Erikson's depiction of shame in this way: "[It] is a vague

12. Wesley, *Journal*, 3:35.
13. Demos, *Little Commonwealth*, 135.
14. Tomkins, *John Wesley*, 14.
15. Heitzenrater, "John Wesley and Children," 283–84.
16. See Demos, *Little Commonwealth*, 138; Capps, "Religious Ritual," esp. 211.
17. Erikson, *Childhood*, 227.

diffuse sense of falling short of some ideal. We feel that our 'fault' (in biblical terms) is a sin of omission; we have left undone that which we ought to have done."[18] Erikson makes this further comment on the nature of shame: "[It] is early expressed in an impulse to bury one's face, or to sink, right then and there, into the ground."[19] The young John Wesley, I suggest, often felt that he had fallen well short of the mark, that he was not even close to attaining his spiritual ideal. In moments of prayerful examination of his Christian living, he found himself too ashamed to "look God in the face."

Doubt is closely linked to shame. It has "much to do with a consciousness of having a front and a back—and especially a behind."[20] The metaphor that captures the experience best is "doing a double take." We will note below that this modality was a prominent feature in Wesley's spiritual life. Though he sometimes convinced himself that he was living a reasonably serious and sincere Christian life, he later experienced times of despair when he adjudged that he had simply been deluding himself. The mental schema that plagued him was this: "I might have thought that I was doing well in serious Christian living, but in moments of absolute honesty I know that I'm not a true follower of Christ."

We will see that John found himself trapped in a vicious cycle. His tendency to shame and doubt drove him to a live a stricter Christian life in the hope of feeling fully assured that he was a real Christian. But the sense of assurance was never quite strong enough, so he launched himself into an even stricter style of Christian living. And so it went on. The operation of this vicious cycle is very evident in his writings pertaining to his time at Oxford.

The Compulsive Pietist: Oxford

The young John Wesley left his school, Charterhouse, in 1720 with a leaving exhibition for Christ Church, Oxford. A study of Wesley during the Oxford period reveals a number of elements in his emerging identity. He was a dedicated and able scholar; he enjoyed socializing with cultured young friends; he worked as a curate; and he had a humanitarian concern. Increasingly, however, Wesley dedicated himself to establishing an identity as a man of holiness. Indeed, the other dimensions of his life were all drawn under the holiness umbrella. He was a young man who became more and more driven in his pursuit of a truly holy life. The young Wesley had an overweening

18. Lowe, *Growth of Personality*, 62.
19. Erikson, *Childhood*, 227.
20. Erikson, *Childhood*, 228.

need for assurance that his regime of piety qualified him as a real Christian. This compulsiveness in piety characterizes the Oxford period. Heitzenrater makes this comment: "The grand scheme of holy living had begun to set the direction of his life. . . . He was increasingly obsessed with a desire for some clear sense of assurance that his approach and method of Christian living would provide adequate grounds for his hope of salvation."[21]

Wesley graduated as a Bachelor of Arts in 1724 and stayed on to pursue a course of study leading to a Master of Arts degree. Ordination was a pre-requisite for embarking on a career as a scholar and tutor. With this, among other things, in mind, John set a course for Orders. He was ordained as a deacon by Bishop Potter on September 19, 1725. He preached his first sermon the following Sunday in the little village church of South Leigh, near Whitney.

The opportunity to receive his reward for his academic achievements came at about the same time that a vacancy arose for a fellow at Lincoln College. Wesley was finally elected to the fellowship on March 17, 1726.

An Oxford don was afforded a great amount of freedom. In fact, from 1726 to 1729 John spent the greater part of his time at Epworth and Wroot (his father had also acquired the living at Wroot), serving as his father's curate. He was ordained to the priesthood at Oxford in 1728.

Late in Michaelmus Time, 1729, Wesley was called back to Lincoln College to serve as tutor. John's return to the college coincided with the foundation of the Holy Club. The club soon constructed a rule of life involving study, frequent attendance at the Eucharist, and regular times of prayer and Bible reading.[22]

There were quite a few who derided the approach of the members of the club. It seems that the major criticism directed at "the Methodists"—as they were sometimes called—was that they showed a lack of balance and were too strict. This criticism fed into Wesley's sense of doubt. "Wesley's view of religion, its requirements and its restrictions, was certainly a minority position at Oxford. Consequently, he was the brunt of a great deal of criticism, even from his friends and family. Under this pressure, Wesley was continually looking for some sense of assurance, some sign that he was truly a Christian."[23]

This criticism was mild, however, compared to what came after the death of William Morgan in August of 1732. John was very concerned about rumors that were circulating concerning the tragic event and decided to

21. Heitzenrater, *Elusive Mr. Wesley*, 51.
22. See Wesley, *Journal*, 1:90, 95.
23. Heitzenrater, *Elusive Mr. Wesley*, 71.

write a letter defending the practices of his Holy Club to William's father, Richard Morgan.[24] Mr. Morgan was convinced by Wesley's arguments and decided to place his other son, Richard Jr., in his care. Richard, however, very quickly found that the strictness of life in the Methodist group was simply too much for him. In a letter to his father he had this to say: "They imagine they cannot be saved if they do not spend every hour, nay minute, of their lives in service of God."[25]

In linking assurance of salvation to sincerity and good works, John followed what seems to be the prevailing theology in the Church of England in the early part of the eighteenth century. With the rise of William Laud to the position of Archbishop of Canterbury in the previous century, an "Arminianising impulse" was introduced into the Church.[26] One Anglican divine of the day expressed the view that "Christ died for all if all will care to perform the condition required by Him."[27] This is putting the matter crudely, but the statement nevertheless gives a sense of the tendency to assign a role to good works in salvation. Rack concludes a survey of seventeenth and eighteenth views on salvation with this assessment: "So, at more sophisticated as well as less sophisticated levels, the old Reformation doctrine of justification by grace through faith had been eroded into a variable balance between grace and works."[28]

If one's hope of salvation is tied to the level of one's sincerity in the pursuit of righteous and assiduousness in doing good, a man like the young John Wesley was bound to be plagued by doubt and anxiety. He was bound to struggle with the questions "Am I doing enough?" "Am I fully sincere in my quest for righteousness?" The cultural factor—the prevailing theology of salvation—and a personal experience—being reared under Susanna's repressive parenting method—interacted to John's disadvantage.

At the end of 1734, Wesley received a call from his father to leave Oxford and the Methodists in order to take over the pastoral reins at Epworth. John wrote a long letter in response setting out carefully his reasons for declining.[29] His main reason was that he thought he had more opportunity of doing good where he was. This conviction notwithstanding, he was on board a ship headed for the American colonies within a year. In September

---

24. See Wesley, *Journal*, 1:101.
25. Wesley, *Letters of John Wesley*, 147.
26. Cromartie, "Mind of Laud," 89.
27. This statement by the Anglican divine of the time is cited in Moore, *John Wesley*, 119.
28. Rack, *Reasonable Enthusiast*, 28.
29. See Wesley, *Letters of John Wesley*, 173.

of 1735, he decided to accept Dr Burton's suggestion that he work as an SPCK chaplain in Georgia.

The Disillusioned Missionary: Georgia

Wesley set out for Georgia from Gravesend in the *Simmonds* on Tuesday, October 14, 1735. Why the turnaround, given his previously stated conviction that his calling was Oxford? No doubt there were a number of reasons. Perhaps chief among them was the thought that taking up missionary work among the Indians was something that only a true Christian, one worthy of the gift of salvation, would do. Indeed, he had this to say in his letter to Dr. Burton, "My chief motive, to which all the rest are subordinate, is the hope of saving my own soul."[30]

It is interesting to note that on the voyage across the Atlantic the *Simmonds* encountered fierce storms and huge waves. Wesley was terrified that the ship would sink, and he would drown. By way of contrast, the Moravian immigrants displayed tranquility of spirit in the face of imminent doom displayed by the Moravians. Upon observing this, Wesley felt ashamed.[31] After the long and sometimes difficult trip, the good ship Simmonds reached its destination on February 5, 1736.

John had close contact with the Moravians who so inspired and challenged him. He had profound respect for the way in which they lived the Christian life; indeed, he was almost in awe of their piety. While the ship was lying off Tybee Island, James Oglethorpe, founder of the colony, brought on board the leader of the Herrnhut settlement in Georgia, August Gottlieb Spangenberg. Wesley was to hold a series of thought-provoking and enlightening conversations with Spangenberg. In one of their conversations, the Moravian leader put this very direct question to Wesley: "Do you know Jesus Christ?" "I know He is the Saviour of the world," came the answer.[32] The Moravian, however, was probing Wesley to see if he had a deep and abiding *personal* assurance of salvation: "But do you know that He has saved you?" Finally, John was able to declare that he did indeed have a personal assurance. In the *Journal* we find this interesting comment: "But I fear these were vain words."[33]

We have seen that Wesley was motivated to go to Georgia in no small measure by a desire to save his own soul through dedicated missionary work

30. Wesley, *Letters*, 188.
31. See Crutcher, *John Wesley*, 41.
32. Wesley, *Journal*, 1:151.
33. Wesley, *Journal*, 1:151.

amongst the Indians. In actuality, he spent most of his time in parish ministry in Savannah. He would leave Georgia a very disillusioned young man. It has to be said that his two-year project failed to reach any great heights. Indeed, that is putting it mildly. His dream of establishing a mission to the Indians remained just that, a dream. On the chaplaincy front, his rigid Catholic discipline alienated many of the colonists. To top it off, he badly mishandled his broken relationship with Sophy Hopkins. His exit was a hasty flight from rough colonial justice. Wesley had not found the assurance that he longed for. Instead, he found himself languishing in a state of despair.

John had plenty of time for soul-searching on board the *Samuel* as he headed for England. His reflections give an indication of just how disconsolate and gloomy he felt at this time: "I went to America to convert the Indians; but oh, who shall convert me?"[34] He seemed to be doubting the very foundations of his faith: "But in the storm I think, what if the gospel be not true? Then thou art of all men most foolish."[35]

This was clearly crisis time for the young John Wesley. He desperately needed to know with much greater clarity and conviction that he was a righteous man of faith and accepted by God.

The Assured Preacher: Aldersgate and Bristol

Wesley arrived at Deal Harbor on February 1, 1738. He was very disillusioned and more entangled than ever in self-doubt. A brighter day, however, was about to dawn.

Tuesday, February 7, was for him "a day much to be remembered."[36] This was the day Wesley met the man who was to be a catalyst in the process that led to a new faith experience, namely the Moravian, Peter Bohler. The two would spend a good deal of time together over the next few months.

During the ensuing weeks, Wesley was gripped by the doubt that we have become accustomed to expecting. In his diary, for example, he had this to say: "Leave off preaching. How can you preach to others, who have not faith yourself?"[37] His Moravian companion, however, recommended a strategy for dealing with his faith crisis: "Preach faith *till* you have it; and then, *because* you have it, you *will* preach faith."[38] John dutifully followed

---

34. Wesley, *Journal*, 1:418.
35. Wesley, *Journal*, 1:418.
36. Wesley, *Journal*, 1:436.
37. Wesley, *Journal*, 1:436.
38. Wesley, *Journal*, 1:442.

the wise counsel, and it was beginning to work. He found that now he "had no objection to what [Bohler] said of the nature of faith."[39]

Early in May, Charles Wesley was led by Bohler to a conviction of the truth of the doctrine of salvation by grace through faith alone.[40] A few weeks later, on May 24, 1738 John would himself feel a strong personal assurance that by grace his sins were forgiven and that sin and death no longer had power over him. At Aldersgate his heart was "strangely warmed."

There has been significant debate over what the Aldersgate experience meant for Wesley. Gordon Rupp is convinced that what happened on May 24 was indeed deeply significant for Wesley. In support he quotes Wesley's proclamation the next Sunday to those gathered in the house of Rev. John Hutton that five days before he was not a Christian.[41] Tomkins considers that the impact was short-lived: "[Aldersgate] seems to have had little long-term importance in Wesley's spiritual journey as genuine assurance actually came to him through a much steeper climb."[42] Rack concludes his survey of various psychological interpretations of the experience in this way: "It seems reasonable to accept that Wesley's prolonged adolescence and recurring difficulties in attaining autonomy and maturity might be a reasonable summary of the situation. . . . The idea that Wesley failed to gain a permanent inward sense of joy and assurance and that the problem was resolved by observing the fruits of faith in others . . . appears to be soundly based."[43]

However we should interpret Aldersgate itself, it seems clear that it should be placed in the context of a series of events if we are to understand properly the process that led to greater assurance. The most important of these is the success of Wesley's field preaching at Bristol.

In the summer of 1738 Wesley made a short visit to the Moravian communities at Herrnhut and Marienborn.[44] He saw this trip largely as an opportunity to do some further testing of the Moravian spirituality.

John returned from Germany in September. A few months later, George Whitefield, who had recently returned from a highly successful preaching tour in the American colonies, attempted to enlist Wesley as a leader in a mission he had started in Bristol. Initially Wesley was quite resistant to the proposal. For him, preaching the word of God is appropriately performed in

---

39. Wesley, *Journal*, 1:454.
40. See Wesley, *Journal*, 1:459.
41. See Rupp, *Religion in England*, 357.
42. Tomkins, *John Wesley*, 61.
43. Rack, *Reasonable Enthusiast*, 152.
44. Wesley, *Journal*, 1:3–62.

a church. Finally, however, he gave into the pressure and preached his first address before a crowd of about three thousand.

Wesley's preaching was in fact very well received; indeed, a number of people manifested physical reactions after hearing an address, so moved were they. The positive reception from the folk in the field at Bristol provided a significant boost to the growing sense of affirmation and assurance that Wesley was feeling. Aldersgate and Bristol together produced a significant change in him. He was able to break out of the cage of shame and doubt that had so long held him captive. Albert Outler makes this telling observation: "It is most impressive to observe the marked effect this success at Bristol had on Wesley's spiritual equilibrium. Up to this point the story is full of anxiety, insecurity, futility. Hereafter, the instances of spiritual disturbance drop off sharply and rarely recur, even in the records of a very candid man."[45]

Two critical events—Aldersgate and Bristol—worked together to bring Wesley to a point of greater spiritual and psychological equilibrium. Though the attacks of shame and doubt would return, they would be much less frequent. Wesley took with him a greater sense of confidence and assurance as he launched himself into the task of stirring up faith in eighteenth-century England.

Conclusion

I have attempted a psycho-theological reading of the parable of the prodigal son and of certain significant events in the life of John Wesley. I have argued that the prodigal wrestled with moral shame and that young John Wesley suffered from a propensity for shame and doubt. In the psychotherapeutic literature it is routinely acknowledged that acceptance is what the person suffering from shame needs most. Both the wayward son and Wesley were privileged with a deep experience of grace-as-acceptance. In one of his sermons, Paul Tillich said something that is profoundly true. He noted that many today struggle to grasp the true meaning of divine grace. Here, he suggested, the psychotherapist can help us out. Grace is much like acceptance or unconditional positive regard.[46] Christian joy springs from the knowledge that in faith we can rely absolutely on the wondrous gift of God's acceptance of us in Christ through the power of the Spirit.

45. Outler, "Introduction," 17.
46. See Tillich, *Shaking of the Foundations*, 158.

Bibliography

Cairns, Douglas. "Representations of Remorse and Reparation in Classical Greece." In *Remorse and Reparation*, edited by Murray Cox, 171–78. London: Kingsley, 1999.
Capps, Donald. *The Depleted Self: Sin in a Narcissistic Age*. Minneapolis: Fortress, 1993.
———. "Religious Ritual and the Excommunication of Ann Hibbins." In *Christian Perspectives on Human Development*, edited by Leroy Aden et al., 209–23. Grand Rapids: Baker, 1992.
Clarke, Adam. *Memoirs of the Wesley Family*. New York: Bangs and Mason, 1824.
Cromartie, Alan. "The Mind of William Laud." In *England's Wars of Religion, Revisited*, edited by Glenn Burgess and Charles Prior, 75–100. London: Routledge, 2011.
Crutcher, Timothy J. *John Wesley: His Life and Thought*. Kansas City: Beacon Hill, 2015.
Demos, John. *A Little Commonwealth: Early Life in Plymouth Colony*. New York: Oxford University Press, 1970.
Erikson, Erik H. *Childhood and Society*. 2nd ed. London: Triad, 1977.
———. *Identity: Youth and Crisis*. Rev. ed. New York: Norton, 1994.
———. *Insight and Responsibility*. New York: Norton, 1964.
Fowler, James. *Faithful Change: The Personal and Public Challenges of Post-modern Life*. Nashville: Abingdon, 1996.
Goodliff, Paul. *With Unveiled Face: A Pastoral and Theological Exploration of Shame*. London: Darton, Longman & Todd, 2005.
Heitzenrater, Richard P. *The Elusive Mr. Wesley*. Vol 1, *John Wesley His Own Biographer*. Nashville: Abingdon, 1984.
———. "John Wesley and Children." In *The Child in Christian Thought*, edited by Marcia J. Bunge, 279–99. Grand Rapids: Eerdmans, 2001.
Karen, Robert. "Shame." *Atlantic Monthly*, February 1992.
Lowe, Gordon R. *The Growth of Personality*. Harmondsworth: Penguin, 1972.
Moore, Robert L. *John Wesley and Authority: A Psychological Perspective*. Missoula: Scholars, 1979.
Outler, Albert C. "Introduction." In *John Wesley*, edited by A. C. Outler, 3–33. New York: Oxford University Press, 1980.
Pattison, Stephen. *Shame: Theory, Therapy, Theology*. Cambridge: Cambridge University Press, 2000.
Pembroke, Neil. *The Art of Listening: Dialogue, Shame, and Pastoral Care*. Edinburgh: T. & T. Clark, 2002.
Peristiany, John George, and Julian Pitt-Rivers. "Introduction." In *Honor and Grace in Anthropology*, edited by J. G. Peristiany and J. Pitt-Rivers, 1–18. Cambridge: Cambridge University Press.
Rack, Henry D. *Reasonable Enthusiast: John Wesley and the Rise of Methodism*. London: Epworth, 1989.
Rupp, Gordon. *Religion in England 1688–1791*. New York: Oxford University Press, 1986.
Siebert, Johanna, *The Construction of Shame in the Hebrew Bible: The Prophetic Contribution*. London: Sheffield Academic, 2002.
Thrane, Gary. "Shame." *Journal for the Theory of Social Behavior* 92 (1979) 139–66.
Tillich, Paul. *The Shaking of the Foundations*. Harmondsworth: Penguin, 1966.
Tomkins, Stephen. *John Wesley: A Biography*. Oxford: Lion, 2003.
Wesley, John. *The Journal of John Wesley*. Vol. 1, *From October 14, 1735, to November 17, 1746*. Edited by Nehemiah Curnock. London: Epworth, 1938.

———. *The Journal of John Wesley*. Vol. 3, *From December 13, 1760, to September 13, 1773*. Edited by Nehemiah Curnock. London: Epworth, 1938.
———. *The Letters of John Wesley*. Edited by John Telford. London: Epworth, 1931.
Wurmser, Leon. "Shame: The Veiled Companion." In *The Many Faces of Shame*, edited by Donald Nathanson, 64–92. New York: Guilford, 1987.

www.ingramcontent.com/pod-product-compliance
Lightning Source LLC
Chambersburg PA
CBHW050849230426
43667CB00012B/2216